Intellectual Property: Licensing and Joint Venture Profit Strategies

SUBSCRIPTION NOTICE

This Wiley product is updated on a periodic basis with supplements to reflect important changes in the subject matter. If you purchased this product directly from John Wiley & Sons, Inc., we have already recorded your subscription for this update service.

If, however, you purchased this product from a bookstore and wish to receive (1) the current update at no additional charge, and (2) future updates and revised or related volumes billed separately with a 30-day examination review, please send your name, company name (if applicable), address, and the title of the product to:

Supplement Department
John Wiley & Sons, Inc.
One Wiley Drive
Somerset, NJ 08875
1-800-225-5945

For Customers outside the United States, please contact the Wiley office nearest you:

Professional and Reference Division
John Wiley & Sons Canada, Ltd.
22 Worcester Road
Rexdale, Ontario M9W1L1
Canada
(416)675-3580
1-800-263-1590 in Canada

John Wiley & Sons, Ltd.
Baffins Lane
Chichester
West Sussex PO19 1UD
United Kingdom
(44)(243)779777

Professional, Reference and Trade Division
Jacaranda Wiley Ltd.
PO Box 174
Ryde, NSW 2113
Australia
(02)805-1100

Intellectual Property: Licensing and Joint Venture Profit Strategies

Gordon V. Smith

Russell L. Parr

John Wiley & Sons, Inc.

New York • Chichester • Brisbane • Toronto • Singapore

This text is printed on acid-free paper.

Library of Congress Cataloging in Publication Data:

Smith, Gordon V., 1937–
Intellectual property : licensing and joint venture profit strategies / Gordon V. Smith, Russell L. Parr.
p. cm.
ISBN 0-471-57445-7 (cloth : alk. paper)
1. License agreements—United States. 2. License agreements—Economic aspects—United States. 3. Joint ventures—United States. 4. Intellectual property—United States. 5. Intellectual property—Economic aspects—United States. I. Parr, Russell L. II. Title.
KF2979.S646 1993
346.7304′8—dc20
[347.30648] 92-39298

Printed in United States of America

10 9 8 7 6 5 4 3

For Carlye Smith and Sam Clemmer,
the world is a much brighter place
since you arrived.

For my beautiful wife Jane Parr
and our brilliant sons John
and James.

About the Authors

GORDON V. SMITH is President of AUS Consultants and has advised clients in valuation matters for 30 years. His assignments have included appraisals of nearly every type of tangible and intangible asset as well as consultations relative to royalty rates and the economic life of property. Clients have been many of the Fortune 500, as well as research and educational institutions, regulatory bodies, and the U.S. government. He has served as an expert witness on numerous occasions regarding valuations and valuation theory.

Mr. Smith, a graduate of Harvard University, has lectured widely on valuation subjects in the United States and internationally, including regular guest lectures at the Franklin Pierce Law Center. He is an Accredited Senior Appraiser of the American Society of Appraisers, and a member of the United States Trademark Association, Licensing Executives Society and the International Fiscal Association. He has written many professional papers and articles that have appeared in professional publications here and abroad.

He has authored three books, published by John Wiley & Sons, titled:

Corporate Valuation: A Business and Professional Guide

Valuation of Intellectual Property and Intangible Assets (co-author)

Intellectual Property: Licensing and Joint Venture Profit Strategies (co-author)

RUSSELL L. PARR is a Vice President of the Valuation Services Group of AUS Consultants and expert at assessing the value of intellectual property and intangible assets. He advises clients about the investment value of patents, trademarks, copyrights and other intangible assets to help accomplish strategic mergers, acquisitions, licensing transactions, and joint ventures. Mr. Parr also advises banks about the use of intangible assets as loan collateral and has served as an expert witness regarding intellectual property infringement damages.

Mr. Parr is also publisher of the highly respected *Licensing Economics Review* which is dedicated to reporting detailed information about the economic aspects of intellectual property licensing and joint venturing. Mr. Parr has a bachelor of science (BS) in electrical engineering, and a masters in business administration (MBA) from Rutgers University. He is currently pursuing a Ph.D. in International Business Management at Rutgers. His professional credentials include designations as a Chartered Financial Analyst and an Accredited Senior Appraiser of the American Society of Appraisers. Mr. Parr is a member of the New York Society of Security Analysts and Licensing Executives Society. He is also on the Board of Directors of the Rutgers Alumni Association and a regular guest lecturer at the Franklin Pierce Law Center.

Among Mr. Parr's writings are four books, published by John Wiley & Sons, titled:

Investing In Intangible Assets: Finding and Profiting From Hidden Corporate Value

Valuation of Intellectual Property and Intangible Assets, (co-author)

Intellectual Property: Licensing and Joint Venture Profit Strategies (co-author)

Intellectual Property Infringement Damages: A Litigation Support Handbook

Preface

This book is about ideas and money—their interaction and interdependence. Ideas need money capital in order to grow and bear fruit. Without this earth and water, the seeds of innovation will wither and die. Everyone who picks up this book owns some intellectual property. Everyone has thought of a story, a character, or a design that is new. Every business enterprise has several innovations within it. Some are buried; some are on the surface. What does it take to turn these innovations into a profitable product in the marketplace? Money (one's own, or someone else's) and the tools to know "the wheat from the chaff". . .

This book is about what happens in that boundary area between creation and commerce. This boundary zone is inhabited by those of us who are neither creatures of the deep (creativity) or of the land (commerce). We seek to provide a bridge between, and the skills that are required are varied indeed. There are matters of law (since intellectual property exists through the law), and there are matters of economics, investment theory, business, and plain common sense. The need for these skills grows daily, as the cutting edge of technology widens and moves ever faster. Our primary focus is to provide some tools for those who operate in this "Twilight Zone" between the inventor, artist, writer, technician, or photographer, the law, and the business enterprise within which all this happens.

Each day, the business press reports another major licensing deal or joint venture that is centered on intellectual property. This is because the most important business strategy for the next decade and beyond involves optimal exploitation of intellectual property using unique arrangements like licensing agreements and joint ventures. This book will focus on the most important aspect of this trend—economic returns from the exploitation of intellectual property. Our focus is the financial earning power of patents, trademarks, copyrights, and other forms of proprietary know-how.

Surprisingly, this is a most neglected subject. Books, magazines, and trade journals are providing excellent coverage about the legal and strategic aspects of licensing and joint ventures, but very little has been written about the economic considerations that are so crucial to successful intellectual property exploitation.

The primary objective of the book is to answer two vital questions: 1) How much should I get for contributing my intellectual property to a joint venture?, and 2) How much royalty should I get for letting someone else use my intellectual property as part of a licensing arrangement?

The audience for this book includes licensing executives, strategic planners, patent attorneys, accountants, litigation attorneys, research and development executives, scientists and inventors. This book will help business leaders to optimize the exploitation of intellectual property. Specific objectives of the book are to:

1) examine and analyze the business economics of strategies involving intellectual property; licensing and joint venturing

2) provide flexible analytical models that can be used to determine fair royalty rates for licensing transactions
3) provide flexible models that can be used for determining equity splits in joint venture arrangements
4) present examples of exploitation strategies being used by major corporations
5) identify the weaknesses associated with royalty rate derivation techniques in common use.

Included in this book are specific industry analyses that isolate the economic contribution of intellectual property, including pharmaceutical technology, industrial equipment, specialty chemicals, cosmetics, world-class trademarks, and other keystone intellectual property. An Appendix also presents a collection of licensing royalty rates that were recently negotiated within a variety of industries.

Corporate value hinges not on the operation of production assets, but on the optimal financial exploitation of intellectual property. We provide in this book a disciplined approach to quantifying royalty rates and joint venture equity splits.

GORDON V. SMITH *Moorestown, NJ*
RUSSELL L. PARR *Yardley, PA*

Contents

1

Emergence of Intellectual Property Exploitation Strategies

Strategic alliances will dominate the corporate landscape far into the future as the primary strategy for creating corporate value. At the core of these strategies will be intellectual property—especially technology and trademarks. Licensing deals and joint ventures will become the dominant forms for optimizing intellectual property exploitation strategies.

When a trademark or patent is licensed to another corporation, continuing royalty payments are usually part of the transaction. When intellectual property assets are contributed to a joint venture company, equity ownership is usually the reward. This book is all about royalty rates and joint venture financial structuring. This book presents quantitative methodologies for answering two vital questions: How much royalty should a licensor get?, and How much equity should an intellectual property contributor expect from a joint venture?

Intellectual properties, such as patented technology and world class trademarks, are at the very core of corporate success. These assets capture huge market shares, command premium prices, and hold customer loyalty. They are also in scarce supply and expensive to create. Companies that possess such assets will grow and prosper. Those without access to intellectual property will stagnate for awhile in low-profit commodity businesses and eventually fade out of existence.

In *Microcosm: The Quantum Revolution in Economics and Technology*, George Gilder explains that wealth is no longer derived from possessing physical resources. "Wealth and power came mainly to the possessor of material things or to the ruler of military forces capable of conquering the physical means of production: land, labor, and capital." Gilder explains that: "Today, the ascendant nations and corporations are masters not of land and material resources but of ideas and technologies.''

D. Bruce Merrifield, Professor of Entrepreneurial Management, The Wharton School of the University of Pennsylvania, echoed this theme in an article entitled ''Economics in Technology Licensing,'' *les Nouvelles,* June 1992: ''Wealth no longer can be measured primarily in terms of ownership of fixed physical assets that can be obsolete in a few years. . . Wealth instead will be measured, increasingly, in terms of ownership of (or time-critical access to) knowledge-intensive high value-added, technology-intensive systems.''

Of special interest is Prof. Merrifield's parenthetical highlighting of the time-sensitive nature associated with intellectual property. Not only do companies need these knowledge-based assets, but they need them right now. Time is one of the primary forces that will be featured throughout this book as driving the trend towards strategic alliances. Time is also a major force that drives royalty rates and joint venture equity splits.

Before analyzing the more subtle forces driving companies into strategic alliances, the following few graphs will show the fundamental reason that intellectual property has become the central issue in strategic planning; intellectual property is responsible for superior stock performance. Companies possessing proprietary intellectual property are creating corporate value.

CORPORATE VALUE COMES FROM INTELLECTUAL PROPERTY

A comparison of stock market value with accounting book value for selected companies indicates that the investment community recognizes the value of intellectual properties in a big way. Expenditures that are made for land, factory buildings, office headquarters, truck fleets, and manufacturing equipment are all capitalized and presented as assets on the balance sheet. Funds spent to acquire or build these assets become part of the equity of the company to the extent that their value exceeds liabilities. Stock prices typically include the value of these assets. A question arises, however, about the extent to which the market price of a stock reflects the intellectual properties of trademarks and technology. Just like fixed assets, funds are expended to build trademarks through advertising. Other funds are used to create trade secrets and technology through research and development efforts. The expenditures, however, are not recorded onto the balance sheet, but the assets are indeed quite real. The market recognizes these assets, and reflects their value in stock prices, as shown in the following analyses.

A ratio of the market price of a common stock divided by the accounting book value of the same stock yields the market-to-book ratio. If intellectual properties are not present at a company, then the price of a stock would very likely be close to the book value. The ratio of market price to book value would equal approximately 1.0. Utility companies are an excellent example. The earnings of electric and gas utilities are regulated by governmental agencies. The companies are allowed to set prices for their services at a level that earns a fair rate of return on the net book value of the assets that are used in the business. Intellectual properties are not typically considered as a part of the rate base, so only the fixed asset investment can serve as the basis for the earning power of the company. Utility stocks, as a result, tend to trade at a price that is approximately equal to the book value of the investment.

When valuable technology, trademarks, or other intellectual properties are present among unregulated businesses, they contribute to the earnings of the company far above the contribution of the fixed assets. Stock prices reflect this earnings power and trade above the book value of the stock, sometimes substantially.

TRADEMARKS DELIVER CORPORATE VALUE

A regression analysis of advertising expenditures was conducted to see if the market recognizes the long-term value of the trademarks that are being created and maintained by advertising expenditures. The analysis compared the market-to-book value ratio of selected companies with the amounts spent on advertising. The analysis shows that advertising expenditures are seen as asset-building investments that deserve recognition in the stock price. Figure 1.1 shows that as the amounts of advertising expenditures (shown as a percentage of revenues for each company) increase, the price of the stock above book value also increases. The companies selected were taken from a list that annually

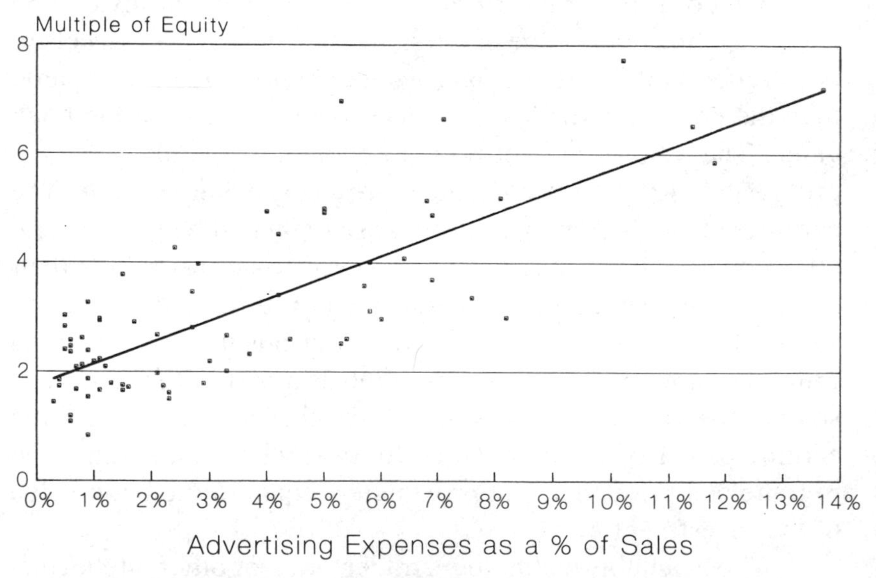

Figure 1.1 Market Multiples Related to Advertising Expenses

Source: Gordon V. Smith and Russell L. Parr, *Valuation of Intellectual Property and Intangible Assets, 1992 Cumulative Supplement* (New York: John Wiley & Sons, 1992), p. 21. Reprinted by permission of John Wiley & Sons, Inc.

appears in *Advertising Age* of companies which have spent the most amount of money on advertising. As advertisement spending increased, the market-to-book value increased.

A lack of correlation would have indicated that the market did not recognize the value of the trademarks. But the trademarks that are created by advertisement spending are highly valued intellectual property.

Companies that spend the most on advertising are either creating or maintaining valuable trademarks. It follows that companies spending the most money have some of the best known names. The question is: "Do well-known trademarks contribute to stock performance?" The answer is definitely "Yes."

The following analysis first appeared in *Investing in Intangible Assets—Finding and Profiting From Hidden Corporate Value,* published by John Wiley & Sons in 1991. It shows that, without a doubt, intellectual property contributes to high stock prices and the creation of corporate value.

Each year, *Advertising Age* compiles a list of the "100 Leading National Advertisers." To make the list in 1990, companies had to spend over $108 million in the prior year. Philip Morris took the number one spot by spending over $2.0 billion in advertising to support its portfolio of famous trademarks. In aggregate, the Top 100 spent $32.2 billion in 1989. This spending created and maintained well-known trademarks. This spending, and the trademarks that are created, translates to positive stock performance.

A regression analysis is presented in Figure 1.2. It shows the relationship between advertisement spending and investment rates of return. For each company in the Top 100, advertising expenses were calculated as a percentage of company sales. This spending level was then compared to the investment rate of return achieved from a ten-year investment in the company stock. Figure 1.2 shows that higher amounts of advertising on trademarks yields higher investment returns.

Over the last ten years, the companies in the Top 100 have remained relatively stable. Consistent advertising is fundamental to nurturing and maintaining a trademark. As an example, the Top Ten advertisers have changed little:

Consistent Advertisers

Top Ten 1980	Top Ten 1990
Procter & Gamble	Philip Morris
General Foods	Procter & Gamble
Sears, Roebuck	General Motors
General Motors	Sears, Roebuck
Philip Morris	RJR Nabisco
K Mart	Grand Metropolitan
RJR Reynolds	Eastman Kodak
Warner-Lambert	McDonald's
AT&T	PepsiCo
Ford Motor	Kellogg

General Foods is still among the Top Ten as part of Philip Morris, which acquired the company in the mid-1980s. RJR Reynolds is also still in the Top Ten, but it is currently a private company that is combined with NABISCO trademarks. Many companies have combined operations during the mergers boom, but the Top 100 advertisers are still mostly comprised of the same club members with the same valuable names, regardless of ownership. Analysis of the stock performance of the companies that own famous trademarks reflects the contribution to investment performance made by trademarks.

The analysis could not include all of the Top 100. Over half

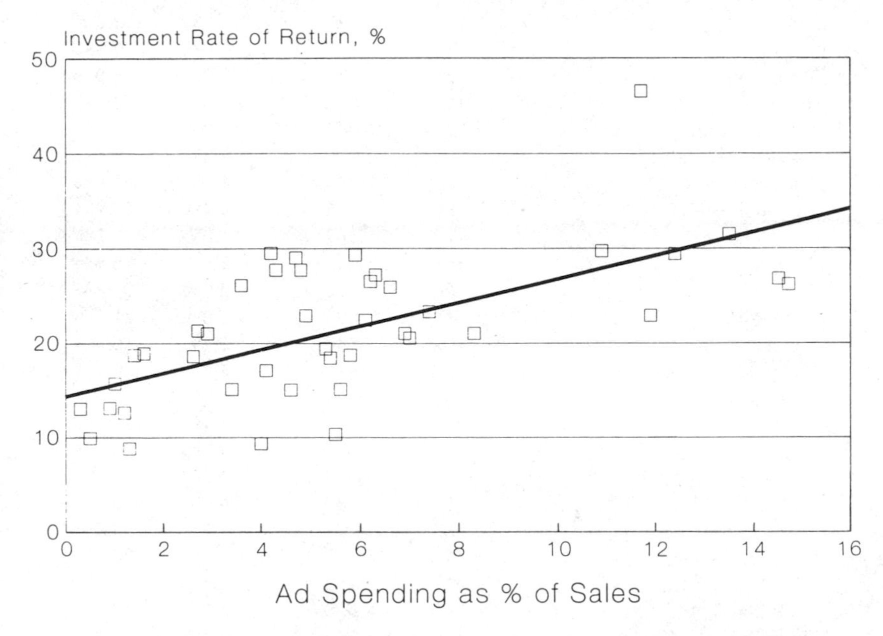

Figure 1.2 Ad Spending and Investment Returns

of the big spenders had to be eliminated because they were private companies without public stock price information, like Mars, Inc., or they were nonprofit institutions, such as the Dairy Farmers Association. The trend presented in Figure 1.2 clearly indicates that trademarks are associated with superior investment performance. The companies that comprise the trend data are listed in Figure 1.3.

Over the same ten-year period the S&P 400 index showed a compound rate of return of 11.8%. A ten-year investment in the Dow Jones Industrial Average of 30 stocks would have provided a compound return of 12.0%. Of the 43 companies that were ultimately included in the study, all but three showed significantly better stock appreciation. The 40 winners have famous trade-

Company	1990 Ad Spending ($ millions)	1990 Revenues	Ad Spending as a % of Revenues	R O I
Mobil	156	55,432	0.3%	13.0%
IBM	214	41,586	0.5%	9.9%
Ford Motor	570	82,879	0.7%	26.0%
Dow Chemical	157	17,600	0.9%	13.1%
American Express	247	25,047	1.0%	15.7%
General Motors	1,294	109,610	1.2%	12.6%
Goodyear	125	10,869	1.2%	8.8%
American Brands	169	11,921	1.4%	18.7%
Chrysler	474	30,567	1.6%	18.9%
Seagram	143	5,582	2.6%	18.6%
CPC Intl.	134	5,103	2.6%	21.3%
Whitman	112	3,895	2.9%	21.0%
Marriott	120	3,546	3.4%	15.1%
Campbell Soup	203	5,672	3.6%	26.1%
Eastman Kodak	736	18,398	4.0%	9.3%
Pfizer	230	5,672	4.1%	17.1%
Gillette	161	3,819	4.2%	29.5%
Coca-Cola	385	8,966	4.3%	27.7%
MCA	154	3,382	4.6%	15.0%
Philip Morris	2,058	44,759	4.6%	29.0%
PepsiCo	712	15,242	4.7%	27.7%
Bristol-Myers Squibb	431	9,189	4.7%	22.9%
American Cyanamid	256	4,825	5.3%	19.4%
Time Warner	410	7,642	5.4%	18.4%
Tandy	232	4,181	5.5%	10.3%
SmithKline Beecham	264	4,749	5.6%	15.1%
American Home Products	393	6,747	5.8%	18.7%
H.J. Heinz	340	5,801	5.9%	29.3%
Colgate-Palmolive	307	5,039	6.1%	22.4%
Anheuser-Busch	635	10,284	6.2%	26.5%
Ralston Purina	421	6,658	6.3%	27.2%
Walt Disney	301	4,594	6.6%	25.9%
Johnson & Johnson	469	6,757	6.9%	21.0%
Procter & Gamble	1,507	21,398	7.0%	20.5%
Quaker Oats	423	5,724	7.4%	23.3%
Schering-Plough	262	3,158	8.3%	21.0%
Clorox	148	1,356	10.9%	29.7%
Hasbro	165	1,410	11.7%	46.5%
McDonald's	728	6,142	11.9%	22.9%
Hershey Foods	299	2,421	12.4%	29.4%
Wrigley	134	993	13.5%	31.5%
Warner-Lambert	609	4,196	14.5%	26.8%
Kellogg	683	4,652	14.7%	26.2%
S&P 400				11.8%
DJIA 30				12.0%

Figure 1.3 Advertisement Spending Related to Investment Performance

marks, all of which powerfully contributed to superior stock returns.

TECHNOLOGY DELIVERS CORPORATE VALUE

Another example using research and development expenditures confirms that the marketplace reflects the value of intellectual property in stock prices. Figure 1.4 shows a regression analysis of R&D spending (as a percentage of revenues) for selected pharmaceutical companies with the market-to-book value ratio for the same companies. As spending levels grow, the market rewards the company price with a higher market to book multiple, not because investors reward endless spending, but because valuable intellectual properties are being created.

The primary benefit derived from continually nurturing intellectual properties is best exemplified by the technology of the pharmaceutical industry. An analysis of six pharmaceutical companies shows that continued support of research efforts are rewarded. The number of patents awarded to these companies when compared to the ten-year compounded rate of return earned by investors shows that superior investment returns are associated with the research efforts that yielded patents. Figure 1.5 shows the number of patents that were granted to six companies between 1979 and 1988. The total number of patents for the entire period is also presented, along with the ten-year investment returns earned by holding the stock of these companies.

Warner-Lambert shows the highest rate of return at 24.4%. Second place goes to Merck with the highest number of patents, but investors only achieved a 23.9% return. Merck received 1283 patents between 1979 and 1988, but investors in the stock earned slightly less. The slight advantage of Warner-Lambert may be attributed to the rapid pace at which the company obtained patents since 1984, when it obtained only 49 patents. By 1989, it obtained 113.

Upjohn received 1178 patents during the period, but only provided a 21.0% rate of return to investors. Of all the companies, Upjohn received the lowest number of patents in the most recent year, 1988. As the number of patents falls, the rate of return is lower. Generally, the relationship between recently obtained patents and investment returns prevails, providing another example of the vital role that intellectual property plays in delivering corporate value.

Huge value comes from possessing proprietary intellectual property. Without it, all that remains is an idle manufacturing plant where employees aimlessly wander.

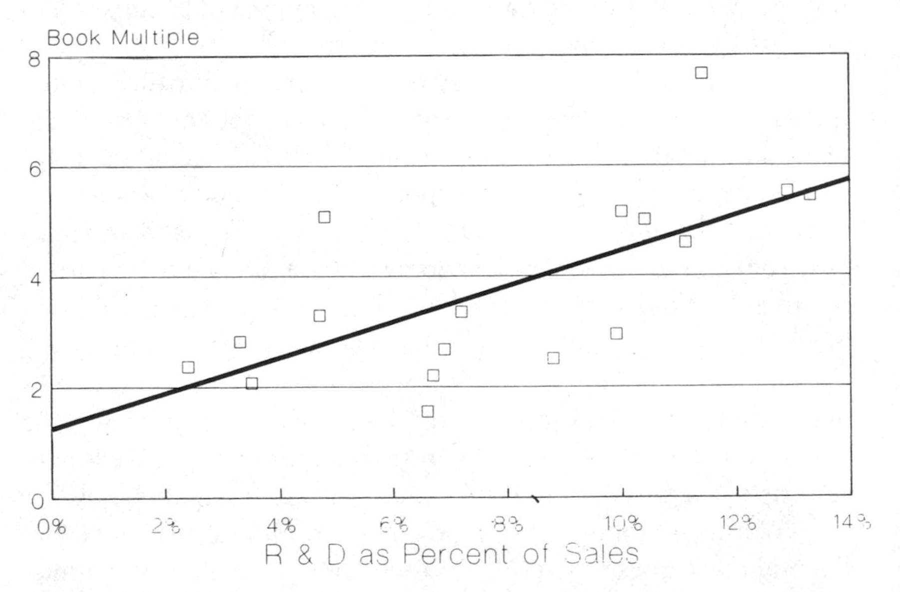

Figure 1.4 Market Multiples and R&D Spending: Pharmaceutical Industry

Source: Gordon V. Smith and Russell L. Parr, *Valuation of Intellectual Property and Intangible Assets, 1992 Cumulative Supplement* (New York: John Wiley & Sons, 1992), p. 22. Reprinted by permission of John Wiley & Sons, Inc.

Company	Total Patents 1979–1988	Compound Investment Return	NUMBER OF PATENTS ISSUED PER YEAR									
			1988	1987	1986	1985	1984	1983	1982	1981	1980	1979
Warner–Lambert	622	24.4%	113	118	101	73	49	34	25	37	36	36
Merck	1283	23.9%	125	123	103	105	135	114	135	160	156	127
Upjohn	1178	21.0%	15	26	66	66	107	73	122	337	170	196
Eli Lilly	881	20.7%	68	85	82	107	80	74	104	112	85	84
American Home Products	444	20.5%	69	46	38	49	32	24	43	52	52	39
Pfizer	728	17.3%	63	67	72	72	89	61	72	92	75	65

Figure 1.5 Drug Industry: Patents and Investment Returns

THE FACTORS THAT DRIVE STRATEGIC ALLIANCES: TIME, COST, RISK

Companies are seeking to expand product lines, increase market share, minimize new product development costs, expand market opportunities internationally, and reduce business risks. Companies are seeking to create corporate value for investors. The prior analyses show that intellectual property can powerfully contribute to corporate value. But intellectual property is even more important. Without intellectual property, profits are low, growth is lacking, and corporate value is lost. Corporate managers realize more than ever that access to intellectual property is key to their ability to create corporate value, and more importantly, key to continued corporate survival. The forces driving the licensing and joint venturing of intellectual property include time savings, cost controls, and risk reduction.

TOO EXPENSIVE ON YOUR OWN

Even the largest companies cannot fund all of the intellectual property programs that they may desire. Research programs can run into hundreds of millions of dollars annually, and trademark development costs can reach billions of dollars. A major force behind the desire to form strategic alliances is the high level of investment needed to create new intellectual properties. The list below provides an indication of the amounts required to create, acquire, or protect keystone intellectual property:

- Pharmaceutical companies spend almost $250 million to develop and commercialize a new drug.
- Hoffman LaRoche paid $300 million to Cetus Corporation for the Polymerase Chain Reaction technology.

- American Brands paid $372.5 million to acquire seven liquor brand names from Seagram.
- Philip Morris spends over $2 billion annually on advertising programs to support the continuing recognition of its portfolio of brand names.
- A film producer paid $9 million for the television rights to the new book *Scarlet*.
- At auction, Doubleday made the winning bid of $4 million for the memoirs of Sam Walton.

One of the first major joint ventures of the 1990s was the combination of pharmaceutical product lines from DuPont with the distribution network of Merck & Co. The new joint venture company is equally owned by the two companies. Its name is DuPont–Merck. DuPont had a product line of drugs, but needed help with international distribution. The time and cost needed to create their own network of sales staff was a formidable obstacle to fast growth and return on the research effort that DuPont had in the new drug line. Part of DuPont's worries included the remaining patent life associated with some of their drug products. By the time a self-created distribution network was established, some of the valuable products would be off patent. Full exploitation of patents required that sales be maximized during the premium price years that would exist before generic products hit the market. DuPont needed a way to tap its full market potential fast.

Merck has annual sales that run above $6.5 billion. It also has one of the largest research and development budgets in the world. Even so, Merck has limitations as to the number of new drugs that it can discover, investigate, develop, and commercialize. Access to a new line of already commercialized products was a great attraction to Merck.

The DuPont–Merck joint venture saved DuPont both time and money. It gave DuPont immediate access—a vital point made by Prof. Merrifield—to an international distribution network. Merck gained immediate access to a whole new product line that would have cost enormous amounts of time and money to develop. This joint venture is a classic case of how the factors of time and cost drive strategic alliances which are founded on access to intellectual property. It also illustrates how strategic combinations of key intellectual property can reduce the investment risk associated with new strategies. If DuPont had attempted to build its own international distribution network, the cost would have been high, the time needed long, and there was no assurance that it would successfully construct a network that could move the goods. Merck enjoyed a reduction in investment risk by gaining access to the profits associated with the DuPont product line. If Merck had embarked on its own plan to duplicate the DuPont product line, there was no assurance that they would have been completely successful. Further, there existed the risk that the Merck product line could have ultimately infringed on the DuPont product line. The two companies saved research funds, gained immediate access to commercialized intellectual property, and reduced business risk. Judy Lewent, Chief Financial Officer at Merck & Co., told *The Wall Street Journal* that the Merck–DuPont deal "added about a third to our research capacity" ("Financial Prescriptions for Mighty Merck," *The Wall Street Journal*, June 30, 1992, p. A17).

The cost to establish and maintain world-class trademarks is no different. Huge sums of money are required, and customer recognition takes time. One of the first mega-launches of a new product in the cosmetics industry was Yves Saint Laurent's 1978 "OPIUM" party to introduce his new fragrance. In attendance were Cher, Truman Capote, BBC correspondents, the crew of *60 Minutes*, and leaders of the fashion industry. The party cost $250,000, which in 1978 was a staggering amount for a single party to launch a new product. The total launch budget was $500,000. In turns out that those were inexpensive times. Similar launch budgets now run between $20 and $25 million. Joseph Spellman, Executive Vice President at Elizabeth Arden, said: "Today everything is global . . . The competitive level is way up. The packaging, concept, advertising, staging—all of it has to be fabulous. The attention is always on big productions, so launches have escalated to mega proportions."

The reason for the high costs to launch new product names was simply and accurately described by Edith Weiner, President of Weiner, Edrich, Brown, Inc., trend trackers and marketing strategists, when she told *Mirabella* magazine, "There's a product glut . . . It's getting harder and harder to get people's attention."

First quarter spending during 1991 shows the huge sums needed to maintain the top ten mega-brands. The amounts:

Top 10 Mega-Brands
1991 First Quarter
Advertisement Spending

MCDONALD'S	$95 million
FORD	$90 million
CHEVROLET	$89 million
KELLOGG	$77 million
AT&T	$67 million
TOYOTA	$66 million
SEARS	$63 million
KRAFT	$55 million
OLDSMOBILE	$47 million
PEPSI	$46 million

These amounts represent ad spending for only three months of 1991. McDonald's might spend $400 million before 1991 ends.

These are the amounts being spent to maintain and nurture well-established world-class brands. It is no small wonder that brand name licensing at almost any price is less expensive and far less risky than building a new name from the ground up.

CUSTOMER ATTITUDES IN THE 1990s HAVE CHANGED

Product companies have learned the hard way that the congenial relationship between mass production and mass consumption is at an end. The large homogeneous market that propelled the old mass manufacturing model is gone. In its place is a new fragmented market with highly specialized niches comprised of very sophisticated consumers. Instead of a mass production driven system where consumers wanted whatever was produced, the world has shifted to a market that is dominated by mass customization. Custom products possessing quality and priced to deliver "value" are in demand. Products are now required to deliver high utility at reasonable prices. During the 80s, faster, shinier, larger, golder products ruled the day at any price. In fact, price was part of the reason for a lot of the product demand. Now, a more mature and sober population of consumers is forcing companies to deliver performance at a realistic price—"value." This new market demands innovation and differentiation. Service companies are not immune either. Demand for flexible financial planning products has accelerated too. Whole life insurance policies just do not make it anymore. Highly specialized policies are required: the kind that have different investment options, different pay-out options, and reflect in their premium the improved risk of nonsmokers. Companies reacting to these fundamental changes are finding that they do not always possess all of the technological and marketing skills needed to quickly address the new demands of consumers. They need help. They are strategically aligning to fill the gaps.

> Affluent double-income baby boom couples, who spent a lot of money in the 1980s on things like expensive consumer electronics, personal gadgets, BMWs and Club Med, are now shifting their spending to their homes and families.—*Ira Kalish, an economist with Management Horizons, a market research company.*

> *We are seeing different parents than we served [even] five years ago . . . We're serving clients who are 28 to 35, the second half of the baby boom. They are more pragmatic, less idealistic and more stressed out.—John Kaegi, Senior Vice President for Kinder-Care Learning Centers.*

To compete in such a market environment, companies are forced to optimize their particular skills and know-how while quickly filling gaps that they are discovering in their capabilities. This new and demanding environment is forcing many companies, lost in the change-resistant, not-invented-here mentality, to accept their limitations and seek out partners to help them quickly, efficiently, and safely respond to the dramatically changing marketplace.

IMPOSSIBILITY OF MASTERING ALL THE NECESSARY TOOLS

A new battery that stores electricity mechanically instead of chemically may be the breakthrough needed to make electric powered automobiles a reality. The new technology may possibly power a car for 600 miles on a single charge. Conventional chemical-based batteries currently available have a range potential of 100 miles at the most. The technology is the product of American Flywheel Systems, a company comprised of former scientists from the Environmental Protection Agency and military aerospace researchers. The new battery is referred to as a flywheel electromechanical battery which stores energy kinetically. It operates on the same principle that drives the ancient potter's wheel. A heavy mass rotates at a very high speed inside a vacuum enclosure suspended by magnetic bearings and controlled by sophisticated electronics.

The first electric car was created 100 years ago. But chemical batteries required frequent recharging. The old batteries also involved toxic wastes, subjected other car components to corrosives, and introduced an explosion potential. Flywheel batteries were studied in the 1970s, but could not be perfected until recently. Advanced technological development in three separate fields of science were required before the flywheel battery could become viable. Advances in composite materials, computers, and electromagnetics were all required to make the flywheel battery a reality.

A confluence of three critical technologies was needed to make the flywheel battery a viable technology. Lightweight but strong materials, such as graphite, DuPont's KEVELAR, the Japanese-made TECHNORA, and fused silica, have come into being recently. In 1990, the Army tested a flywheel battery which used graphite components having a tensile strength of 52,000 pounds per square inch. Graphite now has a tensile strength of 1 million pounds per square inch. The second critical breakthrough has occurred in computer power. Faster computers allow the performance of millions of calculations and the simulation of thousands of prototypes. This breakthrough allows scientists to more quickly turn ideas into working machines. The third direct scientific advance involved the development of magnetic bearings. These electromagnetic fields allow objects to spin in vacuums without friction.

All of these technologies are needed for one product idea. But what company can master all the necessary science alone? None. And that is why we are seeing more strategic alliances.

The critical technologies that will cause major and fundamental restructuring in major segments of business are highly complex and cost vast sums to investigate and develop. According to Prof. Merrifield and others, they include:

Advanced Materials

- Electronic materials
- Ceramics
- Composites
- High-performance metals
- High-performance alloys

Biotechnology

- Diagnostics
- Medical instruments
- Drug delivery systems
- Molecular biology therapies

Information Processing and Storage

- Microelectronics
- High-performance computer networks
- Data storage

- Sensor and signal processing
- Computer simulation

Manufacturing Techniques

- Computer integrated processing
- Microfabrication capabilities
- Systems management technologies
- "Smart" processing equipment

Transportation Systems

- Aeronautics
- Surface transport technologies

Energy and Environmental Technologies

- Long-distance power transmission
- Pollution minimization systems
- Waste management technologies

Technology is becoming more complex. Investigating any one of these critical technology areas requires a multidiscipline understanding of a wide variety of sciences such as physics, chemistry, and electronics. Advanced knowledge in each discipline is required, not just one specialty and a superficial understanding of the others. Corporations are a lot like people. A professional architect with expertise in marina design cannot cope with the complexities of modern life without outside assistance. Tax preparation services, medical treatment, lawn services, and many other areas of individual expertise must be acquired from others in order for the architect to cope. Corporations, too, have their specialized areas of expertise, but to deliver the products of tomorrow, these specialized corporations will need to incorporate into their products advanced aspects of different technologies. This will require specialized knowledge that they do not possess, and will require them to get outside assistance through strategic alliances.

Speaking to *The Wall Street Journal* about pocket-size cellular telephones, where wireless telecommunications technology must be integrated with portable computing, information services, and satellite technological know-how, John Sculley, Chief Executive Officer of Apple Computer, Inc., said: "no one can go it alone anymore" ("Getting Help; High-Tech Firms Find It's Good to Line Up Outside Contractors," *The Wall Street Journal*, July 29, 1992, p. A1).

A SHORT HISTORY OF CORPORATE STRATEGIES

How did we get here? Most of the time, the primary goal of business strategies has been to create corporate (shareholder) value. The big question is: How did we get to a new era where intellectual property is at the center of business strategies? The trail includes stops at:

- Management science magic, where large egos thought they could rule the day and run any company anytime.
- Acquisition fever, where large egos thought that they saw unrealized value while everyone else was asleep.
- Financial management magic, where, once again, egos bellowed that this time the trick to higher value was higher risk tolerance.

MANAGEMENT SCIENCE MAGIC

In the 1960s, business strategies were driven by diversification and integration strategies. Diversification spread economic risks among many businesses to counter the negative effects of being too focused in cyclical industries. Integration merged manufacturing, raw materials suppliers, and distribution networks to bring control and profits from indirectly related activities under one corporate roof.

Manufacturing companies acquired raw material suppliers. Then finance companies and other vaguely related businesses became desirable. As acquisitions hit stride in the 1960s, completely unrelated businesses were combed into a portfolio of diversified business investments. Anything and everything was a potential acquisition target.

The underlying notion was that acquirers would introduce *management* science and centralized control, thereby enhancing the value of all of the portfolio components. Management science would be the missing element of magic that would make the combined entities more powerful, successful, and profitable than when the businesses were independent. "Conglomerate" was a descriptive term that managers eagerly sought to have bestowed upon their company. It carried images of power and expansive management skills. With superior organizational skills founded in management science, the acquirers of the 1960s thought that they could manage any business. Understanding the nature of the business did not matter. Overreaching occurred, and conglomerate builders found that more than a little knowledge about the business was needed.

> Gulf & Western started life as a manufacturer of automotive parts, but following the fad of the 60s, the company embarked on a buying binge which eventually included completely unrelated business interests—Par-

amount Pictures, Desilu Productions, South Puerto Rico Sugar Company, Provident Washington Insurance, Consolidated Cigar Company, and Madison Square Garden.

ITT managed international telephone systems and manufactured telephone equipment when the portfolio acquisition fever struck in the early 1960s. Before the decade was out, the following dissimilar businesses were part of the ITT conglomerate—Continental Baking, Avis Car Rental, Sheraton Hotels, Hartford Steam Boiler Insurance, and Grinnell.

In the 1970s, United Airlines sought to build a travel company empire. Acquisitions were made that would integrate all aspects of travel. The collection included Hertz Rental Car Company, Hilton Hotels, and Westin Hotels.

Huge and unwieldy corporate structures were needed just to monitor the performance of the unrelated businesses which comprised these conglomerates. Long delays occurred in decision making, and strategy meetings with *Corporate* killed any inventive ideas that were developed at the operating level. Often, the accounting systems used to monitor one of the conglomerate components was completely unworkable for monitoring other components. Management time was spent studying the portfolio rather than managing the business. Instead of gaining investment performance from portfolio diversification, the centralized control structures introduced anti-synergistic costs of time and money. In almost all cases, the conglomerates have failed. Stock performances for these portfolios of management science were dismal. Companies soon learned that management science magic was a false deity. Conglomerates were dismantled, and managers did everything possible to shed the dark shadow that accompanied the once coveted descriptive word—conglomerate.

EXCESS ASSET MAGIC

Acquisitions of the late 70s and early 80s focused on the value of excess assets. These assets were on the balance sheet, but were not adequately reflected in the stock price. They included real estate, cash hoards, and resource reserves like timberland and oil, especially oil.

Companies that had excess assets were the delight of acquirers who wanted to restructure and enhance. If the excess asset was cash, the company could be acquired, and then the cash was issued as a special dividend or used to pay-down the debt associated with the purchase of the company. In some cases, the target company's own cash was used to finance part of the takeover. If the excess asset was real estate, then after acquiring the company, sale–leasebacks were put into effect. Valuable land and buildings were sold to institutional investors as safe investments providing the acquired company with cash. A long-term lease allowed the company to continue to use the property.

In the case of oil, acquirers went on a binge. T. Boone Pickens, Jr. was trained as a petroleum geologist. In the late 1970s, the cost to find oil was about $15 per barrel, and oil prices were rising as fast as the OPEC nations could schedule price-fixing conferences. The stock exchange became an easier place to search for oil reserves than in the Indonesian jungles. The stock market was perceived to be undervaluing the stocks of asset-rich companies. On the stock exchange, the cost could be as low as $5 per barrel if the deal were priced right.

As with all good ideas, other people quickly saw the benefits and joined the party. Bidding wars erupted, bargains disappeared, and the game abruptly ended.

FINANCING MAGIC

The most recent business strategy involving acquisition fever has been fueled by the idea that a little more debt and a willingness to accept just a little more risk would shower profits on those who knew how to introduce financing magic. Acquirers during this period focused on the introduction of financing capabilities, once again not caring about the business they were buying, and often not even understanding the business. Leveraged buy-outs fueled acquisitions during the late 1980s. Raiders looked to enhance investments by using more aggressive financial structures. At times, the restructuring made a lot of sense.

LBOs combined an aggressive leverage strategy with the excess asset concept. Instead of gaining access to particular assets like cash and real estate, takeover artists focused on entire business units that they considered as undervalued or completely unrepresented in the stock price of the target company.

Initially, it can be argued that raiders contributed in a positive way to corporate America. Leverage buy-outs provided a means to get corporate America back on track. Overbloated corporate executives who ignored shareholders just had to go. They spent money on lavish perks, gave themselves extraordinary bonuses, even in poor performance years, and acted more like caretakers. It seemed that the attitude of corporate managers was: Why take risks when mediocrity can get you eight-figure compensation packages?

LBOs provided a means to get rid of these timid managers and return America's business power to the hands of managers who had a financial stake in the business' success. Once again, however, good ideas are often extended far beyond realistic applications. Early successes in LBOs caught the attention of many raiders. Bidding wars erupted again, and the bargains disappeared. Watching the devastating effect of "just a little" more debt is going to be a sad legacy of the 1980s.

CHANGING STRATEGIES

The earliest strategy was industry domination. A growth company would capture a huge market position, and the value of the company would soar along with growing sales volume. The next step led to vertical and horizontal integration of operations. Suppliers were acquired, and distribution outlets were also folded into the dominating company's portfolio. Stock prices continued to rise until all forms of integration were optimized. Mature markets led to stagnation, and stock prices stopped rising.

From industry domination, the next strategy was to build a conglomerate. Managers could be heard to say: "I can dominate my core business and all others that I choose." The strategy involved doing for new acquisitions what the managers had done for their core business. Unwieldy portfolios of unrelated companies could not be controlled, and stock prices not only stopped climbing—they dropped.

Since core operations were optimized and conglomerate building did not work, the next playground, after divestitures erased the conglomerate, was to turn on the financial strategy. Managers yelled from penthouse offices: "I can tolerate risk and leverage my way to riches." This disastrous strategy was taken to the extreme, as usually happens with a good idea, and it almost seems that the ground still shakes when a leveraged balloon of a company comes crashing down.

Have we finally grown up? Maybe so. The failures of the past business strategies coupled with new global pressures have caused managers to focus on what they know best and to get assistance to fill corporate capability gaps. Managers are heard to say, although with less fanfare than the previous announcements, "I can't do it all alone—I need help." Hence, we are entering the age of strategic alliances where licensing deals and joint ventures rule. The focus has finally changed—"You help me and I'll help you."

LOOK AT WHAT THEY WANT NOW—THE MAGIC OF INTELLECTUAL PROPERTIES

Reviewing the annual reports and other public statements of business leaders shows that the paths being taken by successful corporations will include strategic alliances centered on intellectual property exploitation.

From the 1991 annual report of Imo Industries, Inc., a leading manufacturer of analytical and optical instruments used in the industrial and defense industries. . .

> Our increasing focus on international markets is underscored by the fact that almost 40% of IMOs overall revenue comes from outside the United States. . . Around the globe, we are increasingly utilizing joint venture structures to develop opportunities.

From a press release quoting Sidney Taurel, Executive Vice President of Eli Lilly & Company, a leading pharmaceutical maker. . .

> Strategic alliances, co-marketing agreements, and licensing agreements have become vital to the continued success of the pharmaceutical industry and an important part of Lilly's strategic direction.

From a press release quoting Dr. Glen Bradley, Chief Executive Officer of Ciba Vision Worldwide, a vision care company. . .

> The combination of internal research and development at Ciba and licensing agreements, such as the newly announced 3M license, allows Ciba Vision to fulfill our mission of developing quality products and services

> which will best satisfy our customer needs and expectations.

From the 1991 annual report of The Liposome Company, Inc., a leading-edge biotechnology company. . .

> The Liposome Company has licensed TLC ABLC (a new antifungal therapy) to Bristol-Myers Squibb. Pharmaceutical development and manufacturing scale-up have been a co-development effort of the two companies. Bristol-Myers Squibb is responsible worldwide for conducting all clinical trials and will handle all sales, marketing and commercial manufacturing. The Liposome Company will be paid royalties on all sales of the product, worldwide.

As the 90s unfold, company executives are going to find that outright acquisition of intellectual property will be difficult and expensive. But access to the new coveted crown jewels of corporate empires—marketing expertise, research capabilities, manufacturing know-how, international networks, and world-class trademarks—will be available by licensing arrangements and joint ventures.

STRATEGIC PLANNING WITH AN INTANGIBLE BASIS

Popular forms of strategic alliances include:

- Technology licensing,
- Trademark licensing,
- Research and development contracts,
- Marketing agreements,

- Manufacturing contracts,
- Supply agreements, and
- Minority equity purchases.

The trend is not at all limited to small companies that might be expected to be the most needy. Usually, lack of capital, distribution networks, manufacturing expertise, or other proprietary know-how relegates small companies to the arms of strategic partnerships with large companies. But huge multinational corporations are embracing the new trend. Four of the most active participants in strategic alliances during 1991 were IBM, AT&T, Hewlett-Packard, and Digital Equipment Corporation. The following chart was presented in the First Quarter 1992 issue of *Corporate Venturing,* a publication of VENTURE ECONOMICS of Newark, NJ. It shows the number of strategic alliances in which the ten most active companies engaged during 1991.

Leading Strategic Alliance Partners 1991

Corporation	Number of Agreements
IBM	136
AT&T	77
Hewlett-Packard	65
Sun Microsystems	45
Daimler-Benz AG	44
Motorola	43
General Electric	42
Mitsubishi	41
Siemens	39

The same issue of *Corporate Venturing* reported that the most active strategic partnering industry was the computer software and service industry, which completed 661 of the 5080 deals that were monitored during 1991. Industrial products and equipment took second place with 625 deals. Polymers, industrial chemicals, and specialty metals are also hot areas for strategic alliances.

Strategic alliances with foreign-based companies are growing, and Japan is the most active partner as U.S. companies seek to gain access to the Japanese marketplace. In 1991, 753 deals were counted between U.S. and Japanese companies involving semiconductors, therapeutic biotechnology, and mobile communications.

Dow Chemical Corporation is making strategic alliances a cornerstone of its growth plans. The Dow Board of Directors felt that the company possessed a portfolio of projects and businesses that addressed relatively mature markets. It was decided that growth would only come from aggressively searching for new opportunities founded on emerging technologies. The company identifies discontinuities throughout the world, and then develops products that fill gaps. The search for product technology includes developing alliances with universities, start-up companies, and federal laboratories.

Upjohn realized that it could not entirely rely on internal sources to support new product development. So it created The Technology Partnership Program (TPP) to seek out strategic alliances with development-stage companies that possess technologies and products related to health care therapeutics. TPP has the mission of gaining access to technologies that will complement existing licensing and acquisition programs. Under the program, Upjohn gains access to technologies. In return, its partners get a variety of benefits that can include financial assistance, manufacturing capabilities, access to marketing prowess, and research assistance.

Genentech created the Technology Venture Program in order to take advantage of emerging technologies from around the world. The program focuses on gaining access to promising technologies in commercial gene therapy products. The goal of the program is to: 1) expand the current product portfolio of the company where Genentech's commercialization expertise can take emerging technology to market, 2) seek partners with complementary technology which would allow Genentech to accelerate the introduction of products that are being internally developed, and 3) participate in technological areas which are outside of the current Genentech focus of expertise.

It seems that management leaders have finally returned to a tight business focus. Possibly, the LBO debt burdens hanging around many necks has forced clear thinking as to how to get the most out of the businesses that they know how to run best.

LEGAL ATTITUDES ENHANCE VALUE

When intellectual property laws were administered inconsistently, owners of trademarks, and especially technology, were lucky to get requests for license deals. Infringement did not carry the same potential for financial ruin as it does today. When a potential licensing partner approached, the leverage needed to demand high royalty rates was not very strong. Enhanced legal protection around the world has made patented technology and trademarks more valuable than ever before. As such, royalty rates for licenses and joint venture equity splits are moving to much higher levels, and intellectual property owners are less interested in outright sales of their valuable properties.

In the United States, the patent system was dramatically strengthened with the creation of the Court of Appeals of the Federal Circuit (CAFC). It is the only court in the nation that handles patent and trademark case appeals. The continuity of the court's thinking and decisions has strengthened the rights of patent and trademark owners. It has made willful infringement a very risky proposition. Damage awards by courts are higher than ever before. Lost profit awards of up to 60% of the infringing sales have been upheld by the CAFC. Damage awards based upon a reasonable royalty have used royalty rates as high as 25% of sales. Several decisions have upheld damage awards that have bankrupted the infringer. Patent rights have been reinforced to such an extent that the value of patents has risen to new heights. The exploitation opportunities of licensing are greatly enhanced, and royalty income has risen as a result.

Recent court decisions have encouraged owners to vigorously defend their property. IBM has seen billions of dollars go to the makers of personal computers that mimic the original IBM PC. The company has recently served notice that its legal department will descend on anyone who flirts with the distinguishing features of its Personal System/2 machines without licensing.

The enhanced protection has trebled the avenues by which intellectual property can be safely exploited. Instead of only deriving profits from internal use, the licensing option is now well protected, and joint venture projects are becoming common. Instead of deriving only one stream of income from intellectual property, we are more likely to see three: internal use, licensing, and joint ventures. Each of these represents another source of earnings growth which adds to the value of companies.

Legal protection of intellectual property is not at all limited to the United States. Germany, Great Britain, Japan, and France are all providing strong legal protection for intellectual property. Even the third world recognizes the importance of protecting these vital assets. IBM was recently successful in stopping five companies within the People's Republic of China from assembling knock-offs of their IBM PC. More than 3,800 trademark infringement cases were processed last year in five of China's provinces. Legal protection around the world is advancing in recognition that intellectual property is the most important asset and must be protected. Much of the recent GATT treaty negotiations focused on the proper means for protecting internationally exploited intellectual property. The value of patents and trademarks as a result are enhanced, along with the opportunities to expand economic exploitation.

CHAPTER SUMMARIES

The rest of this chapter provides a summary of the contents of the book. Remember, the focus of this book is directed at financial strategies for exploiting intellectual property. The derivation of proper royalty rates for license deals is the focus, along with the determination of proper equity splits for joint ventures. This book cannot tell readers where their technology gaps lie or which candidate is the best joint venture partner in Europe. The book does, however, provide the tools necessary to cut the best deal and maximize the value of intellectual property and corporate value.

It is not necessary to read this book from front to back to get a new idea or two. Some of the chapters present stand-alone ideas. The following summaries are provided to help readers find the sections of this book that are of most interest.

Chapter 2, "Introduction to Exploitation Strategies," identifies and discusses the two most common intellectual property exploitation strategies being used. The nuts and bolts of each strategy, along with the potential pitfalls, will be presented. It also talks about how each of these value-creating strategies couples intellectual property with complementary intellectual properties. This chapter will center on license transactions and joint ventures.

Chapter 3, "Economic Analysis of Exploitation," presents

a basic review of investment analysis techniques. Value is defined as the present value of a future stream of economic benefits. The time value of the money concept is also reviewed. When read in conjunction with Appendix A, "Investment Rate of Return Requirements," the reader will have absorbed a solid foundation of the basic concepts on which the rest of this book relies.

Chapter 4, "Economic Contributions of Intellectual Property,"reviews the ways in which intellectual property enhances profits, and ultimately corporate value. This chapter serves as the foundation for the technical presentation about royalty rates and joint venture profit splits. The discussion is expanded to explain the interplay of enterprise assets: net working capital, fixed assets, complementary intangible assets, and intellectual property.

A detailed economic analysis is presented in this chapter about the economic contribution of specific intellectual property. Two different companies are dissected to illustrate the economic contribution of trademarks. The excess earnings of the GILLETTE CORPORATION are contrasted and compared to the financial performance of GOODY PRODUCTS INC. Both companies are in the same industry and serve the same customers. One of the companies possesses world-class trademarks, and the other is relatively unknown. The level of enhanced earnings is extraordinary. The same technique can be adapted to isolate the earnings contribution of keystone patents.

At the end of the chapter, royalty rate techniques that are in common use are exposed as having severe inadequacies for pricing intellectual property.

Ten industries are studied in Chapter 5, "Intangible Returns in Key Industries," with graphs prepared for each to show the excess earnings that are available for licensing royalties. These earnings can also be looked on as the contribution provided by intellectual property as part of joint ventures. This chapter can serve as a handy reference for anyone who is considering a license or joint venture in one of the ten featured industries.

The industries featured include:

- Specialty chemicals
- Pharmaceuticals
- Electronics
- Food products
- Medical products
- Computer hardware
- Computer software
- Industrial machinery
- Cosmetics and personal hygiene products
- Mega-brands

Chapter 6, "Risks of Exploitation," fully addresses the risk of intellectual property exploitation. Technology becomes obsolete, and trademarks can fade in popularity. Just look at the difficulty that some of the chic brand names are having. Sociological trends have turned consumers away from glitz towards products that optimize the quality for value equation. Technology risks are also rising. Obsolescence used to take seven years, then five, then three. Now many electronic products have an economic life of 18 months. This chapter shows the risks and explains the economic implications of intellectual property exploitation.

Chapter 7, "Licensing Economics & Royalty Rates," discusses how royalty rates are effected by the terms of license agreements, i.e., exclusive licenses carry higher royalty rates. Chapter 7 lists key licensing agreement clauses and shows the effect that they have on royalty rates.

Chapter 8, "Joint Venture Equity Allocations," discusses the accelerating trend towards joint venturing, and presents a detailed analytical model that demonstrates the economic contribution of technology and trademarks. Some companies bring money to a joint venture. Other companies bring technology. Other partners bring distribution networks. This chapter will show how readers can derive a fair split of joint venture ownership.

Chapter 9, "Global Exploitation of Intellectual Property," highlights the role that licensing and joint ventures will play in getting U.S. companies into more markets, at less cost, with controlled risks. The global economy is here to stay, and the exploitation strategies discussed in this book are ideally suited to advance the exploitation of intellectual property around the world. Different intellectual property laws and tax practices around the world can have a significant effect on the economic success of licensing and joint ventures. This chapter will identify the countries where intellectual property investment risks are higher. It will also tell readers what to do about the added risks. Highlights will include:

1. A discussion about how U.S. companies use licensing strategies and joint ventures as a prelude to international acquisitions.
2. A discussion about how different accounting rules can help and hurt licensing and joint ventures.
3. A discussion describing the important emerging issues of taxation due to cross-border transfer prices.
4. A discussion of unique aspects of international business that increase risk.

Chapter 10, "Exploitation Begins With Mapping," explains that you cannot begin to license or joint venture intellectual property until you know what you posses. The greatest business challenge in the future will be to assure that intellectual property is optimally exploited. The goal is complicated because many companies are not aware of all of the intellectual property that they possess. This section of the book will talk about procedures that can be used to identify and evaluate all of the intellectual property and the intellectual properties that are making profits for a company.

Checklists and detailed procedures are included in this chapter to show exactly how to MAP the intellectual property of a company. The steps include:

- Identification
- Location
- Strategic plan coordination
- Routing for internal exploitation
- Identifying gaps
- Routing for external exploitation.

Appendix A, "Investment Rate of Return Requirements," shows how to determine an appropriate weighted average cost of capital for use in evaluating investment projects. These same rate of return requirements are used in the investment models that derive royalty rates and joint venture profit splits. This Appendix provides detailed investment return theory, and includes a list of important references.

Appendix B, "Financial and Business Information Sources," is a presentation of information sources that we have found to be helpful over the years. Licensing and joint venturing require some knowledge about other lines of business and other companies. Sometimes this information is difficult to obtain, but this chapter should point you in the right direction.

Appendix C, "Licensing Transaction Examples and Royalty Rates," is a listing of actual royalty rates that were negotiated during 1991 and early 1992. The information provided identifies the:

- intellectual property involved in the transaction.
- industry in which the intellectual property will be used:
  identity of the licensor
  identity of the licensee
  amount of license fee, if any, and
  royalty rate and calculation base.

The information is grouped by industry, and was provided by *Licensing Economics Review*, a monthly publication that reports royalty rates for technology, trademarks, and copyrights.

ONWARD

The remainder of this book will delve into critical factors that impact the exploitation of intellectual property. Almost all of the factors are fundamentally driven by time, cost, and risk reduction forces. The proper derivation of royalty rates for licensing deals and equity splits for joint ventures is the central focus of this book. Our discussion and examples concentrate on exploitation strategies involving technological know-how and trademarks. The same techniques can also be applied to the analysis of exploitation strategies for all types of intellectual property.

2

Introduction to Exploitation Strategies

Facing the challenges that businesses face today as described in Chapter 1, we now turn to a discussion of specific strategies for the exploitation of intellectual property to meet those requirements.

SOME HISTORY

It was during the Renaissance that what we know today as intellectual property first began to flourish within organizations that were the precursors of the modern business enterprise.

As the period began, craftsmen individually exploited their know-how and trade secrets in the production of goods and services. Knowledge that provided a competitive advantage was then no less jealously guarded than it is today. The craftsman's enterprise grew by "sweat equity, and he made his own tools, gathered his own raw materials, and accomplished the entire manufacturing process alone or with the help of his family.

A realization of the financial limitations of being a "one-man band" led to the emergence of the apprentice system. Typically taking seven years or so, an apprentice progressed from beginner through journeyman status and, if skill and fortune permitted, to master craftsman. Perhaps this arrangement between craftsman and apprentice was an early form of license. A master craftsman exchanged the loss of the exclusive use of his proprietary know-how for the economic advantage of additional labor and a greater quantity of product to sell. There was some protection in that the larger business that resulted increased the craftsman's market power, and so the competitors he was training in the apprentice system would likely go elsewhere to set up their enterprises if they became skilled enough to do so. The system worked as long as technology advanced at a relatively slow pace and travel and communications were such that markets were kept small and local.

At the beginning of this time, legal protection of intellectual property was largely lacking, although there came to be informal protection through the guilds. It was within the guild system that trademarks began to be recognized as the "hallmark" of a craftsman, especially in gold and silver goods, in the form of a monogram or emblem; they began to receive strict legal protection.

ENTER TECHNOLOGICAL CHANGE

As markets expanded and technology development gathered momentum, the enterprise was increasingly forced to go outside itself for capital and labor. Lenders and investors provided money capital, other enterprises became the source of raw materials, tools, transportation, and distribution, and the enterprise had to hire labor which was paid for in cash or goods rather than know-how. Paying for labor obviated the need to reveal proprietary technology, and so the intellectual property of the enterprise stayed within it, as in a walled fortress. This mentality was to persist for many years.

This "do it yourself" system of intellectual property exploitation no longer works. Why? Several very important aspects of business have undergone drastic change.

Technology

It may well have been possible for an Archimedes to have personal knowledge of a good portion of the world's newest technology. That time is long gone, with technology growing and subdividing like an amoeba gone berserk. Now even a large enterprise cannot possess all of the technology it requires, and must look to outside sources.

This vast explosion of technology has created an equally long "cutting edge" which results in a geographically diffused proliferation which is occurring at a bewildering speed. This makes it impossible for an enterprise, even if it controls the technology it requires for current operations, to depend exclusively on a strategy of internal development.

Markets

The ability to communicate completely and instantaneously with one another, ignoring national boundaries, has created a world marketplace, and therefore world competition. John Ruskin exemplified the insularity of his time when, asked to comment on the then new England to India cable, he said: "What have we to say to India?" A great deal, as we now know! It becomes impossible for an enterprise to "stake out" a territory free of competitors. An enterprise cannot rest on its laurels and be comfortable in what appears to be a market niche. Good niches do not last long, and the interloper can come from anywhere. An enterprise needs to have a "full pipeline" of new or enhanced products and/or services in order to survive.

Cost

Most of the modern advances in technology, such as the electric light, the telephone, and the camera, were developed without extensive material resources. We do not intend to denigrate the financial sacrifices of the inventors, which were at times substantial. Thomas Edison, responding to one who commented on the large number of failures in his search for a new storage battery, replied, "Results? Why, I have gotten a lot of results. I know fifty thousand things that won't work!" The Wright brothers' historic flight was made in a craft designed and manufactured using their own skills and capital. Today, however, even small advancements in technology are gained only at great cost, notable examples being in the computer and biotechnology fields. IBM estimates that a manufacturing facility for the next generation of 64-megabit chips will cost $1 billion. At the very least, an enterprise must be able to assure itself of being able to quickly reach a gigantic market if it is to commit the resources necessary to develop a new technology or product. One can no longer afford to "run a product up the flagpole to see who buys it"; it costs too much to create the flag, and the risks of nonacceptance are too great.

Significant gains are, for the most part, beyond the resources of even the largest enterprises. This is an obvious oversimplification—there will continue to be inexpensive innovation, and sometimes it will represent a "breakthrough." Elias Howe nearly ran out of money and ideas while wrestling with the location of the needle's eye in a sewing machine he was developing. One night he dreamed he was being led to his execution for this failure, and he saw that the guards surrounding him carried spears that were pierced near the tip. He woke up and rushed to his workshop where, by the next morning, the design of the first sewing machine was near completion. Today, for better or for worse, progress has largely been left to the giants, corporate or governmental, or to consortia of smaller enterprises that have the wit and timing to assemble the necessary resources.

The path from idea to marketplace has therefore become a very costly one, and competition has made it a short one as well. Those who negotiate it successfully have mastered the ability to quickly gather and deploy the massive amounts of labor and capital necessary. Intel has been successfully compressing its chip development cycle by beginning research on a following generation before its predecessor is brought to market. The list of those who have been successful is as long as those who have fallen by the wayside. Few, if any,enterprises by themselves have the resources to meet these market challenges of speed and cost.

CREATION OF INTELLECTUAL PROPERTY

To understand exploitation strategies, it is useful to review how intellectual property is created and its relationship with the business enterprise. Since the business enterprise can be a large and complex organization, we will, for the purposes of this discussion, equate it to a single product which has been developed and successfully introduced to the marketplace. The essential elements, for our purposes, are the same. Every product (or service) is supported by three types of assets.

Monetary Assets

Sometimes referred to as "working capital," this element comprises cash and cash equivalents, accounts receivable, inventories, prepayments, taxes and other accruals, and accounts payable. Monetary assets can be quantified by subtracting current liabilities from current assets, as shown on a typical balance sheet.

The need for working capital arises because, in commerce, there is always some mismatch between when funds are received from the sale of product and when expenses for running the business are incurred. Generally, expenses precede sales revenue, and so some capital must be made available to the enterprise to cover this requirement.

Tangible Assets

Every product or service requires some tangible assets to support it. These may be extensive manufacturing or research facilities including land, buildings, machinery, and equipment, or in the case of a service enterprise, office furniture and equipment or improvements to leased property.

Intangible Assets and Intellectual Property

Every product or service is also supported by intangible assets such as an assembled workforce, contracts, records, computer software, and elements of a going concern. It may also be supported by intellectual property such as patents, trademarks, proprietary technology, or copyrights.

We think of a business enterprise (or an individual product or service as described above) as a *portfolio* of assets very much like a portfolio of securities. The objective of assembling either type of portfolio is to earn a profit. Securities are assembled in order to reflect the owner's tolerance for risk—to avoid having to put one's "eggs all in the same basket." The portfolio of assets assembled in a business enterprise comes about as a result of the desire to maximize profits. An enterprise that lacks essential assets suffers from earnings malnutrition. An enterprise that has excess assets is slowed by obesity. Earnings are maximized when the correct complement of assets is deployed to meet the needs and wants of the marketplace. The essence of what our business schools teach is how to obtain and deploy the optimal mix of assets.

ECONOMICS OF EXPLOITATION

Intellectual property is so called because it is a "*product of the mind*" and is capable of *ownership*. That ownership equates to the right to possess, use, and dispose of the property, to the exclusion of others. Unlike other intangible assets, such as an assembled workforce or a favorable contract, intellectual property can by itself be purchased, sold, given away, traded, leased, used as collateral, or bequeathed. We are here concerned with the rights that are provided by law to the owner of intellectual property, not the physical embodiment of the intellectual property. We can own a BUICK automobile, but that ownership does not give us the right to copy its design, trademark, or any patented components that may have physical existence in the vehicle.

Intellectual property rights are analogous to those connected with other kinds of property of a more familiar nature. We can describe these rights by paraphrasing these concepts as they apply to real property (land and/or improvements).

Fee Simple Interest

When one possesses a fee simple interest, ownership is complete and includes the entire "bundle of rights" associated with the property.

A patent, trademark, or copyright owner is automatically granted this full bundle of rights when that intellectual property is recognized by government. If the owner is an individual, that person is the sole owner of the interest.

It is important to remember that this interest represents the totality of property rights. Those rights can be contractually divided among parties in an infinite number of ways (to create co-owners of the fee simple interest), but *the sum of the parts always equals this whole*.

Mortgager's Interest

When property is pledged as security for repayment of a loan, the lender receives a portion of the fee simple interest in the form of a right to receive interest and principle payments and the right to force the sale of the property to liquidate the debt.

It is increasingly common for intellectual property to be pledged in this fashion, although the form of that pledge can vary, along with the specific rights conveyed to the mortgagee.

Lessee's Interest

When property is leased, a portion of the fee simple rights are transferred to the lessee, usually in the form of the right to use the property in a defined way for a specific period of time. The rights of lessee and lessor when added together constitute the whole, or are said to be complementary.

This is the essential form of what we will refer to hereafter as a "license," as it applies to intellectual property.

Intellectual property is therefore very much the same as other forms of property relative to the means of its description, form of ownership, and its exploitation. For a more complete discussion of particular property definitions and ownership rights, the reader is referred to *Appraisal Principles and Procedures* by Henry A. Babcock, 1980, American Society of Appraisers.

Basic economic theory does not dwell on the role of intellectual property within the business enterprise, presumably because when it evolved, intellectual property did not loom large as a producer of profits. If this consideration had been made, however, we believe that intellectual property would have been seen as a source of so-called "monopoly profits," at least during the period of its legal protection. These monopoly profits can be seen as a form of rent, since the asset, likened to land, is not reproducible during the period of protection. Economist David Ricardo discussed *rent* in an 1891 publication [1]:

> as that portion of the produce of the earth, which is paid to the landlord for the use of the original and indestructible powers of the soil . . . [as opposed to] . . . the interest and profit of capital. . . employed in ameliorating the quality of the land and in erecting buildings. . .

We think that this description fits intellectual property as well. The rights enjoyed by the owner of a trademark have an "original and indestructible" flavor. The capital and labor employed to "ameliorate its quality" (research or manufacturing technology) and (perhaps through advertising) to build a brand on its foundation to add to the value of trademark rights enhance its earning power.

These profits are also described by economists as "tending to capitalize." That is, the value of the enterprise is increased by the capitalized amount of the monopoly profits. We concur with those economists who define intellectual property as "intangible capital." This definition allows us to examine the ways in which intellectual property can be deployed within the framework of the exploitation of other forms of capital which may be more familiar.

DEVELOPMENT OF INTELLECTUAL PROPERTY

How intellectual property assets come into existence and how they interact can best be illustrated by an analysis of a product or service in development. We will examine two situations. One is a case in which a completely new product has sprung from innovation. The other is where a product or service is commercialized to fill a perceived discontinuity in the marketplace.

Innovation Product

Some products begin with an idea or the development of a technology. In 1845, Christian Friedrich Schonbein was experimenting with sulfuric and nitric acid in his kitchen, a practice understandably forbidden by his wife. When he spilled some of the mixture on the table, he quickly mopped up the liquid with his wife's cotton apron. Hanging it near the fire to dry so his experimentation would not be detected, it exploded. Schonbein, the chemist, subsequently invented, marketed, and exploited smokeless gunpowder, known as guncotton.

Another example could be the concept of combining scrap plastic and wood chips or sawdust to make artificial fireplace logs or formed molding products for construction. This concept is attractive because it is environmentally positive (using two waste materials that are difficult and costly to dispose of) and because of the potential profitability resulting from the use of very low cost raw materials.

Beginning with the concept, the development moves to literary research on plastics (physical properties, availability, environmental concerns), and from there, perhaps to modest experimentation with small quantities. At some point, however, successful development will have reached a milestone where:

It appears technically possible to combine the two materials.

The problems of combining dissimilar plastics can be overcome.

Adequate supplies of material are determined to be available.

The cost of raw materials and processing appears to be reasonable vis-à-vis the possible market for the product.

The prototype products appear to meet the standards of the marketplace.

To this point, nominal amounts of money for monetary and tangible assets have been required. Development has begun with intellectual property. Whether this is in the form of proprietary technology or becomes patented technology is not relevant for this discussion. Further development will, however, require significant capital and labor as the product moves through pilot plant production, testing, market research, and finally production for the marketplace. This progression can be illustrated as shown in Figure 2.1.

Niche Product

Some business enterprises are created in order to fill an opportunity created by geography, population growth, price opportunities, or some other discontinuity in the market—an opportunity that comes about because of a need unfulfilled. The enterprise arises not from a new concept, but from a market opportunity.

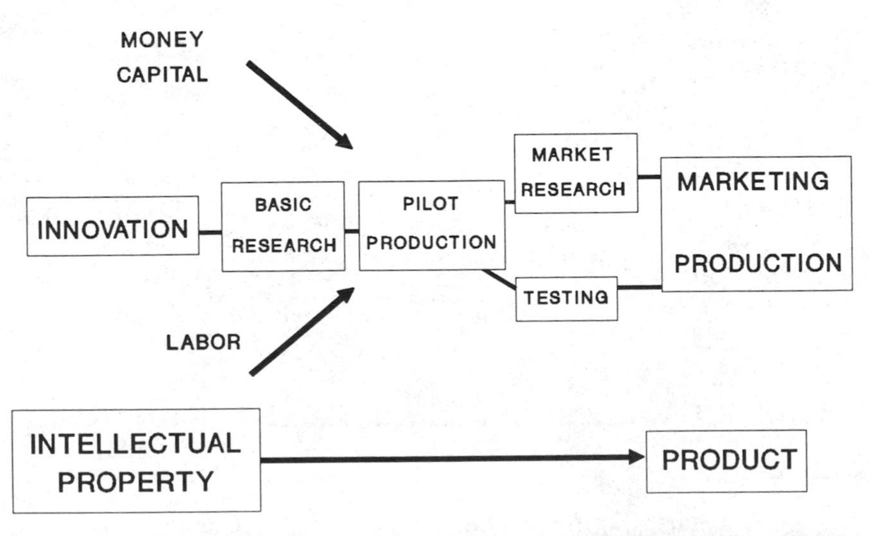

Figure 2.1 Intellectual Property Development

The innovation has already been done; the concept exists. The first order of business for this entrepreneur is to assemble capital and labor to enter the market. There are many examples of this in the retail business segment. BEN & JERRY did not invent ice cream, and MRS. FIELDS did not invent chocolate chip cookies. These entrepreneurs recognized a potential market segment, enhanced and individualized existing products, accumulated the capital, converted it to monetary and tangible assets, obtained labor, and were successful in entering the market.

In this case, the creation of intangible assets and intellectual property, in the form of market position, trademarks, and all of the other intellectual property assets associated with a brand, generally followed that of monetary and tangible assets. In this situation, the formation of the enterprise is illustrated in Figure 2.2.

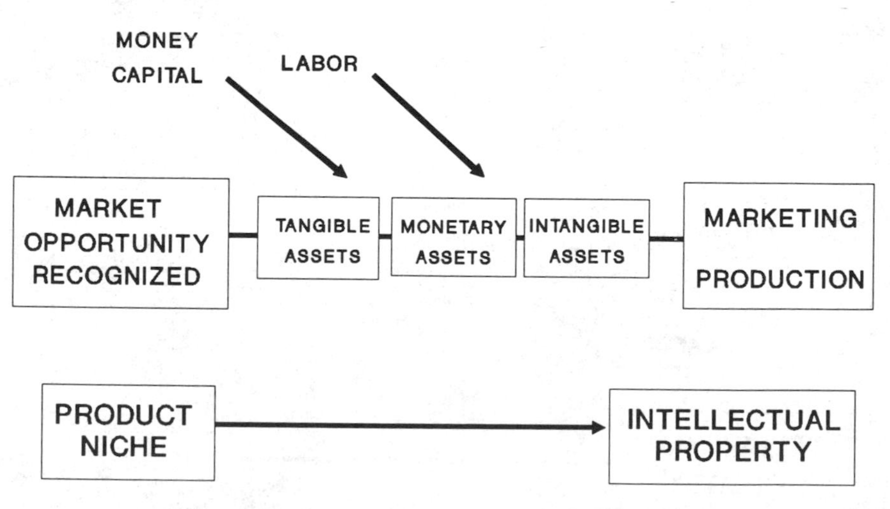

Figure 2.2 Intellectual Property Development

SOURCE OF PRODUCTION FACTORS

At every intermediate point along either of these two paths, decisions must be made about how to obtain the necessary resources. We can easily transplant the situations described above to the corporate world, where the exact same conditions arise. The research efforts of the IBMs and Mercks of the world continually produce innovations. Their marketing people continually observe opportunities in the marketplace. By whatever path these opportunities come to management, however, decisions must be made as to *how* these opportunities will be exploited, or *whether* they will be exploited.

Until relatively recently, the corporate world had a "do it yourself" approach to every such situation. This corporate xenophobia dictated that ideas were to be kept "in the family," hoarded, and nurtured privately. Even those not pursued were kept in the vault to gather dust. Long an innovative leader in the chemical industry, DuPont for many years firmly adhered to this policy. It has, along with the rest of the corporate world, however, come to the realization that no company has a "lock" on anything anymore. Enterprises in touch with innovation and/or the marketplace have come to the realization that they cannot "go it alone." The long cutting edge of technology development has created a veritable flood of opportunities. If an enterprise depends for exploitation on its own resources alone, so few of these opportunities can be dealt with that it inevitably drops behind in the race.

In the 1990 annual report of Sumitomo Chemical Company is a section describing significant events of the company's year. Twenty-seven such events are noted, and included are:

> Ten joint ventures started or expanded, several internationally, involving a total of 23 partner companies.

A contract to support a research program at Massachusetts General Hospital/Harvard University.

A joint marketing agreement with a U.S. company.

A license from a U.S. company.

Even this giant company, with annual sales of $7.9 billion and assets of $8.8 billion, extensively employs external exploitation strategies.

We next examine the alternatives among the strategies that are available to marshal the resources necessary to stay in the race.

INTERNAL STRATEGIES

Grow Your Own

While the necessity for intercompany collaboration has been recognized, the option of developing a product or service "in-house" is still valid, and if it is the fastest and most economical way, desirable. After all, 100% ownership and control of a promising innovation is still the best option, provided one has the resources to commercialize it by providing the most efficient research, development, design, production, marketing, sales, and distribution. The Greek philosopher Thales once bought up all the olive presses in Miletus at a time when his knowledge of meteorology told him a bumper crop of olives was on the way. He was right, and he charged monopolistic prices for the use of his presses, becoming wealthy in one year.

The most obvious course is therefore to internally create the factors of production that the enterprise needs. If research in a commodity chemical company has brought forth a drug patent in a new and unfamiliar field, manufacturing facilities and a distribution system can be built and organized. If the marketing staff has identified a potentially profitable opportunity, research resources may have to be created or redirected to augment the product line.

The advantage of this approach is that the new element will be created "in the image" of the rest of the enterprise. There will be no clash of corporate cultures. Complete control will be maintained. There can be assurance of adequate protection of the intellectual property from competitors. The new venture or element will provide career opportunities for existing staff. There may be currently underutilized resources that can be put to work in the expansion.

The disadvantages relate primarily to speed and ability.

Speed

Obtaining intellectual property resources by self-development is the slowest path, if they already exist elsewhere and are accessible by some means. Developing a trademark and a market position is a slow endeavor.

Ability

One would question the ability, as an example, of the commodity chemical company noted above to develop the manufacturing and distribution capability following the patenting of the drug. There are simply too many practical barriers to overcome. Its manufacturing personnel, skilled though they may be, have never dealt with FDA standards, its marketing staff would be unfamiliar with the distribution channels for drugs, and so forth.

It is for this reason (as well as a lack of financial resources) that universities and research organizations rarely elect to internally develop the means to exploit the technology that they continually produce.

The *cost* of internally developing resources may not be very different from obtaining them externally, if there is a knowledgeable marketplace. To illustrate: if I have the manufacturing capability sought by the commodity chemical company with the new drug patent, I am certainly aware of what it costs to build and staff such a plant. Even though it might involve little *incremental cost* to add the manufacture of the new product to my existing complement of products, I will most certainly *price* that manufacturing function based on the *value* of that service, rather than the cost of providing it.

THE ENTREPRENEURING CORPORATION

Corporations have adopted a number of strategies attempting to retain total control over the development of intellectual property while obtaining benefits which otherwise might have to come from outside the organization. Large organizations are notably poor at creating an atmosphere of innovative thought and deploying resources rapidly. The new strategies combine a creation of the entrepreneurial climate for innovation with the existing development resources of a large corporation. Names such as "intrapreneuring" or "internal venturing" have been used to describe these techniques. These techniques are designed to encourage innovation from within by a system of policies, performance measures, and rewards or by establishing autonomous "skunk works" within the organization, as IBM did to develop its line of personal computers. Most often, early-stage development of new products is the objective. Kodak, 3M, and Monsanto have all had a run at this strategy.

In 1988, Xerox Corporation created an internal venture capital operation—Xerox Technology Ventures. The objective was to enable the exploitation of technology developed in-house, but for which the decision had been made at the corporate level not to commercialize. Scientists and engineers who develop such technology can approach the Ventures group for funding a start-up development company. If accepted, they form an enterprise on company premises, and if commercialization is successful, they receive a portion of the new company's stock. Several of the ventures have been successful.

The advantage of these strategies is, of course, that total control and ownership is maintained. The disadvantages are several:

> In spite of best efforts otherwise, many organizations are simply unable to tolerate this "intrusion," and there is a dampening or extinguishing of the spirit necessary for this to succeed.
>
> Compensation schemes are put awry. To maximize the entrepreneurial spirit, it is beneficial to give the occupants of the "skunk works" an opportunity to financially share in the success of a project. Other employees probably do not mind if the development is unsuccessful, but if the reverse is true, problems can arise.
>
> Another question is where to locate the operation within the organization. No product manager, whose compensation may be dependent on product line profitability, wants to have a nonearning development team as part of his or her group. Beyond that, start-ups absorb an inordinate amount of management time and energy.
>
> At the corporate level, these operations are a drag on earnings per share, and the short-run outlook of the financial markets makes this a serious consideration.
>
> There is also the added risk that the failure of a fledgling product could tarnish the image of the larger entity.

ACQUISITION

Another strategy is to obtain intellectual property or the elements to exploit it by acquisition. This usually involves the purchase of an entire enterprise, although product lines are occasionally exchanged. We classify this as internal because the result is 100% control through ownership. This can be the quickest way to obtain intellectual property or access to a market. As we noted above, it likely will not be the least cost solution. When this strategy is employed to obtain early-stage technology, the serendipitous combination of a small, entrepreneurial organization with the financing and resource power of a large one will often produce success.

There are disadvantages to this strategy as well:

If the target enterprise becomes aware of the strategic need for what it has, the price will be high, factoring in the time value of being able to supply to the buyer a "ready-made" solution.

When the objective is to obtain innovative entrepreneurship, the target enterprise is usually small, relative to the buyer. Small businesses are different from large ones in many ways besides size. The small business corporate culture (if it can be called that) is likely to be vastly different, and the people who gravitate to such an atmosphere tend to have different motivations and needs. The result is that there is a high likelihood that, in spite of best efforts, a marriage of large and small enterprises will fail. The small enterprise will be swallowed up in the larger, and the characteristics that originally made it so attractive will disappear (along with the people).

Even if the marriage lasts, there is a strong possibility

that the high energy level that was attractive in the target will wane, as the people become "corporatized" (or wealthy, as a result of the purchase).

To acquire the desired intellectual property, the buyer may also receive other undesirable parts of the company and assume unwanted liabilities.

EXTERNAL STRATEGIES

We define external strategies as those in which there is either coownership, collaboration, or a license between otherwise unrelated and sometimes competitive parties for the purpose of exploiting intellectual property or some resource. These arrange ments are often collectively referred to as strategic alliances or strategic partnerships, and they are becoming the primary focus of business development strategies.

Strategic Alliances—General

The business language of the 1990s popularized the term "strategic alliance" to describe a planned state of cooperation between enterprises. Alliances are often between competing businesses. I once asked the proprietor of one of three custom gun shops in a small western Pennsylvania town whether all the competition was a problem. He quickly informed me to the contrary, that gun fanciers came from miles around knowing that their needs would surely be met by one shop or the other. There was close cooperation among the three proprietors, realizing that $1 + 1 + 1 = 5$ in the marketplace. This was a strategic alliance of a very simple and informal sort.

In the corporate world, a common alliance is between a small, start-up enterprise and an industry giant for the purpose of combining innovation and resources. Some alliances are vertical in nature, linking the R&D function of one entity with the manufacturing function of another, or manufacturing with marketing or distribution, and the like. A horizontal alliance would link two, perhaps competing, but complementary manufacturing processes. Increasingly, alliances cross international borders to overcome the barriers of language, currency, or standards. There is an almost limitless variety of strategic alliances, and we will discuss only the more common situations.

We bifurcate strategic alliances into those in which there is some form of shared or cross-*ownership,* and those in which there is only an *exchange* of goods or services.

Exchange Alliances

Alliances of this type are characterized by an exchange at arm's length of goods or services for rights in intellectual property.

Marketing/Distribution Agreement

Some landmark vertical alliances of this kind have occurred in the pharmaceutical industry, in which one company with a strong or strategically placed marketing staff has agreed to sell the complementary products of a competitor. The objective might be to avoid the time and cost of establishing a sales force (perhaps in another country) or to "round out" a product line.

Collaborative Research and Development

Competitors have also agreed to horizontally combine efforts on research or development that are important to each, with the objective of sharing cost or shortening the development cycle.

Joint Bidding

Often, small enterprises will join together to submit a bid in competition with larger entities. This may be needed to assemble the requisite skills or products, or simply to achieve the critical mass that none of them has individually.

Manufacturing Agreements

An enterprise with excess capacity or highly specialized capability may agree to manufacture components for a competitor.

Financial Agreements

There are many permutations available that do not involve cross-ownership. Smaller enterprises chronically suffer from a lack of money capital. Traditional money sources often reject these opportunities because of the perceived risk of default or because they do not, or will not, take the time to understand the underlying intellectual property that may be driving such a business.

Larger enterprises, with access to traditional markets, can serve as a source of money capital. Their price may be some future rights to developed technology, options to purchase it, access to new markets, or the like. This arrangement is quite common between a corporation and a university or research organization.

Licenses

By far the most common of the exchange alliances is the license. A license is directly analogous to the rental of property. The owner of the complete bundle of rights to intellectual property agrees to transfer some of those rights to another in exchange for money, goods, or services. The transfer is contractual, and as in a lease, the terms of the exchange are specified.

There are a number of advantages to licensing as a means of exploiting intellectual property:

> The cash investment is relatively small. This is not to say that one can sneeze at the cost of negotiating a

license, but licensing does not typically require the capital resources of a cross-ownership form of exploitation.

It may not require a long-term commitment. Ideally, if a license turns out to be a "win–win" situation for both parties, it can last for years and lead to close ties between two enterprises. Alternatively, the license form of exploitation can also provide an "out" to either party if the arrangement turns out to be unsatisfactory, giving the technology owner the opportunity of finding another means of exploitation before the economic life of the intellectual property expires.

The owner of the intellectual property licensed retains some rights and control over the property.

It provides an opportunity to exploit intellectual property that is out of the "mainstream" of one's enterprise, or to exploit certain features of intellectual property that would be useful in another business segment.

There are also disadvantages to the licensing strategy:

Control is lost for a time relative to those rights that have been conveyed by means of the license.

The licensee may fall prey to one of a host of evils that may have been unforeseen in the license, and which effectively block the licensor from the exercise of the licensed rights. These can include bankruptcy, capital shortage, environmental problems, or a natural disaster which could prevent the licensee from exploiting the intellectual property while holding the intellectual property captive.

There can be excessive administrative costs, especially in the case of a recalcitrant licensee.

A poorly designed license may, in effect, grant more rights than were originally anticipated.

The licensee might be able to take advantage of knowledge gained as a result of the license to bypass the intellectual property or to improve on it so as to become a competitor.

OWNERSHIP ALLIANCES

The other broad form of alliance involves some type of ownership rather than an exchange of money, goods, or services. Most commonly, the form of that ownership is an investment by one company in the *securities* of another.

As an example, a manufacturing enterprise may have intellectual property that is applicable to some business segment out of its own mainstream. It might seek an alliance with an enterprise that is already in that market, and consummate that alliance by purchasing, in exchange for its intellectual property, some of the common stock of that enterprise. By doing so, it will perhaps receive representation on the Board of Directors, be able to ensure that proper resources are devoted to exploiting its intellectual property, and perhaps receive a share of dividends. It may look forward to selling its holding for a profit in the future.

In another scenario, the parties could form an entirely new enterprise, with common ownership—a joint venture. If that co-ownership involves the receipt of some form of security in another enterprise, an important complexity is introduced. The co-ownership of securities versus property is a situation that has some unique characteristics, and we digress briefly to discuss them.

Type of Security

In the evaluation of this type of arrangement, one must be sensitive to the fact that there is an important difference between the ownership of *property rights* and the ownership of the *securities* of a business enterprise. If one co-owns an acre of land, the rights of each party are commensurate with their pro-rata share of ownership. The securities of a business represent very specific and sometimes limited interests in the enterprise. They are, in a sense, "once removed" from direct ownership, and can take various forms.

Long-Term Debt. Debt securities include bonds, mortgages, or long-term notes. The investment may or may not be collateralized, but will usually have a stated interest rate and term. For the investor (lender), the attraction is receiving payment for the use of the capital, together with its ultimate return (barring default).

As a form of strategic alliance, there is little motivation for one party to provide long-term debt capital to another. There is no potential payoff if success strikes. It is a financing instrument only. When one of the entities or the joint venture is a start-up, as is often the case, the risk is high, and the resulting interest rate would be so high that the business could not pay it anyway. The risk of default would also be so high that an investor would view it as equity.

Preferred Stock. Much the same can be said of this form of financing. Unless there is an opportunity to convert in the future to a security that will share in the upside, there is little reason to use this form of ownership in a strategic alliance.

Common Stock. Common stock ownership is the vehicle most used to form alliances. It has the greatest degree of risk, but that is counterbalanced by the opportunity for future wealth. If the enterprise fails, it is highly unlikely that common stockholders will realize any of their investment, especially if the business was developing high technology. If the enterprise is successful, the common stockholder will reap the largest rewards.

Size of Interest

It is extremely important to understand the impact on value of the size (relative to the total) of a security interest in a business enterprise. This is especially true of common stock holdings, and since they are the most common form of cross-ownership in a strategic alliance, we will concentrate our discussion there.

If one is a co-owner of a fee simple interest in property, as an example a co-author of a book or a co-inventor holding a patent, one's pro-rata share of the benefits of ownership is clear.

Investing in the common stock of an enterprise is altogether a different matter. In this milieu, one consigns the investment to another entity—the enterprise which has its own management. A layer of control over the investment is therefore introduced, with a diminution of the original investor's rights. The degree of loss is generally related to the size of one's investment vis-à-vis the total common equity.

To illustrate, assume that I invest $1 million (or the equivalent goods, services, or intellectual property) in a joint venture, and the parties involved agree that this gives me 10% of the common stock of the new enterprise. If one of the other parties owns 55% of the stock, they have clear control. They have the power to hire and fire management, set policy for the business, buy or sell assets, make acquisitions, make a public offering of the stock, pay or not pay dividends, and change the articles of incorporation or the bylaws of the enterprise. This majority holding can withhold financial information, can issue new stock to dilute my holding, and in a sense, "freeze me out" if they wish. While there are legal remedies for this, they are expensive and time consuming to muster.

In addition, if I reach the point at which I want to sell my interest in a joint venture, then the value of my 10% stock ownership can be expected to be less than 10% of the whole enterprise. Any potential buyer would recognize the possibility of a "tyranny of the majority" and be willing to pay less.

Control, therefore, is a very important consideration in a cross-ownership alliance involving holdings of common stock. An equal division of control between two parties (50–50 stock ownership) could be just as debilitating if the parties become locked in an impasse over policies or direction. Early in his career, Benny Goodman shared a flat with Jimmy Dorsey. Jobs were few, and since they played the same instruments, competition was strong. They agreed that whoever answered the telephone first got the job. There was an occasion, however, when there was a dead heat. As Goodman described it: "Jimmy got the mouthpiece of the phone and accepted the date. But I had the receiver and knew where the job was."

There are also tax consequences to the size of stockholding. If one corporation owns at least 80% of the common stock of another, the results of operation of the two entities can be consolidated for (U.S.) federal income tax computation. The losses to be expected in a start-up could therefore be offset against the profits of the parent, reducing income taxes. If none of the parties to a cross-ownership alliance has an 80% holding, then they must wait until the venture has taxable income before the early-year losses can be utilized.

OTHER LIQUIDITY CONCERNS

There are other factors that must be considered in a cross-ownership alliance. Generally, such an investment is highly illiquid.

First, the common stock of a start-up is rarely publicly traded, so there is no market for it. A private sale of such a stock interest would be time consuming and costly because one would have to seek out a particular buyer who had a particular interest in the enterprise. There may be restrictions as to the sale of the stock so that the original parties have control over who is a stockholder. One can therefore not make such an investment with the idea that: "we can always sell our stock if things don't work out."

It is also important to consider preemptive rights in order to preserve one's original pro-rata share of assets, earnings, and voting power. These rights give a shareholder the right of first refusal on additional stock if it is necessary to raise additional equity capital (a not unlikely situation for a start-up venture).

Market Risk and the Discount for Lack of Marketability

In his book, *Valuing A Business: Analysis and Appraisal of Closely Held Companies,* Shannon Pratt begins his chapter on discounts for marketability by saying:

> All other things being equal, an interest in a business is worth more if the interest is marketable . . . .

Benjamin Graham is often referred to as the father of modern investment analysis. He stated in his famous book, *Security Analysis,*

> . . . it is obviously better to own a readily marketable security than one with a poor market.

It can be argued that many forms of intellectual property have very limited characteristics of marketability. Trademarks may be limited to a specific industry with few participants.

During the late 1960s, many registered investment companies invested in restricted stocks (those which cannot be actively traded on a stock exchange or over the counter). During the early 1970s, investor confidence was severely eroded by high inflation and a no-growth economy. As investors clamored to redeem their shares, many of the mutual funds ran into substantial liquidity problems. One of the problems was the inability to liquidate their restricted investments. At a time when investors wanted to liquidate, they found that a lack of marketability forestalled their ability to limit further decline in the value of their investments.This lack of marketability clearly increased the risk of their investment.

One method that allows a means by which to measure the discount on investment value because of illiquidity is to study the private placements of restricted stocks. Restricted stocks are often common stocks of a publicly traded corporation. The restricted securities are identical to securities that are registered in every way, except that the restricted securities are not able to be traded in a public market. Since the only difference between the two investments is the ability to publicly trade the security, analysis of the price differentials between a trade of the registered stock and a trade of the restricted stock on the same day provides an indication of the value of marketability.

During the Spring of 1983, Standard Research Consultants compared the placement prices of restricted securities to the market price of the identical publicly traded security. The difference in price represented the negotiation between the buyer and seller in the private transaction and the value associated with the illiquidity of the restricted securities. The study indicated a median discount of 45%.

In an article published in the March 1973 issue of *Taxes,* Moroney presented the results of another study of the prices paid for restricted securities by ten registered investment companies. The study showed that the average discount for illiquidity was 35%.

Yet another restricted stock study completed by J. Michael Maher and published in the September 1976 issue of *Taxes* presented a conclusion that the proper discount was about 35%, with discounts in specific cases ranging between 10 and 90%.

It must be remembered that the amount of discount indicated in these studies reflects the fact that the underlying corporation has similar securities that are indeed marketable, and that the restricted stocks contain provisions most often to arrange for their registration in a few years. Thus, the restricted securities will enjoy liquidity in the future. The private transaction prices used in these studies therefore reflect the positive fact that active trading in the public marketplace will be possible. An investment that does not possess this near-term marketability characteristic might well be discounted even further.

The discount to the publicly traded price is the same as requiring a higher rate of return on the illiquid investment. The market sees lack of immediate marketability as an additional risk beyond the risks already discussed, and requires a higher return to compensate for the added risk.

While the studies cited above are based upon marketability discounts of common stock, the same principle is valid for all investments, including an investment in intellectual property.

The market for intellectual property may be very limited. The number of corporate investors that possess the needed complementary assets of plant and equipment may be few. Further, if the intellectual property for which a market is desired is unfinished, embryonic technology, the possibilities for recovering the research investment may be more limited. A lack of marketability introduces higher risks, and a higher rate of return is appropriate.

ESTABLISHING A CROSS-OWNERSHIP ALLIANCE

There are several common scenarios for joint venturing:

Purchase of Equity. One option is to simply purchase with cash an equity position in a new enterprise (joint venture), along with another entity. The only difference between this and an initial public offering of a new company is that one is assured of the existence of only one other stockholder. The assumption is that the ownership will be divided between two entities, and that those entities have enough common interest that the focus of the enterprise will remain as envisioned by the parties originally.

Presumably, the value of contribution will be measured by the cash invested in the enterprise. If the other party put up cash, the share of ownership between us is clear. If the other party put up goods or services, then the question of our share of ownership is not clear, and it depends on the value of that investment.

Contribution of Equity. Very often, a portion of the equity of the new venture is in the form of goods or services. It could be intellectual property as yet undeveloped for the marketplace, manufacturing capacity, a contract for the supply of raw materials, an agreement to market or distribute the developed product, research and development resources—only the imagination limits the possibilities. If those same possibilities apply to the contribution of the other party, then we have a real problem determining the relative ownership in the outcome of the enterprise.

Contingent Contributions. Sometimes, the partners agree upon an initial contribution, and also agree to make further contributions as the enterprise develops or as milestones are passed. This presents a ''moving target'' in terms of relative ownership, and the preemptive rights discussed above become important.

The benefits and problems associated with joint ventures are more fully discussed in Chapter 9, where we also present the financial tools to evaluate them.

SUMMARY

With respect to the exploitation of intellectual property, licensing and joint ventures have the most most advantages, and will be discussed throughout the remainder of this book.

(1) David Ricardo, *Principles of Political Economy and Taxation,* London, George Bell and Sons, Ltd., 1891, 3d ed.

3

Economic Analysis of Exploitation—Underlying Theory

Patents, trademarks, copyrights, and other forms of intellectual property are business assets, just as are land, buildings, and machinery. Prudent managers continually examine the assets under their care to ensure that they are fully and profitably utilized. An outmoded plant is not allowed to drain resources; it is sold, rented, demolished, or modernized. The tools of modern investment theory are used to measure its relative contribution and to choose the appropriate course of action.

The intellectual property of a business requires the same protection and maintenance as the tangible assets, and should also be expected to contribute to the profitability of the enterprise. The same investment measures can and should be used to measure its contribution. While this is not a book on the valuation of intellectual property, the principles of valuation provide important tools that enable us to measure intellectual property's contribution to an enterprise, and to quantify the economic results of various exploitation strategies. Readers possessing a keen knowledge of present value theory might want to skip ahead to Chapter 5, where more complex applications of these basic theories are presented.

UNDERLYING THEORY

We use one form of the definition of fair market value as the basis for this quantifying analysis. Fair market value can be defined as the "present value of the future benefits of ownership." When those future benefits are stated in terms of money, their present value becomes an important tool for comparison.

As an example, let us make the pleasant assumption that,

as a result of some clever basement tinkering, we have designed a putter that unerringly propels a golf ball into the hole. This is an event that most likely defies all laws of the universe. Passing through Rome in 1961, Sam Snead stopped for an audience with Pope John. He mentioned to one of the papal officials that he had putted very poorly for some time, and hoped that the pope might bless his putter. The monsignor commiserated with Snead, commenting that his putting had been poor of late as well. Snead was amazed, and said, "If you *live* here and can't putt, what chance is there for me?" In spite of these daunting obstacles, we have carefully guarded our design and have been awarded a patent. Let us further assume that our decision is to exploit this intellectual property by selling it. We have approached the golf equipment companies, and two of them have made offers. Zing Golf Corporation has offered a cash payment of $550,000. Cougar Club Company has offered $300,000 cash and $300,000 in one year.

The choice would be clear if the two offers were both for cash. The proposed delay in Cougar's second payment complicates the decision. The additional $50,000 is certainly attractive, but we must consider all of the uncertainties surrounding the second offer. Will Cougar Company still be in business a year from now? Will it have the money to make the payment? What if the putter design does not turn out to be the answer to every duffer's prayer and Cougar is unhappy with the deal? What if the design turns out to be very expensive to manufacture and the market will not accept the high price? We must find a way to put the two offers on the same basis so we are able to compare them.

If we are able to do so and decide to accept Cougar's offer with the delayed payment, then we can draw up an agreement that spells out what happens if some of these unforeseen events occur. That is one of the ways that attorneys make a living. The process of reaching a written agreement about the conditions of the second payment may itself resolve some of the uncertainties, making the deal even more attractive. The second payment might be put in escrow or secured by other assets of the buyer, and so forth. The possibilities are endless, *but* as they unfold during the deal, we must be able to evaluate their impact on the worth of the transaction from our standpoint. If Cougar will not agree to any measures to safeguard our position, we might be better off to call it quits and try to reopen negotiations with Zing. In any case, we require some yardstick for comparison, and that is what this chapter presents.

Present Value

What is the essential difference between the offers of Cougar and Zing? It is the concept of the time value of money as measured by its "present value." The present value of a cash offer is obvious, and the comparison of two different cash offers can be made without difficulty. When we introduce the element of time, the complication begins. What is the present value of $300,000 to be received in one year? And what do we need to know about the situation in order to calculate it? The first consideration we must address is how confident we feel that the payment will be made, in full, and on time. If we feel *really* confident about the buyer's integrity and ability to pay, our reasoning could be as follows:

1) If I had the $300,000 today instead of in one year, I could put it in my money market fund and earn 4%. At that rate, the $300,000 would be worth $312,222 (compounded monthly). This calculation uses the basic formula that we learned in early mathematics schooling, $I = Prt$, (interest equals principal times rate times time). To calculate the future amount directly, the formula is transformed to amount $= P(1 + rt)$.
2) Looking at the other side of the coin, we ask ourselves,

How much would I have to put into my money market fund today in order to have $300,000 in one year? The answer is $288,256. This calculation uses another permutation of the basic interest formula, present value = future value/(1 + *rt*).

3) So the present value of the right to receive $300,000 in one year is $288,256, *at an interest rate of 4%.*

If I feel that Cougar Club Company is as financially reliable as the holder of my money market fund, then my analysis is complete. If, on the other hand, I am not so confident about receiving the $300,000 payment on time (or at all!), I would want a greater return for accepting that additional risk. The interest rate in the calculation is the measure of my perceived risk. The present value of $300,000 to be received in one year at an interest rate of *15%* is $258,453. At a rate of *25%*, it is only $234,241. So now a comparison of the prospective sales look like this:

$$\text{Zing's Offer} = \$550{,}000 = \frac{\text{Present Value}}{\$550{,}000}$$

Cougar's Offer =

$300,000 cash	$300,000	$300,000	$300,000
	@4%	@15%	@25%
$300,000 in one year	$288,256	$258,453	$234,241
Total	$588,256	$558,453	$534,241
Zing's offer	$550,000	$550,000	$550,000
Difference	$ 38,256	$ 8,453	$ − 15,759

Armed with this calculation, we can see that, depending on the amount of confidence we have in Cougar making good on the commitment to pay the remaining $300,000 in a year, their offer could either be better or worse. Given the difficulty of precisely quantifying that risk, it might be better, in this circumstance, to accept Zing's offer and head for the bank. It is essential, however, to have some means of quantifying the prospective financial rewards. In the world of intellectual property, it is very important to understand these concepts because the real-world exploitation of intellectual property very often requires the acceptance of future payments or other economic benefits.

What do we require in order to make these calculations? We need to know the *amount* of the delayed payment, *when* it is to be made, and *how much risk* is associated with receiving it. At one time, Thomas Edison was offered $100,000 for one of his inventions by Western Union. This was a mind-boggling sum at that time, and the inventor said, "The money's safer with you; just give me $6,000 a year for 17 years." Edison understood more than he may have thought about the time value of money, although he was a bit generous about the interest rate! Appendix A provides lists of books that discuss present value theory and formulas used in its calculation. Present value tables are included in several of the recommended references.

THE ESSENTIAL INGREDIENTS

Amount of Income

In the example above, the *amount* of the payments to be received is clear ($300,000 now, $300,000 in one year). In the real world, the "amount" portion of the equation can be much more obscure, and can comprise payments to be received as well as expenses to be borne. Building on the same example, let us assume that a third prospective buyer, Golden Shark Enterprises, offered $600,000 if we would videotape a commercial on how we developed the putter. Or, the amount can be other than money. Suppose one of the prospective buyers offered $525,000 cash and free golf equipment for the rest of my life and free tickets to the Masters tournament? In the one case, we would have to calculate the present value of the videotaping expense and net that against the immediate cash payment. In the other, we would have to estimate the present value of the retail cash equivalent of the golf equipment we might want and add that to the immediate cash payment (the value of the Masters tickets would require a more artful judgment!). There are endless possibilities, but all require that we reduce the immediate and future receipts and obligations to a "common denominator," their *present value*. Only then can we compare alternative schemes.

When the Income Is to be Received

Sometimes the "when" of receipts or obligations is clear (as when they are to be made according to a prearranged schedule), but more often they are dependent on other events. When we might receive the benefit of the free golf equipment would depend on how much we play, our health, our skill (how many golf balls will we hit into the woods in a season?), where we live, and so forth.

The "when" is a very important element in present value calculations. The present value of the $300,000 payment to be received at different times in the future can vary as follows:

	1 Year	2 Years	5 Years	10 Years
@4%	$288,256	$276,972	$245,701	$201,230
@15%	$258,453	$222,659	$142,370	$67,564
@25%	$234,241	$182,896	$87,062	$25,266

As illustrated above, the relative effect of "when" is also

greatly altered by the rate of interest assumed. At high interest rates, the deterioration in value is accelerated as receipt is delayed. The present value concept is applicable to any pattern of cash flows as well. At a rate of 15% compounded monthly, all of the following payment schemes have a present value of $300,000:

12 monthly payments of $26,743

$100,000 in cash plus 12 monthly payments of $17,829

11 monthly payments of $19,332 plus $135,649 in one year.

Risk of Achieving the Income

Usually, the most difficult ingredient is the quantification of risk, as measured by the rate of interest, or "discount rate." We will use the term "discount rate" henceforth because expressing the receipt of future benefits in current terms is a process of discounting. There are a number of methods used to estimate an appropriate discount rate, and many of these are discussed in Appendix A. The essence of these, however, is a consensus of returns required by investors on investments of different types in the marketplace.

As an example, investors in United States government securities typically accept rates of return at the lowest end of the range of possible investment returns, currently around 4%. This reflects these investors' perception that this type of investment is nearly riskless. At the other end of the range, investors in the common stock of a start-up, high-technology enterprise may require a rate of return of 30, 40, or 50%. That is, they determine the price of their investment so that the amount expected to be received in the future will be such that they will realize a very high return.

Suppose that an investor in the common stock of a high-risk enterprise expects that a share of the stock will sell for $100 in five years, after new products are developed and successfully introduced to the marketplace. If he or she requires a 40% return on that investment because of the low probability of success (or the high probability of default), then he or she would calculate the present value of $100 to be received in five years at a 40% interest rate to determine an acceptable price, which is $18.59. Stated another way, an investor who pays $18.59 for a share of stock in this enterprise will receive a 40% rate of return if everything goes according to plan and the stock can be sold for $100 in five years. This is risk and its quantification, and later chapters will discuss it in much greater detail as it applies to intellectual property.

DISCOUNTED CASH FLOW

While it has not been called by this term, the process we have illustrated above is the technique of analyzing an investment by discounting cash flows.

Basic Application

The classic illustration of this technique is the purchase of a security, such as a share of common stock. Assume the following:

1) Today's market price of one share of the stock is $45.00.
2) The company currently pays a quarterly dividend of $0.56 per share.
3) Earnings of the company are currently $3.75 per share, and are expected to grow at 8% annually.
4) We expect to hold the stock for three years.

Under these conditions, we could expect that the dividends

paid by the company will grow at 8% per year, and if no market aberrations are expected, the price of the stock will also grow at that rate. If we purchase a share of this stock, the transaction will produce a series of positive and negative cash flows. First, there will be a negative cash flow when we reduce our savings and pay out the $45.00. Then there will be a series of positive quarterly cash flows starting at $0.56 and growing. Finally, when we sell the share of stock in three years, there will be a positive cash flow of $56.69 ($45.00 grown at an 8% annual compound rate for three years).

If all this were to go according to plan, what rate of return would we have achieved on this investment? To calculate this, we need to calculate the summation of the present values of the negative and positive cash flows using different discount rates until they net to zero. Some refer to this as a calculation of the *internal rate of return* (IRR). This is a trial-and-error process best left to a computer or financial calculator. The result of this is the rate of return I would achieve if I entered into this transaction and if the dividends and future stock price were as expected. In this example, the discount rate is 12.37%. As an investor, I must decide whether that rate of return is appropriate relative to what I perceive as the risk of the investment. If it is, I purchase the stock. If it is higher than I require, I purchase it eagerly. If lower, I wait for the price to come down or look for an alternative investment.

Using Discounted Cash Flow Analysis

Discounting cash flows involves using an equation with several ingredients. In the example above, we solved it for the rate of return. If we have decided on an appropriate rate of return and have made an estimate of future cash flows, we can solve for the price (or the present value of the transaction). This is the way we will most often use the discounted cash flow technique. As a shortcut we usually calculate the *net* cash flows:

	Year 1	Year 2	Year 3
Cash Inflow	$1,000	$1,200	$900
Cash Outflow	500	1,400	600
Net Cash Flow	$ 500	$−200	$300

The present value of the net cash flow is the sum of the present values of each year's amount. We will calculate this by multiplying each year's net cash flow by a discount factor, in this case, at a rate of 15%:

Net Cash Flow	$500	$−200	$300
Discount Factor	0.928	0.800	0.689
Present Values	$464	$−160	$207
Sum of Present Values =	$511		

By using this technique, we can compare one potential transaction with another, even though they have different cash flows, different timing of those cash flows, and a different perceived risk. The alternative with the largest present value is the most attractive.

Income Statement Format

Cash flow forecasts are typically structured in the form of a modified income statement. They are usually more detailed than the income statement that one would find in the annual report of a company, and they contain additional information in that the objective is to estimate cash flows, not net income as defined by Generally Accepted Accounting Principles (GAAP). A typical GAAP income statement might appear as shown in Figure 3.1, beginning with Sales Revenue and ending with Net Income.

Note that this business shows a loss in its first three years of operation. It depicts a start-up situation in which the revenue from the early sales of a product is insufficient to offset research and development and marketing expense. A cash flow forecast adds line items that are required to calculate net cash flows during the forecast period:

Depreciation. Depreciation is shown as a current expense in GAAP income statements as a means to allocate the cost of tangible property over the periods during which it is used up in the production of income. Amortization, when that is shown, accomplishes the same purpose for intangible assets or other previously incurred costs. These are "noncash" items (the cash has already been spent), and so we add them back into the cash income stream.

Working Capital Additions. Net working capital is the difference between the balance sheet amounts of current assets and current liabilities. For most enterprises, this is a positive amount, and represents capital required to cover near-term expenses of the business. As a business grows, the amount of net working capital usually grows with it. This additional capital is either generated from outside the business or by diverting profits that would normally be available to investors back into the business. In either case, if the forecast includes enterprise growth, the additional net working capital is a reduction from cash flow.

Capital Expenditures. Capital expenditures in the cash flow

YEAR	0	1	2	3	4	5	6	7	8	9	10
Sales	0	2,500	24,000	75,000	180,000	224,640	280,351	349,878	436,647	544,936	680,080
Cost of Sales	0	2,000	15,000	35,000	72,000	89,856	112,140	139,951	174,659	217,974	272,032
Gross Profit	0	500	9,000	40,000	108,000	134,784	168,211	209,927	261,988	326,962	408,048
Operating Expenses:											
General & Administrative	250	300	2,880	9,000	21,600	26,957	33,642	41,985	52,398	65,392	81,610
Research & Developement	1,000	500	0	0	0	0	0	0	0	0	0
Marketing	0	2,000	2,400	7,500	18,000	22,464	28,035	34,988	43,665	54,494	68,008
Selling	0	500	4,800	15,000	36,000	44,928	56,070	69,976	87,329	108,987	136,016
Operating Profit	(1,250)	(2,800)	(1,080)	8,500	32,400	40,435	50,464	62,978	78,596	98,089	122,414
Income Taxes	0	0	0	3,230	12,312	15,365	19,176	23,932	29,867	37,274	46,517
Net Income	(1,250)	(2,800)	(1,080)	5,270	20,088	25,070	31,287	39,047	48,730	60,815	75,897

Figure 3.1 Pin-Point Products: Strategic Business Unit Value

projection are very similar to net working capital additions, except that they arise from the need to add to property, plant, and equipment. As such, they represent a reduction in cash flow *and* cause a corresponding increase in depreciation expense since they add to the depreciation base.

With these additional items reflected, our cash flow forecast now appears as in Figure 3.2.

In this forecast of cash flows, the early operating losses are exacerbated by the need to commit additional capital to support the projected growth.

APPLICATION TO INTELLECTUAL PROPERTY

The discounted cash flow technique illustrated above is the basic form of a model that we will be using throughout this book. It assembles all of the elements of a business enterprise and allows us to examine their effect on the earning power of the enterprise. This technique is especially applicable for the economic analysis of intellectual property because intellectual property finds its value as part of a business enterprise. Intellectual property may be only one element in the portfolio of assets within a business, or it may be responsible for the creation of a whole new enterprise. Either situation can be addressed by this methodology. This technique also permits a sensitivity analysis related to the elements that are primary to driving the amount of present value.

The discounted cash flow technique is also uniquely appropriate because it facilitates *changes* in the underlying assumptions of a forecast as a potential transaction is structured and, when used with computer spreadsheet software, provides an instantaneous result. We therefore highly recommend its use in the context of the economic analysis of intellectual property.

YEAR	0	1	2	3	4	5	6	7	8	9	10
Sales	0	2,500	24,000	75,000	180,000	224,640	280,351	349,878	436,647	544,936	680,080
Cost of Sales	0	2,000	15,000	35,000	72,000	89,856	112,140	139,951	174,659	217,974	272,032
Gross Profit	0	500	9,000	40,000	108,000	134,784	168,211	209,927	261,988	326,962	408,048
Operating Expenses:											
General & Administrative	250	300	2,880	9,000	21,600	26,957	33,642	41,985	52,398	65,392	81,610
Research & Developement	1,000	500	0	0	0	0	0	0	0	0	0
Marketing	0	2,000	2,400	7,500	18,000	22,464	28,035	34,988	43,665	54,494	68,008
Selling	0	500	4,800	15,000	36,000	44,928	56,070	69,976	87,329	108,987	136,016
Operating Profit	(1,250)	(2,800)	(1,080)	8,500	32,400	40,435	50,464	62,978	78,596	98,089	122,414
Income Taxes	0	0	0	3,230	12,312	15,365	19,176	23,932	29,867	37,274	46,517
Net Income	(1,250)	(2,800)	(1,080)	5,270	20,088	25,070	31,287	39,047	48,730	60,815	75,897
Cash Flow Calculation:											
+ Depreciation	0	26	242	753	1,804	2,251	2,810	3,506	4,374	5,458	6,811
- Working Capital Addtns	0	313	2,688	6,375	13,125	5,580	6,964	8,691	10,846	13,536	16,893
- Capital Expenditures	250	250	2,150	5,100	10,500	4,464	5,571	6,953	8,677	10,829	13,514
Net Cash Flow	(1,500)	(3,337)	(5,676)	(5,452)	(1,733)	17,277	21,562	26,909	33,581	41,908	52,300

Figure 3.2 Pin-Point Products: Strategic Business Unit Value

Some Examples

In the following paragraphs, we present some of the more typical situations in which one can could benefit from the use of the discounted cash flow technique relative to the exploitation of intellectual property. These examples are greatly simplified in order to illustrate the breadth of the technique. In subsequent chapters, we will present in detail the complex elements that must be considered in order to apply it meaningfully.

Sell (Buy) Outright Versus Payments. This is the golf club transaction used above, and the decision process is the same.

Sell (Buy) Outright Versus Conditional Payments. This adds the complexity of forecasting the elements of the purchaser's business that control the time and amount of payment. This might be levels of sales (in dollars or units), expense reductions, or levels of market penetration.

Sell Versus License Out. A discounted cash flow model can be constructed to emulate the business of the *licensee* so that an estimate can be made of the earnings resulting from the licensed intellectual property, and therefore the potential cash flow from incoming royalties (to the licensor). The comparison is between the present value of this income stream and the potential selling price.

Buy Versus License In. This is similar to the example above, except that the licensee is forecasting its *own* business, which should permit a more precise forecast and perhaps less risky discount rate.

License Out (In). This is potentially the most complex of the discounted cash flow analyses because one is attempting to quantify the economic effect of various licensing schemes. The basic comparison is between the present value of the licensor's (licensee's) business with and without the effect of the license rights. Again, the exercise is quite different for licensor and licensee because each has proprietary information unknown to the other. Chapter 7 presents a detailed discussion of this analysis.

Joint Venture. This can be complex as well because of the many forms of joint venture. The joint venture could be an entirely new enterprise, in which it would be necessary to construct a model that will encompass its complete operation. The comparison is between the present value of the complete operation and its value without the contribution of one of the partners. This form of exploitation is discussed in Chapter 8.

Many joint ventures introduce a new element into an existing enterprise, such as additional sales resulting from a marketing agreement. In this case, one adds the new elements into a "base case" model to observe the value of the enterprise with and without the joint venture agreement.

Internal Exploitation. This is similar to the joint venture situation, except that the additions to the "base case" model must include all of the elements of an enterprise, such as sales, cost of sales, operating and G & A expenses, working capital, and capital additions. In addition, one must consider the "side effects" on the base business such as erosion of existing sales, shortage of capital or labor resources, and the like.

In Chapters 4–6, we will discuss the ways to analyze intellectual property exploitation schemes so as to quantify the essential three elements necessary to the discounted cash flow technique—the *amount* of cash flow, the *timing* of the cash flow, and the *risk* of achieving the cash flow.

4

Economic Contributions of Intellectual Property

Fully expanded, this chapter title is really asking the question: "How much of the earnings of a business enterprise are derived from intellectual properties such as patents, trademarks, and copyrights?" The answer to this question is the foundation on which licensing royalty rates and joint venture profit splits are based.

This chapter first discusses the basic ways in which intellectual property delivers enhanced amounts of corporate earnings. Then a detailed example is provided that shows the earnings contributions derived from a world-class trademark. The analysis focuses on the earnings power of the trademarks that are exploited by Gillette. When these earnings are contrasted with the meager earnings of an unbranded personal care products company, Goody Products, Inc., the earnings power of intellectual property is demonstrated. The analysis presented in this chapter provides a framework for isolating the earnings contribution of almost all forms of intellectual property. It serves as the basis for negotiating royalty rates in licensing transactions and equity splits for joint ventures. Also presented in this chapter are the weaknesses associated with commonly used royalty rate derivation methods.

INTELLECTUAL PROPERTY CONTRIBUTES POWERFULLY TO EARNINGS

Delivering a product or service to customers involves costs. Rent, maintenance, utilities, salaries, raw materials, sales commissions, and advertising are just some of the costs involved with delivering a product or service. When these costs are kept below the amount that customers pay for the product or service, a profit is earned.

The mere existence of profit, however, is not enough to justify company investments in intellectual property. Before creating, buying, or licensing intellectual property, its contribution to the overall earnings of the enterprise in which it will be used must be determined. Earnings derived from operations must be of an amount, on a consistent basis, to yield a fair rate of return on investment. A huge investment in fixed assets must be justified. Raw materials inventory, industrial land, delivery trucks, manufacturing buildings, and production equipment cannot be justified if the funds that were used to acquire these assets could generate a higher return from alternate investments. When T-bills produce a 4% return, a plant and equipment investment must deliver an investment rate of return that exceeds the safe rate of 4% by an amount necessary to compensate for the added investment risk.

INTELLECTUAL PROPERTY SUSTAINS SUPERIOR EARNINGS

In our competitive economic environment, profits are eventually driven downward to the lowest level at which a fair return can still be extracted from participation in a mature market. Above-average profits are not often sustainable for long periods. Competitors are quick to recognize and enter high-profit markets. New entrants in a high-profit market force lower selling prices and squeeze profitability. This microeconomic process is efficient in general, but can be bumpy for market participants along the way. Attractive profit levels often attract more competitors than the market will bear. When supply exceeds demand, the corresponding reduction in selling prices can make the entire industry unprofitable in which to continue competing. After the inevitable shake-out, the profitability of the industry tends towards the lowest price at which a fair return can still be earned. Previous glories of above-average profits become only memories. Keystone intellectual property, however, can help deliver sustained superior profits.

ACTIVE INTELLECTUAL PROPERTY

When above-average profits are generated on a consistent basis, intellectual properties are responsible. Active intellectual properties are categorized as those that are directly responsible for generating sustained amounts of above-average profits. Active intellectual properties work to control costs of production or introduce product characteristics that command premium selling prices. Sometimes, intellectual property contributes by commanding a premium selling price on a consistent basis regardless of competitor actions. Well-recognized trademarks are good examples. Two polo shirts of identical material and construction quality can differ in selling price by as much as $25. Customers are willing to pay, on a consistent basis, more money for the "POLO" logo. The same can be said to be true for other consumer goods like TOSHIBA personal computers, SONY television sets, TORO lawn mowers, MAYTAG kitchen appliances, and some of the Japanese automobile offerings. As long as the entire amount of premium is not spent on image-creating advertisements, net profits are enhanced.

Premium selling prices are not only associated with trademarks. Patented products can also command premium prices. An example is the ulcer drug, "TAGAMET." Generally, the production equipment investment that is needed to manufacture medicine tablets is similar to the equipment needed to make other medicines like aspirin. Patented drugs, however, are likely to sell at $1.00 or more per tablet, while aspirin costs under $0.10 per tablet.

Production costs savings are another example where active intellectual properties are a source of enhanced earnings. There are various ways that intellectual property can directly contribute to controlling production costs, including:

1) Reduction in the amount of raw materials used.
2) Substitution of lower cost materials without sacrifice of quality or product performance.
3) Increases in the amount of production output per unit of labor input.
4) Improved quality that reduces product recalls.
5) Improved production quality which reduces waste or finished product rejects.
6) Reduced use of electricity and other utilities.
7) Production methods that control the amount of wear and tear on machinery, and thereby reduce the amount of maintenance costs and production down-time for repairs.
8) Elimination of manufacturing steps and the machinery investment previously used in the eliminated process.
9) A process that reduces or eliminates effluent treatment.

When above-average profits are earned on a consistent basis, some form of intellectual property is responsible. Figure 4.1 illustrates two ways in which active intellectual property contributes to earnings.

The middle set of bars presents the *standard* profitability for a product that is associated with a mature market. The selling price is competitively determined in a mature industry at a level that allows market participants to earn a marginally fair rate of

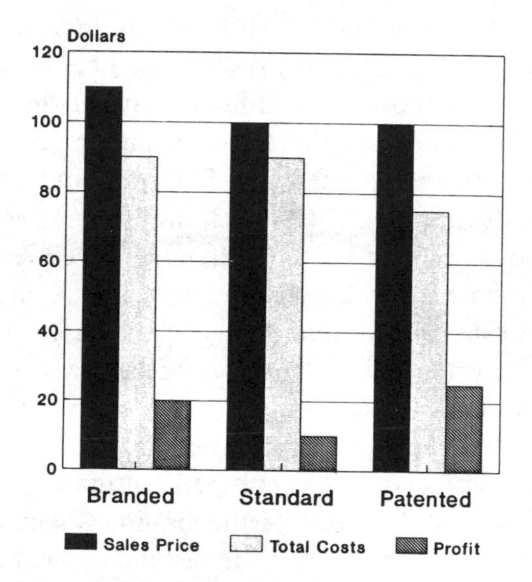

Figure 4.1 Intellectual Property Earnings Enhancement

return on their fixed asset investment, but above-average profit levels are not possible. Costs of production and overhead costs associated with administration, selling, and general expenses are shown at a hypothetical 90% of the selling price. The remaining 10% represents operating profits before taxes. In a mature market, net profits, after paying income taxes, are typically 4–6% of sales or less.

The set of bars on the right shows the enhanced profitability that might be contributed by a *patented* process. Excluding use of the process by competitors allows the company to sell at the competitively determined market price, but at the same time enjoy higher profits due to production cost savings. Operating profits are enhanced by the exact amount saved in production costs. Total costs in this example are reduced from the standard 90% of the selling price to 75%. The earnings contribution derived from the patented process is represented by the enhanced profit margin of 15%.

The set of bars on the left shows a product that can consistently command a higher selling price in an otherwise competitive market. All of the costs of producing and selling the branded product are the same, but the higher selling price allows enjoyment of above-average profits. The 10% premium price translates directly to a 10% increase of operating margins. This example might be associated with a product that has a well-regarded trademark for which people are willing to pay the premium price shown. The brand name intellectual property contributes directly to enhanced earnings, but this is only true if the higher price that the brand image commands can be obtained without higher advertising expenses. Most likely, the reason that a higher selling price can be commanded in a competitive market is because an image has been established for the brand. Image creation and maintenance requires huge advertising budgets, but as long as the additional advertising expenses are not greater than the earnings enhancement from better selling prices, then the brand name intellectual property can contribute directly to earnings.

A combination of the two forces is also quite possible. A combination of intellectual properties can provide a premium price and also allow lower production costs, producing a compounding of enhanced earnings.

PASSIVE INTELLECTUAL PROPERTY

Enhanced profitability can also be derived from passive intellectual property where profits are not directly enhanced from premium selling prices or cost savings. These intellectual properties can be just as valuable, but their contribution to earnings enhancement is more subtle. Even when active contributions to earnings are not present, intellectual property can provide a company with above-average profits. A dominant position in a market allows a company to enjoy a large sales volume on a consistent basis. Manufacturing and operating synergies can then enhance profits. Patented processes are not necessarily responsible for higher earnings. Costs are saved very often just from operating efficiencies associated with large-scale production. Only because of passive intellectual property, however, is this possible.

When large and reliable amounts of production volume consistently go through an organization, synergistic advantages are possible, and they generally lead to enhanced profits. Some of the typical synergies associated with large production volumes include:

1) Raw materials can be purchased at large-order discounts. Suppliers are likely to offer discounts to customers that place large orders. A cost savings is the result.
2) Manufacturing efficiencies can be introduced throughout each step of the process.
3) Selling expenses might be more controllable, with fewer sales people covering large accounts.
4) Retail efficiencies can include special arrangements with distributors or discounts in the purchase of shelf space at retailers.
5) Regulation and compliance costs can be spread over a larger production base, along with other fixed overhead costs.
6) Large volumes can allow companies to provide utility companies with guaranteed energy purchases which could be obtained at a bulk rate discount.

Each synergistic benefit combines to provide enhanced profits, which is made possible by market-dominating intellectual property like trademarks and distribution networks.

ENHANCED PROFIT MARGINS DO NOT TELL THE WHOLE STORY

Active and passive intellectual properties can deliver enhanced profits. The incremental increase can be looked on as indicating the earnings contribution associated with intellectual property that is being considered for a licensing or joint venture project. Unfortunately, an analysis that ends after only studying the profit margins can be wholly incorrect. A more proper method must study the total earnings of a business enterprise relative to the investment in monetary and fixed assets. Only then will it be possible to identify the contribution that was delivered by the intellectual property.

Intellectual property assets rarely generate economic benefits alone. Rather, complementary assets, in the form of working capital and tangible assets, are typically combined into a business enterprise. This portfolio of business assets generates an overall economic return. Allocation of the total company returns among the asset categories that comprise the portfolio can isolate the amount of return that is attributable to the intellectual property.

HOW MUCH DID THE INTELLECTUAL PROPERTY EARN?

A comparison of two companies is presented in this chapter to show the earnings contribution of intellectual property. The following analysis allocates the total return derived from the two business enterprises among the integrated assets that are used in the businesses. The allocation of earnings is conducted relative to the amount invested in each asset category and the investment risk associated with each asset category.

Two companies that design, manufacture, and sell personal care products are compared. The products that they manufacture and sell possess commodity-like characteristics, but one of the companies possesses a world-class portfolio of brand names—*Gillette*. The other company, *Goody Products*, does not possess any significant brand names. We attribute the excess earnings enjoyed by Gillette to the ownership and exploitation of its brand name intellectual property. The following analysis provides an indication of the amount of excess earnings that are contributed by the intellectual property of Gillette.

Isolating the stream of economic benefits that are derived from intellectual property is the key to fairly compensating companies that enter into strategic alliances. The required analysis allocates the anticipated economic benefits from the overall business enterprise to the asset categories that are employed in the generation of these benefits.

As stated earlier, delivering a product or service to customers involves investment and costs. Rent, maintenance, utilities, salaries, raw materials, sales commissions, fees, and advertising are just some of the costs involved with delivering a product. When these costs are kept below the amount that customers pay for the product or service, a profit is earned. The mere existence of profit, however, is not enough to justify company intellectual investments. Earnings derived from operations must be of an amount, on a consistent basis, to yield a fair rate of return over the term of the investment in the intellectual property, as well as the complementary monetary and fixed assets. A huge investment in fixed assets must be justified. Raw materials, industrial land, delivery trucks, manufacturing buildings, and production equipment cannot be justified if the funds that were used to buy and build these assets could generate a higher return from alternate investments. Excess earnings go to the companies that possess intellectual property. Otherwise, the most that a company can expect is to earn a fair rate of return on the working capital and fixed plant investment.

In allocating earnings to intellectual property, a fair return must first be allocated to nonintellectual property assets. The allocation must address two important factors;

1) the relative amount of each asset category involved in the business, and
2) the appropriate rate of return to associate with each asset category.

Business enterprises are comprised of monetary assets, tangible assets, intangible assets, and intellectual property. Economic benefits are generated from the integrated employment of these complementary assets: net profits. Each asset contributes. Based upon the relative importance of each asset category and the risk associated with each asset category, the aggregate net income of the enterprise can be allocated to its components. Figure 4.2 shows the composition of a typical business enterprise that was presented earlier.

Each of these asset categories contributes to the overall achievement of earnings. Before it is possible to allocate the enterprise earnings, we must first determine an appropriate rate of return to associate with each of the component parts. Starting

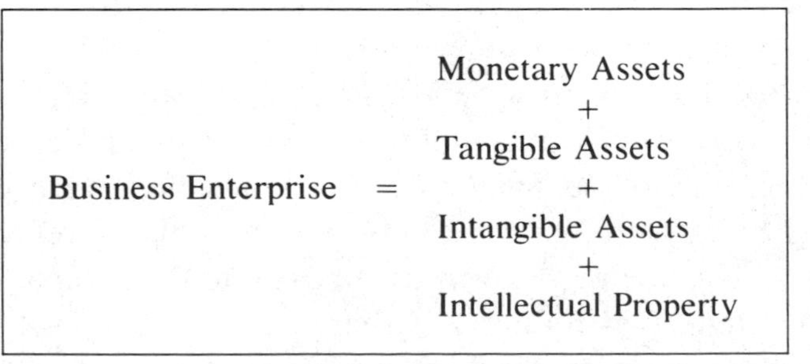

Figure 4.2 Composition of a Business Enterprise

with the rate of return requirement for the overall enterprise, an assignment of rates of return for each asset category can be estimated.

A NOTE ABOUT EARNINGS

Throughout this analysis, a broad definition of earnings is used. Debt-free operating net income is used to eliminate, wherever possible, some of the artful manipulations to net income that are used by creative and sometimes desperate company managements. It represents the income from operations of the company. The use of the term "earnings" throughout this analysis is meant to describe, in broad terms, economic benefits that a company derives from its commercial activities. Earnings, as used here, are not used strictly to describe the accounting concept of net income. Earnings contributions from intellectual property should be studied independently of all interest payments that are associated with a company. Interest expenses are associated with the financing decisions of company management which can substantially affect the overall company earnings. Debt ratios are a fundamental and important factor to analyze when studying investments, but should be considered separately from the analysis of intellectual property contributions. Intellectual property contributions are independent of financial structures and should be studied in that manner.

Debt-free operating net income can be looked upon as the total economic benefit that the business enterprise, and the assets of which it is comprised, generates from continuing operations. Absent from this measure of economic benefits are extraordinary items that are not expected to recur in the future. Unusual bad debt write-offs are an example, as are windfalls from large one-time-only contracts.

The use of debt-free operating net income as the measure of economic benefits still, however, accounts for all of the variable, fixed, selling, administrative, and overhead expenses that are required to exploit intellectual property. Omission of any of these expenses overstates the amount of economic benefits that may ultimately be allocated to the intellectual property.

In a comparison of two items of intellectual property, the property which generates sales, captures market share, and fosters company growth while using less selling and/or support efforts is more valuable than the one which requires extensive advertising, sales personnel, and administrative support. The economic benefits generated by the property are most accurately measured after considering all production, selling, and support efforts associated with the business.

In a comparison of two items of intellectual property, the property which generates sales, captures market share, and fosters company growth while using less monetary and tangible assets is also more valuable than the one which requires higher fixed asset investment.

The analysis presented below captures the contribution of intellectual property relative to both cost control and optimized fixed asset investment.

RATE OF RETURN REQUIREMENTS FROM THE INTEGRATED PORTFOLIO OF BUSINESS ASSETS

Corporate investments typically must pass hurdle rates in order to be considered as viable opportunities. Since debt and equity funds are used to finance these investments, the return that is provided must be sufficient to satisfy the interest due on the debt, and also provide a fair rate of return on the equity funds. The hurdle rate must be the weighted average cost of capital

(WACOC)[1] in order to earn a fair rate of return on invested capital. The cost to the company of the invested capital equals the rate of return that the investors expect to receive less any tax benefits that the company enjoys, such as the deductibility of interest expenses on debt.

Invested capital is defined as the summation of the fair market value of equity funds and debt obligations. The capital structure of the company might be a complex collection of bonds, notes, subordinated debentures, common stock, warrants, and preferred stock. Nonetheless, the total fair market value of the debt obligations and the various equity capital components represents the total invested capital of the business enterprise. These are the funds that were used to obtain the complementary assets of the business, including land, buildings, machinery, truck fleets, office equipment, patented technology, and net working capital.

GOODY PRODUCTS—COMMODITY EXAMPLE

Goody Products, Inc. is basically a commodity products manufacturer. It designs, manufactures, and sells hair care accessory products such as barrettes, rollers, combs, hairbrushes, ponytail holders, bobby pins, and shower caps. Very little technological

[1] The weighted average cost of capital is a weighting of the investment rates of return required by equity investors and debtors of the corporation based on the percentage of each in the capital structure of the company. It represents the minimum amount of return that should be generated by a corporate investment. It is often referred to as the "hurdle rate." A thorough discussion is provided in the book *Financial Theory and Corporate Policy* by Thomas E. Copeland and J. Fred Weston, published by Addison-Wesley Publishing Company. A specific discussion about the topic as it applies to intellectual property is contained in Appendix A, "Investment Rates of Return Requirements."

advantages are evident in their products, and very little brand name recognition is involved with demand for these products. The aggregate value of stockholders' equity at the time of this writing was $104.9 million, and the value of long-term debt can be fairly approximated at the book value of $53.5 million. The total value of the overall business enterprise was therefore $158.4 million.

An allocation of the invested capital to the asset categories of Goody Products is presented in Figure 4.3.

The source of values for the Goody Products asset value allocation are described in Figure 4.4.

A comparison of the market value of the invested capital of Goody Products with the values of monetary and fixed assets leaves little room for any intellectual property value. Based upon the earnings of the company, growth prospects, and investment risk characteristics, the investment marketplace is not placing a premium value on the company. The value placed on the company represents a fair value for the monetary and fixed assets. The earnings of the company are not to support a higher value for any intellectual property.

Income from operations for the year ending December 31,

Goody Products Asset Category Values

	($ Million) Value	Percent of Total
Working Capital	71.0	44.8%
Fixed Assets	69.5	43.9%
Intangible Assets	15.8	10.0%
Intellectual Property	2.1	1.3%
Total	158.4	100.0%

Figure 4.3 Allocation of Assets Equals Invested Capital

Asset Category	Source of value.
Net Working Capital	Book value as reported in the company financial statements.
Fixed Assets	Average of the gross and net amounts shown in the financial statements. Net value is considered to understate the operating value of assets due to aggressive depreciation policies.
Intangible Assets	Estimated at 10% of the total value of invested capital.[2]
Intellectual Property	Residual amount of invested capital after allocation to the other assets listed above.

Figure 4.4 Goody Products Asset Category Values

1991 are estimated to be approximately $7.5 million after reversing interest expenses and extraordinary, nonrecurring items. This represents a current yield, on the $158.4 million of invested capital, of only 4.7%. Even after factoring in growth, the return on investment leaves very little to attribute to intellectual property. All of the earnings from company operations are consumed by a required rate of return on monetary and fixed assets.

This financial analysis supports a qualitative analysis of the company. Its products are commodity items, plainly blister-

[2] The intangible assets of Goody are comprised of a trained work force, an established distribution network, management information software, and other corporate practices and procedures. The value presented in this chapter is estimated from years of consulting experiences involving mergers and acquisitions. Precise methodologies for valuing this category of assets are presented in the book *Valuation of Intellectual Property and Intangible Assets* by Gordon V. Smith and Russell L. Parr, published by John Wiley & Sons.

packed and sold from peg hooks on the walls of discount stores. A comb is a comb is a comb. Rarely do consumers rush to *Target* stores to look exclusively for Goody combs, barrettes, or hairpins. Obviously, there is little technological innovation possessed by this company. The company has an insignificant advertising budget for the support of brand names, and an equally small amount allocated for technological research and development.

In a licensing deal or joint venture, it is doubtful that anyone would pay much of a royalty for use of the Goody name or for use of its product technology. Goody does not have any, and the financial analysis bears out this conclusion.

GILLETTE IS ANOTHER STORY

Gillette Company manufactures and sells a wide range of personal care products including razors, razor blades, electric shavers, toiletries, cosmetics, dental products, and writing instruments. The majority of products are sold under internationally known brand names such as Braun, Parker Pen, Oral B, and its flagship brand—Gillette. Gillette-branded products accounted for about 37% of sales and over 60% of net income recently. During 1990, $677 million was spent on advertising and sales promotion in support of the continued customer recognition of the Gillette brand name portfolio. This represents approximately 15.6% of 1990 sales. In 1989 and 1988, advertising and promotion expenses were 17.2 and 16.9% of respective sales. Technology is not ignored either at Gillette. The new *Sensor* razor technology is reported to have required $300 million in research and development.

The differences between Goody Products and Gillette are not as strong as they initially appear. Both companies sell their products in chain drug stores, discount stores, and convenience markets. Both companies sell low-priced merchandise that is mostly a staple. Both companies therefore sell a low-priced commodity product to a mass market in a competitive environment. The difference is that Gillette has nurtured and supported world-class trademarks and Goody has not. The remainder of this chapter will show how the trademarks payoff by isolating the economic returns that are contributed to the enterprise.

THE INTELLECTUAL PROPERTY OF GILLETTE

Gillette has a total value of invested capital of $12.7 billion comprised of $11.2 billion of equity and $1.5 billion of long-term debt (both equity and debt are valued at market prices). The company is comprised of various asset categories, just like Goody Products, which must equal the value of the invested capital. Figure 4.5 allocates the total amount of invested capital amount among all of the assets used by Gillette using the same procedure as used for Goody Products.

The economic contribution from the Gillette intellectual property requires an allocation of the total debt-free net income of the enterprise. Based on the value of the different assets used in the business and the relative investment risk associated with each, the intellectual property contributions can be isolated. The weighted average cost of capital (WACOC) for Gillette is the key factor. The weighted average cost of capital is based upon the market value of equity and the value of long-term debt. WACOC represents the minimum amount of investment return that should be considered as acceptable from operating the business. When the cost of these capital components are weighted by their percentage of the total capital structure, a weighted average cost of capital for Gillette of 14.7% is the result. This is the amount of return that the company must earn on its overall investment as comprised of the monetary assets, tangible assets, intangible

Gillette Company Asset Category Values

	($ Million) Value	Percent of Total
Working Capital	957.0	7.6%
Fixed Assets	931.0	7.3%
Intangible Assets	1,268.1	10.0%
Intellectual Property	9,525.2	75.1%
Total	12,681.3	100.0%

Figure 4.5 Allocation of Assets Equals Invested Capital

assets, and intellectual property. Each asset component must provide a portion of the overall return relative to the risk associated with that asset. The tax deductibility of interest expense makes the after-tax cost of debt only 60% of the stated interest rate for the corporation. It pays a combined state and federal income tax of 40%. Equity returns are in no way tax deductible.

The weighted average cost of capital requirement can be allocated among the assets that are employed within the business enterprise. The allocation is conducted with respect to the amount of investment risk that each component represents to the business enterprise. Just as the weighted average cost of capital is allocated among the debt and equity components of the invested capital, it is also possible to allocate a portion of the WACOC to the asset components, with consideration given to the relative risk associated with each category of assets.

APPROPRIATE RETURN ON MONETARY ASSETS

The monetary assets of the business are its net working capital. This is the total of current assets minus current liabilities. Current assets are comprised of accounts receivable, inventories, cash, and short-term security investments. Offsetting this total are the current liabilities of the business such as accounts payable, accrued salaries, and accrued expenses.

Working capital is considered to be the most liquid asset of a business. Receivables are usually collected within 60 days, and inventories are sometimes turned over in 90 days. The cash component is immediately available, and security holdings can be converted to cash with a telephone call to the firm's broker. Further evidence of liquidity is the use of accounts receivable and/or inventories as collateral for loans. In addition, accounts receivable can be sold for immediate cash to factoring companies at a discount of the book value.

Given the relative liquidity of working capital, the amount of investment risk is inherently low in comparison to that of the other asset categories. An appropriate rate of return to associate with the working capital component of the business enterprise is typically lower than the overall WACOC. A surrogate rate of return can be used to estimate a proper amount to associate with the working capital; that which is available from investment in short-term securities of low risk levels. The rate available on 90-day certificates of deposit or money market funds can serve as a benchmark. While net working capital may be more risky than bank deposits, it is still much less risky than the other assets categories. As an alternative, a corporation could earn a low-risk short-term rate of return on working capital if it were not invested in the operating business. As such, the operations of the business must earn at least that amount on working capital.

APPROPRIATE RETURN ON TANGIBLE ASSETS

Tangible or fixed assets of the business are comprised of production machinery, warehouse equipment, transportation fleet, office buildings, office equipment, leasehold improvements, and manufacturing plants. While these assets are not as liquid as working capital, they still possess some elements of marketability. They can often be sold to other companies or used for alternate commercial purposes. This marketability allows a partial return of the investment in fixed assets of the business should the business fail.

Another aspect of relative risk reduction relates to the strategic redeployment of fixed assets. Assets that can be redirected for use elsewhere in a corporation have a degree of versatility which can still allow an economic contribution to be derived from their employment even if it is not from the originally intended purpose.

While these assets are more risky than working capital investments, they possess favorable characteristics that must be considered in the weighted average cost of capital allocation. An indication of the rate of return that is contributed by these assets can be pegged at about the interest rate at which commercial banks make loans, using the fixed assets as collateral. The use of these rates must be adjusted, however, to reflect the equity risk position of the owners, which is slightly riskier than that of the lenders.

Fixed assets that are very specialized in nature must reflect higher levels of risk which, of course, demands a higher rate of return. Specialized assets are those which are not easily redeployed for other commercial exploitation or liquidated to other businesses for other uses. They may be closely tied to the intellectual property and possess little chance for redeployment. In this case, a rate of return similar to that required on intellectual property may be more appropriate. In general, the tangible assets of a business are less risky than the intellectual property.

An alternative fixed asset investment for a company could be the capital leasing of fixed assets to other manufacturers where it would earn a return commensurate with the risk of collateralized lending. When an operating business is chosen as the investment vehicle, then, as a minimum, the collateralized lending rate of return must be earned on the fixed assets that are used.

APPROPRIATE RETURN ON INTELLECTUAL PROPERTY

Intangible assets and intellectual property are considered the most risky asset components of the overall business enterprise. Trademarks can become out of sync with the attitudes of society, and patents can be made obsolete by the advancing technology of competitors. These assets may have little, if any, liquidity and poor versatility for redeployment elsewhere in the business. This increases their risk. Customized computer software that is installed and running on a company's computer may have very little liquidation value if the company fails. The investment in a trained work force may be altogether lost, and the value of other elements of a going concern are directly related to the success of the business. A higher rate of return on these assets is therefore required. Since the overall return on the business is established as the weighted average cost of capital, and since reasonable returns for the monetary and tangible assets can be estimated, we are then in a position to derive an appropriate rate of return to be earned by the intellectual property.

Each of these assets contributes to the overall required rate of return. For Gillette, the overall required return was determined to be 14.7%. Based upon the relative risk discussion presented earlier, Figure 4.6 assigns different levels of required return to the different asset categories.

The weighted average cost of capital requirement can be allocated among the assets that are employed within the business enterprise. The allocation is conducted with respect to the amount of investment risk that each component represents to the business enterprise. Just as the weighted average cost of capital is

Asset Category	Asset Value	Percent of Total	Required Return	Weighted Return	Percent of Weighted Return	Allocation of DFNI	DFNI as Percent of Sales
Net Working Capital	957.0	7.5%	8.0%	0.6%	4.1%	21.7	4.1%
Fixed Assets	931.0	7.3%	12.0%	0.9%	6.0%	31.6	6.0%
Going Concern	1268.1	10.0%	15.5%	1.6%	10.6%	55.9	10.5%
Intangible Assets	9,525.2	75.2%	15.5%	11.7%	79.4%	420.6	79.4%
	12,681.3	100.0%		14.7%	100.0%	529.8	100.0%

Figure 4.6 Allocation of the Required Rate of Return Among the Gillette Enterprise Assets ($ Millions)

allocated among the debt and equity components of the invested capital, it is also possible to allocate a portion of the WACOC to the asset components, with consideration given to the relative risk associated with each category of assets.

As a result of these investment rate of return requirements, the intellectual property of Gillette accounts for almost 80% of the total debt-free operating net income of the company. Of the $529.8 million of debt-free operating net income generated by the company, $420.6 million is attributed to the intellectual property. Without intellectual property, the company could be expected to have earned only $108 million.

Excess returns were earned from the employment of intellectual property.

As a percent of sales, the excess returns of $420.6 million represents almost 9% of 1991 sales of $4.68 billion. This is calculated on an after-tax basis. Since royalties are a pretax expense, the pretax indication of intellectual property royalties that Gillette could afford to pay is 15%. If we attribute most of the excess, intellectual property returns to the brand names of Gillette, then an appropriate royalty rate is 15% of sales.

Gillette generated enough earnings to provide a fair rate of return on the complementary assets, and still has excess earnings generated from intellectual property. In comparison with Goody, the analysis shows that the intellectual property of Gillette is the source of excess earnings contributions.

ADJUSTED GROSS PROFITS CAN ALSO INDICATE INTELLECTUAL PROPERTY CONTRIBUTION MARGINS

A comparison between the gross profit margins of Gillette and Goody Products can also be viewed as a shortcut indication of the contribution of key intellectual property. Presented in Figure

4.7 is the recent history of gross profit margins for both companies adjusted for advertising and promotion expenses. Gross profit margin comparisons can indicate the contribution of intellectual property. Brands can contribute to high gross profit margins by commanding premium selling prices. They also can capture huge amounts of market share which allow for manufacturing economic synergies. When compared to a company that does not enjoy these same benefits, an indication of the economic contribution of intellectual property results.

An adjustment to the gross profit margin for expenses associated with advertising and promotion is considered to be appropriate. Companies that possess brands and the associated benefits do not get the benefits for free. The cost is represented by the continuous need to support the value of the brand. As such, the gross profit margins for Gillette and Goody Products are adjusted for historical advertising expenses. The adjustment was especially easy for Goody because they do not spend any significant amounts on brand advertising and promotion.

Figure 4.7 presents the adjusted gross profit margins for Gillette.

Figure 4.8 presents the adjusted gross profit margins for Goody Products.

Figure 4.9 shows the economic advantages of having a

Year	Gross Profit Margin	Advertising Expenses	Adjusted Gross Profit Margin
1991	59%	15.6% est.	43.4%
1990	58	15.6	42.4
1989	58	17.2	40.8
1988	58	16.9	41.4

Figure 4.7 Gillette Gross Profit Margins

Year	Gross Profit Margin	Advertising Expenses	Adjusted Gross Profit Margin
1991	35.1%	0% est.	35.1%
1990	33.5	0	33.5
1989	30.3	0	30.3
1988	33.5	0	33.5

Figure 4.8 Goody Products Gross Profit Margins

world-class brand name. The economic advantage of the Gillette intellectual property is calculated as the difference between the adjusted gross margins of Gillette and Goody Products.

It is important to remember that this shortcut method does not specifically address the differences that may exist in the amounts of complementary assets that are employed by the two different companies. This shortcut method is only reliable if the relative amounts of complementary assets for the two companies are similar. In the case of Gillette and Goody Products, the complementary asset similarities are not a safe assumption. Gil-

Year	Gross Profit Margin Advantage
1991	8.3%
1990	8.9%
1989	10.5%
1988	7.9%
Average	8.9%

Figure 4.9 Adjusted Gross Profit Margin Difference Between Gillette and Goody Products

lette displays a fixed asset turnover ratio of 5.0, calculated as sales divided by the gross book value of fixed assets. The company generates $5 of sales for each $1 it has in fixed assets. The working capital turnover ratio for Gillette is 4.8, calculated as sales divided by net working capital. This indicates that the company generates $4.8 of sales for each $1 of net working capital. The fixed asset turnover ratio for Goody is 2.2, and the working capital turnover ratio is 3.0.

A comparison of adjusted gross profits is a very useful method to identify an order of magnitude at which intellectual property contributes to economic advantages. The more detailed method presented in this chapter should be completed as part of preparing for licensing and joint venture negotiations.

COMMONLY MISUSED INTELLECTUAL PROPERTY PRICING METHODS

Some of the more commonly used royalty rate development models are presented in this section, along with highlights of their primary deficiencies.

ARBITRARY ALLOCATIONS OF THE ECONOMIC BENEFIT

One of these calculates a royalty as 25% of the gross profit, before taxes, from the enterprise operations in which the licensed intellectual property is used. At best, this method of royalty determination is too broad. *Gross profit* has never been accurately defined where this rule is discussed. Gross profit based upon a generally accepted accounting principles definition includes the direct costs of production.These include raw material costs, direct labor, manufacturing utility expenses, and even depreciation expenses of the manufacturing facilities. All of the costs and expenses associated with the conversion of raw materials into a final product or service are captured. Since this is most likely the area of greatest contribution from intellectual property, consideration of the amount of gross profit in setting a royalty is reasonable, but it fails to consider the final profitability that is ultimately realized with the licensed property. Absent from the analysis are selling, administrative, and general overhead expenses.

An argument for eliminating these expenses from the analysis might center upon the idea that the value of intellectual property, such as manufacturing technology, should not be measured with respect to royalties by analysis of business areas in which it has no direct input. A more broadened view, however, shows that an intellectual property royalty can be affected by the selling expenses and other support expenses that are part of the commercialization. Intellectual property that is part of a product or service which requires little marketing, advertising, and selling effort can be more valuable than a product based upon intellectual property that requires the use of national advertising and a highly compensated sales personnel.

Two patented products may cost the same amount to produce and yield the same amount of gross profit. Yet, one of the products may require extensive and continuing sales support, while the other does not. The added costs of extensive and continuing sales efforts make the first product less profitable to the licensee. While the two products may have the same gross profit, it is very unlikely that they would command the same royalty.

The profit level after consideration of the nonmanufacturing operating expenses is a far more accurate determinant of the contribution of the intellectual property. The royalty for specific intellectual property must reflect the industry and economic environment in which the property is used. Some environments are competitive and require a lot of support costs which reduce net profits. Intellectual property that is used in this type of environment is not as valuable as property in a high-profit environment where fewer support costs are required. A proper royalty must reflect this aspect of the economic environment in which it is to be used. A royalty based upon gross profit cannot accomplish this portion of the analysis.

The 25% rule also fails to consider the other key royalty determinants of risk and fair rates of return on investment. The percentage of gross profit that should ultimately go to the licenser is considered by most advocates of the 25% rule to be flexible. Where licensees must heavily invest in complementary assets, a lower percentage of gross profit may be more proper. If very little investment is needed, then a royalty based upon the majority of gross profits may go to the licenser.

Intuitively, this seems to be correct, yet it is unsatisfying because the methodology provides no clue as to quantifying a relationship between licensee capital investment and the percentage of gross profit that goes to royalty.

Too many important factors cannot be reconciled by arbitrary allocations of the economic benefit to estimate a royalty rate. Using this method in negotiating a royalty rate is very difficult. There are many factors to be considered in selecting an appropriate split of gross profits. Unstructured consideration of these many factors, without a formalized investment analysis, is bound to omit from consideration the effect of some very important factors.

INDUSTRY NORMS

This royalty rate determination methodology misses even more of the important elements than arbitrary allocations. Here, consideration of the profitability of the enterprise using the intellectual property is lacking, in addition to the other failures noted above. The industry norms method focuses upon the rates that others are charging for intellectual property licensed within the same industry. Investment risks, net profits, market size, growth potential, and complementary asset requirements are all absent from direct consideration. The use of industry norms places total reliance upon the ability of others to correctly consider and interpret the many factors affecting royalties. Any mistakes made by the initial setting of an industry royalty are passed along.

Changing economic conditions, along with changing investment rate of return requirements, also are absent from consideration when using industry norms. A royalty established only a few years ago is probably inadequate to reflect the changes in the value of the licensed property and the changes that have occurred in the investment marketplace. Even if an industry norm royalty rate was a fair rate of return at the time it was established, there is no guarantee that it is still valid. Value, economic conditions, rates of return, and all of the other factors that drive a fair royalty have dynamic properties. They constantly change, and so must the underlying analysis that establishes royalties.

RETURN ON R&D COSTS

When considering a reasonable royalty, consideration of the amount that was spent on the development of the intellectual property could be terribly misleading. The main theme of the analysis presented throughout this book concentrates on providing a fair rate of return on the value of the intellectual property assets. The amount spent in the development is rarely equal to the value of the property. A proper royalty should provide a fair return on the *value* of the asset, regardless of the costs incurred in development.

The underlying value of intellectual property is founded upon the amount of future economic benefits. Factors that can limit the benefits include the market potential, the sensitivity of profits to production costs, the period of time over which benefits will be enjoyed, and the many other economic factors that we have discussed. The development costs do not reflect these factors in any form. Basing a royalty on development costs can completely miss the goal of obtaining a fair return on a valuable asset.

RETURN ON SALES

A royalty that is based upon net profits as a percentage of revenues has several primary weaknesses. The first difficulty is the determination of the proper allocation of the profits between the licenser and the licensee. A precise and quantifiable method for dividing the net profits is rarely specified when this royalty rate methodology is described. Another area of weakness is the lack of consideration for the value of the intellectual property that is invested in the enterprise, as well as a lack of consideration for the value of the complementary monetary and tangible assets that are invested. Finally, this method fails to consider the relative investment risk associated with the intellectual property.

SUMMARY

The determination of a royalty rate for a license agreement or profit split for a joint venture should be at such a level so as to provide an amount which represents a fair rate of return on the value of the investment in the intellectual property with respect to the amount of investment risk accepted. The earnings that are attributed to intellectual property must consider any enhanced earnings that are enjoyed by the business, and must also consider the amount invested in the complementary assets of net working capital and tangible assets.

The royalty must consider at least:

1) Investment rates of return available from alternative forms of investment possessing comparable elements of risk.
2) The value of the intellectual property that is the subject of the licensing.
3) The amount of complementary monetary and tangible assets required to commercialize the intellectual property.
4) The relative investment risk associated with the complementary monetary and tangible assets.
5) The investment risk associated with the intellectual property introduced by factors such as advancing and competing technology, industry economics, governmental regulations, and other factors.

Intellectual properties in the form of trademarks and patents can dramatically contribute to earnings. The return on monetary and fixed asset investments can be propelled to extraordinary levels with the introduction of intellectual property. The comparison of Gillette and Goody Products presented in this chapter showed the economic contribution where brand names are dominant. The same procedure can be used in cases where patents or copyrights dominate.

In the next chapter, an analysis of ten industries is presented that identifies the intellectual property returns that are generated by a sample number of companies in each industry. The intellectual property returns are then correlated with financial performance measures of the selected companies. Interesting insights are the result, and should be useful guidance for establishing licensing royalty rates and joint venture splits.

5

Intangible Returns In Key Industries

In the previous chapter, the economic contribution from intellectual property was defined as intangible earnings, represented by the amount of excess earnings that remain after an appropriate investment return is earned on working capital and fixed plant investments. Once a fair return is allocated, earnings that remain can be attributed to the advantageous economics provided by the intellectual property. This chapter presents an analysis of several hundred companies to show the level of intangible returns that are common to specific industries.

A sample of publicly traded companies for ten different industries was selected. The intangible returns for each company were isolated as a percent of sales using the rate of return analysis presented in Chapter 4. Comparisons between the amount of intangible returns for each company with other performance characteristics provides guidance in assessing the economic value of intellectual property for different industries. The results are presented in a series of graphs for each industry. The graphs can be useful in estimating the royalty rate that should be negotiated in a license deal. The graphs can also be useful in isolating the level of profits brought to a joint venture by intellectual property.

Care must be taken in using these graphs, especially when large investments in fixed assets are involved. The indicated royalty is only valid when a fair return is first available for the working capital and fixed plant investment.

The following industries are analyzed for intangible returns:

Specialty chemicals

Pharmaceuticals

Electronics
Food products
Medical products
Computer hardware
Computer software
Industrial machinery
Cosmetics and personal hygiene products
Mega-brands.

The last analysis focuses on a cross section of industries where the common denominator is exploitation of one or more world-class brand names.

SPECIALTY CHEMICALS ECONOMIC ROYALTY RATES

Companies in the specialty chemicals industry were analyzed to identify and isolate intangible returns. A total of 28 companies was analyzed. Intangible returns for specialty chemicals companies are displayed as a percentage of revenues, and are compared to other operating characteristics such as gross profit margins, debt-free net income levels, and fixed investment returns.

Companies

The companies in this analysis include:

Airgas
American Colloid

Armour All

Balchem

Barrier Sciences

Betz

Cambrex

Chemdesign

Chemed

Crompton Knowles

Detrex

Dexter

Ferro

Flamemaster

Great Lakes Chemical

Hauser Chemical

Hawkins

International Flavor & Fragrances

IVAX

Kinark

Lawter

Learonal

Loctite

Lubrizoil

MacDermid

Nalco Chemical

NCH

Novelles

Petrolite
Sigma Aldrich

Products

The types of products produced by these companies include industrial gases, industrial cleansers, water treatment compounds, fire retardant chemicals, alcohols, pigments, pesticides, plating compounds, fuel additives, oil treatment compounds, adhesives, sealants, waxes, anti-corrosion products, degreasing solvents, metal polishes, lubricating oils, anti-scaling compounds, anti-freeze, and other industrial chemicals.

Industry Conditions

Technological know-how is considered as the primary source of these intangible earnings. Trademarks are considered less important as part of the buying decision for specialty chemicals. Purity, quality, performance, and price are more important marketing forces for a specialty chemical. The intangible returns of specialty chemical companies are therefore attributed to technological know-how and patents. Supporting information can be found in an analysis of advertising expenses and R&D expenditures. While very little effort is placed behind advertising, R&D expenditures are growing. R&D expenditures in the chemical industry for 1989 were 9% higher than the prior year, with still higher growth expected in the future. The current state of the chemicals industry is characterized as being in a new materials renaissance. These include engineered polymers, composites, advanced ceramics, and improved adhesives. All require R&D efforts and yield technological know-how. This is not true of industrial organic and inorganic chemicals. These basic chemicals represent about 25% of U.S. chemical shipments, including bulk compounds such as cholarlkalies, industrial gases, acids, and salts. Very little value-added is associated with this competitive aspect of the chemical business, and intangible returns, if they exist at all, are slim. High indications of royalties are associated with technology-based specialty chemicals.

Intangible Returns Analysis

Intangible returns are not a common phenomenon in specialty chemicals. Four of the companies analyzed, 14% of the total, were not even capable of earning a fair return on their working capital and fixed asset investments. Nothing remained in the way of intangible returns to attribute to intellectual property. These low rates of intangible return are associated with commodity chemicals such as industrial gases. A significant portion of the companies, 35%, would be unable to support a royalty rate of over 3% if their intellectual property had been licensed. Put another way, a licensee would be unwilling to pay a royalty above 3% to obtain use of the technological know-how.

Bright spots, however, exist where extraordinary amounts of intangible profit are generated by some of the companies. These are the specialty products that not only provide value-added compounds, but possess proprietary technology, trade secrets, or patents. After earning a fair return on net working capital and fixed asset investments, a few of these companies generate intangible returns that can represent as much as 20% of sales. In fact, 46% of the companies analyzed generate intangible profits at 10% of sales or higher. The implication for royalty rate negotiations and joint venture profit splits is enormous.

Typical royalty rates that prevail in the chemicals industry hover between 1 and 3% of revenues. While this amount is appropriate in many of the cases, especially amount commodity chemical companies, instances exist where this amount would grossly undercompensate for the use of the underlying technology. Care must be taken to avoid wholesale reliance on royalty rate rules-of-thumb and industry norms. In some cases, extremely valuable intellectual property in the specialty chemicals industry would be almost given away.

Intangible earnings go to the companies that possess the new technologies and can deliver new value-added products. Since a fair return is accounted for on all other assets, intangible returns in our analysis are defined as that amount of earnings that the owner of specialty chemicals technology would expect to receive in a joint venture or licensing arrangement.

Regression analysis of key performance characteristics against intangible returns yielded some interesting insights for specialty chemicals. As might be expected, high royalty rates are associated with high levels of debt-free net profits. Presented in Figure 5.1 is a regression analysis that can serve as guidance for royalty rate determination.

If an estimate of debt-free net profits for a prospective licensed product can be determined, the regression line can indicate an appropriate royalty. A 10% debt-free net profit would indicate a 10% pretax royalty using the graph. The regression data show relatively good correlation, and depending upon particular circumstances, give a good indication of where to begin reasonable royalty negotiations.

A similar analysis compared gross profit margins with intangible returns in Figure 5.2. This was attempted because many royalty rate negotiations focus on gross profits during negotiations. Surprisingly, the correlation of gross profits and intangible returns was poor, indicating that royalty rate negotiations should look beyond estimated gross profitability. Success is ultimately determined by the bottom line. Some products might be manufactured at low cost but involve substantial operating expenses for selling commissions, transportation, quality control laboratories, and process engineering. A royalty based solely

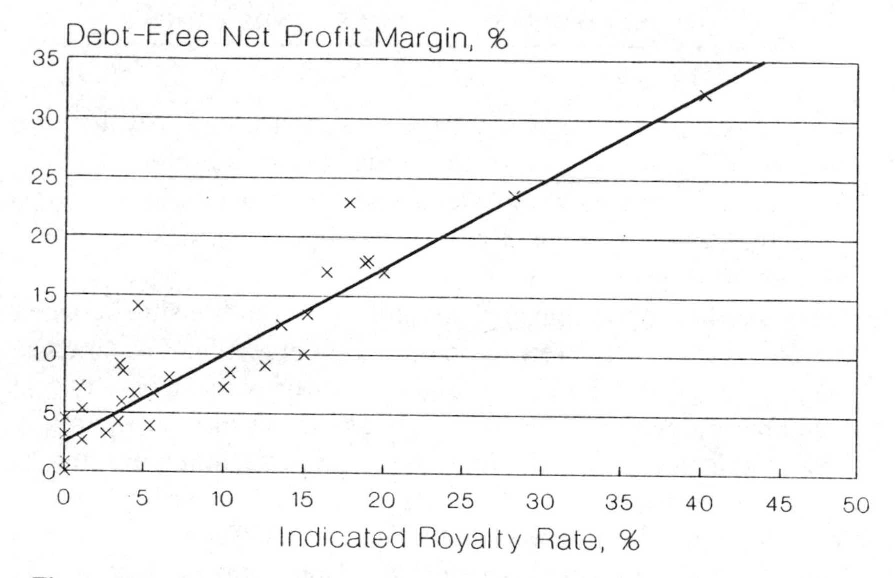

Figure 5.1 Specialty Chemicals: Excess Returns and Debt-Free Profits

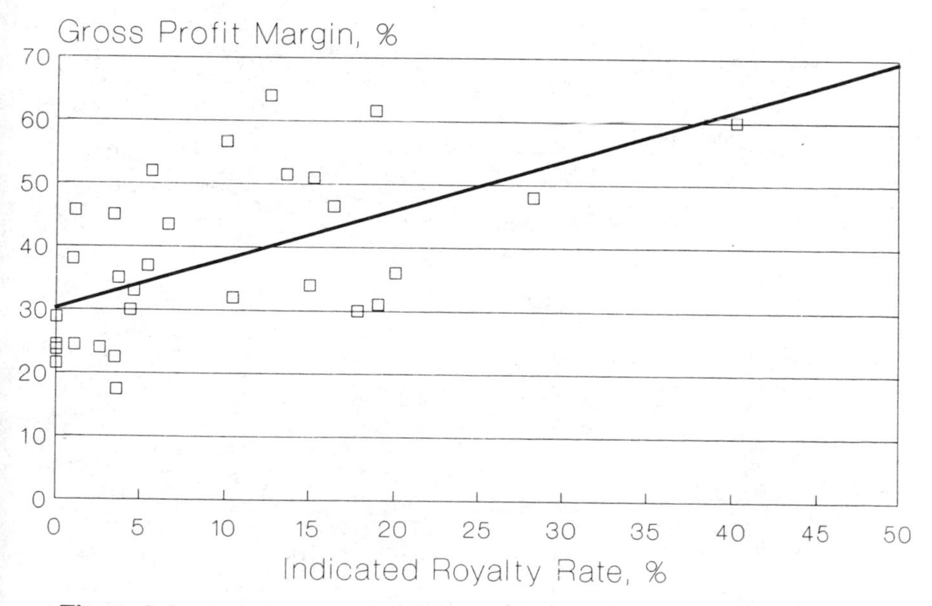

Figure 5.2 Specialty Chemicals: Excess Returns and Gross Profits

upon gross profits might improperly award a high royalty rate to a product that requires substantial overhead support. Conversely, a high royalty rate can still be appropriate for products that generate slim gross profits if overhead support expenses are low.

Another regression analysis shows the relationship between royalty rates and the return on operating investment, defined as net working capital and the original cost of plant, property and equipment. Figure 5.3 shows that as the return on operating investment increases, so does the amount of intangible return available for royalties. A 15% rate of return on operating investment indicates a potential royalty rate of 20%. Technology which allows a high rate of return from fixed plant investment should indeed command higher royalties, but unfortunately, the correlation of the graphed data is low.

Figure 5.3 Specialty Chemicals: Excess Returns and Fixed Return

Another regression analysis was performed to compare the turnover of gross property, plant, and equipment (representing the amount of fixed property needed for each dollar of sales) with intangible returns. Higher values of turnover mean that more sales are squeezed from each dollar that is invested in fixed assets. We had expected to find royalty rates associated with high turnover levels. A technology that can get more revenues out of less plant would be expected to yield high levels of intangible earnings and command a high royalty. A regression analysis in this case showed poor correlation. Extreme data points supported the hypothesis, but the middle data points just muddied the analysis. The concept of relating royalty rates with plant turnover remains unquantified for specialty chemicals.

PHARMACEUTICAL INDUSTRY ECONOMIC ROYALTY RATES

Companies in the pharmaceutical industry were analyzed to identify and isolate intangible returns. A total of 20 companies were analyzed. Intangible returns for these companies are displayed as a percentage of revenues, and are compared to other operating characteristics such as gross profit margins.

Companies

The companies in this study include:

A. L. Laboratories

Abbott Laboratories

Alza Corp.

American Home Products
Amgen Inc.
Bristol-Myers Squibb
Applied BioScience International
Block Drug
Bolar Pharmaceutical Co.
Carter Wallace
Centocor
Elan Corp.
Halsey Drug
ICN Biomedical
Immunex
Incstar
Eli Lilly
Medchem Products
Molecular Biosystems
Mylan International
Merck & Co.
Pfizer
Schering-Plough
Syntex Corp.
Upjohn Co.

Products

The types of products made by these companies include antibiotics, cough remedies, anti-inflammatories, pain relievers, muscle relaxers, amines, acids, salts, esters, tranquilizers, mental drug preparations, depilatories, medicinal chemicals, botanicals, diagnostics, and other pharmaceutical preparations.

Industry Conditions

Product shipments in the pharmaceutical industry reached $55 billion in 1990, with exports representing almost 10% of shipments. Foreign sales are expected to grow as more countries adopt comprehensive intellectual property laws. Domestic sales for products that have generic competition are expected to remain under growth pressures as a national policy for controlling health care costs continues to evolve.

Strategic alliances are being formed at unprecedented rates. Research costs and risks are becoming too extreme for even the biggest billion dollar drug houses. Companies are joining forces in joint development and product promotion. Quite often, the results of the cooperative efforts are shared between the joint venture partners based on geographical allocations, different business applications, or outright purchase by one of the partners.

Research is the backbone of the drug industry. It develops new technology-based products, and serves as the foundation for patents that allow market dominance. R&D spending has grown from 12% of sales in 1980 to almost 17% of sales by 1990. This represents over $8 billion of annual spending on research. The development of a new drug is estimated to cost $250 million. On average, it takes 12 years to develop a new drug, pass regulatory requirements, and bring the new drug to market. The technologies derived from these extraordinary amounts of research spending are vigorously defended against patent infringement. These technologies represent some of the most valuable intellectual property in the world. Pharmaceutical companies indicate the ability to pay higher royalties than any other group of companies.

Intangible Returns Analysis

Extraordinary levels of royalty rates are easily justified. All of the companies studied showed the ability to generate intangible earnings. Sixteen of the companies analyzed, 80% of the total, were capable of earning a fair return on their working capital and fixed asset investments, while still generating intangible returns exceeding 10% of sales. Over 50% of these companies generate intangible returns that exceeded 15% of sales.

A high correlation exists among the companies studied between intangible returns and gross profit margins. Figure 5.4 provides an indication of the magnitude of a fair royalty rate. As an example, if utilization of the licensed technology is expected to generate a gross profit margin of 60%, then the graph shows that a pretax 20% royalty rate would be reasonable. If, instead,

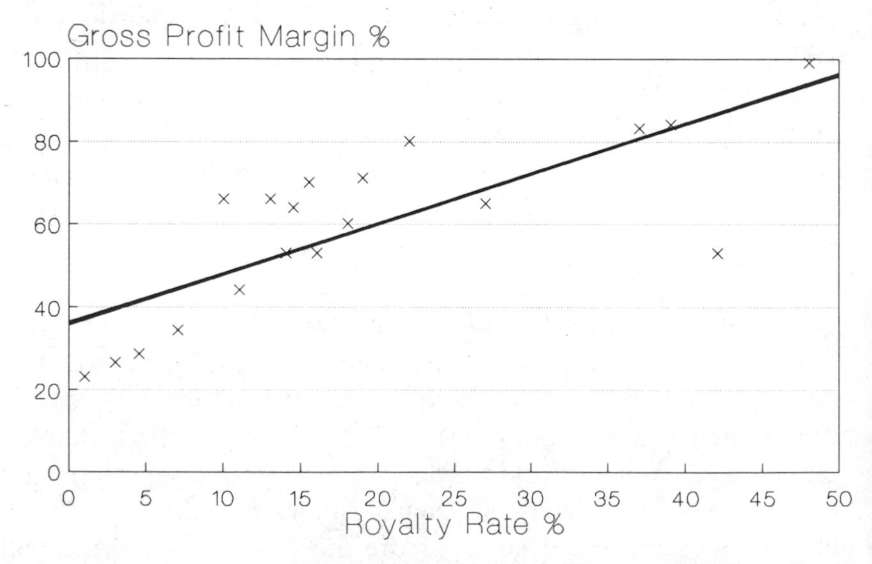

Figure 5.4 Pharmaceutical Industry: Excess Returns and Gross Profit

gross profit margins are anticipated to be 40%, then a royalty rate of under 5% is indicated. Gross profit margins in this industry are typically high. Over 75% of the companies exceeded gross profit margins of 50%. The graph shows a strong correlation between gross profit margins and intangible returns.

Regression analysis of key performance characteristics against intangible returns yielded some interesting insights for pharmaceuticals. Unexpectedly, intangible returns did not correlate well with debt-free net profits. Another regression analysis looked at the turnover of fixed property, plant, and equipment which studied the amount of fixed assets needed for each dollar of sales. Higher values of turnover mean that more sales are squeezed from each dollar that is invested in fixed assets. We had expected to find royalty rates associated with high turnover levels. A technology that can get more revenues out of less fixed property would be expected to yield high levels of intangible earnings and command a high royalty. A regression analysis in this case showed poor correlation. The concept of relating royalty rates with plant turnover remains unquantified for pharmaceuticals, just as in the specialty chemicals industry.

ELECTRONICS INDUSTRY ECONOMIC ROYALTY RATES

Companies in the electronics industry were analyzed to identify and isolate intangible returns. A total of 43 companies were analyzed. Intangible returns for these companies are displayed as a percentage of revenues, and are compared to other operating characteristics such as gross profit margins. The study shows that very few intangible earnings are achieved in the majority of cases.

Companies

The companies in this study include:

Altera
Altron
American Precision Instruments
Andrew Corp.
Augat
Aydin
BMC Industries
Boston Acoustics
Brite Voice Systems
Bytex
California Microwave
Cirrus Logic
Commcable
Comptronix
Cypress Semiconductor
Dallas Semiconductor
Datron
Dynascan
EG&G
Espey Manufacturing
EXAR
General Instrument
Gigatronics
Graham Field Health

GTI
Hadco
Integrated Device
Inacomp
Intermagnetics General
Interpoint
Intel
Invention Design Engineering
Kent Electronics
Methode Electronics
Microcom
Micron
Milgray
Molex Electronics
Plexus
Qume
Reliability
Transmation
Western Digital

Products

Products produced by the companies in this industry include printed circuit boards, antennas, microwave communications equipment, coaxial cable, television transmission equipment, semiconductors, radar systems, multiplexer equipment, space satellite communications equipment, audio systems, audio speakers, voice controls, switches, radar detectors, facsimile machines, answering machines, telephones, radios, integrated circuits, microcircuits, power measuring equipment, electronic test equipment, electronic connectors, and other electronic devices.

Industry Conditions

Electronics describe the simplest coil, and also leading-edge integrated circuits. All aspects of this industry have been hurt by the sluggish economy and overcapacity. Industry shipments are expected to exceed $70 billion in 1992, with greater sales growth coming from export sales. Semiconductors and integrated circuits account for almost 40% of industry shipments. These products are technically the most sophisticated segments of the business, and are also the most volatile. Competition around the world is very strong, and price cutting is a common weapon used in the industry to maintain market share.

Rapid change in electronics makes product lives short. Only ten years ago, the 8086 computer chip was the fastest microprocessor in the world for personal computers. Since then, we have seen the 286, 386, and just around the corner, broad use of the 486 chips. The costs of developing and manufacturing a new integrated circuit can reach $1 billion. Most likely, the new product will be obsolete in four years.

This is a tough industry in which to make money, even when keystone technology is owned. Texas Instruments is making more money from licensing activities than from actual product operations. By some counts, TI has earned $900 million from all of its licensing activities during the past decade. Earnings from product operations are running at significant losses.

Intangible Earnings Analysis

We studied 43 companies that make electronic components or devices. Over 45% did not earn any intangible returns, and many did not earn even a fair rate of return on their working capital and fixed plant investment. Only 13 companies in the group, 30%, achieved intangible returns that exceeded 5% of sales. For an industry with high research costs and sophisticated technology, these results are disturbing but true.

A correlation exists for the companies studied between intangible returns and debt-free net income. Reference to Figure 5.5 provides an indication of the magnitude of a fair royalty rate if the net debt-free profit margin is known or can be estimated. As an example, if utilization of a licensed technology is expected to generate a debt-free net income profit margin of 15%, then an 8% royalty rate on sales is indicated. If the debt-free net profit margin is anticipated to be 30%, then a royalty rate of approximately 23% is indicated, but rarely achieved. The competitive atmosphere of the industry places the majority of companies in a position where little or no intangible earnings are available for

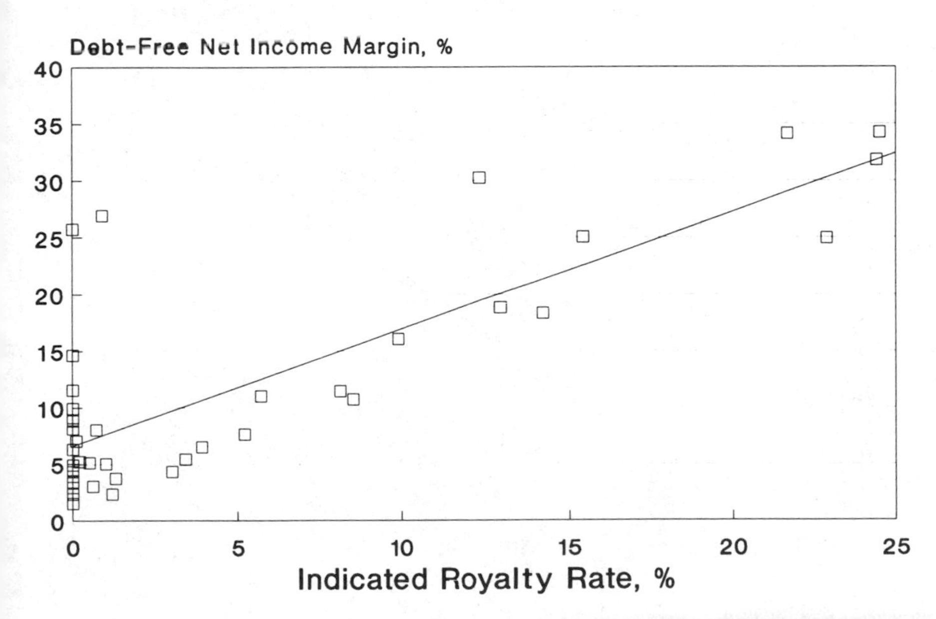

Figure 5.5 Electronics Industry: Excess Returns and Net Profit Margins

royalty payments. Figure 5.5 shows a correlation that is represented by a minority of the cases because the majority of companies showed little or no intangible earnings.

Several companies earned high amounts of debt-free net income, but still did not generate any intangible earnings. This occurs when substantial amounts of fixed plant investment are required to convert the technology into a saleable product. After a fair return is allocated to the fixed plant investment, it is still possible for no intangible earnings to remain, even when a very high level of debt-free profits is generated.

Figure 5.6 represents a similar correlation using intangible returns and gross profit margins. If a 50% gross profit margin is anticipated from using a licensed technology, then approximately 15% of sales is available as intangible earnings to pay royalties. However, more than half of the companies could not generate gross profit margins over 40%.

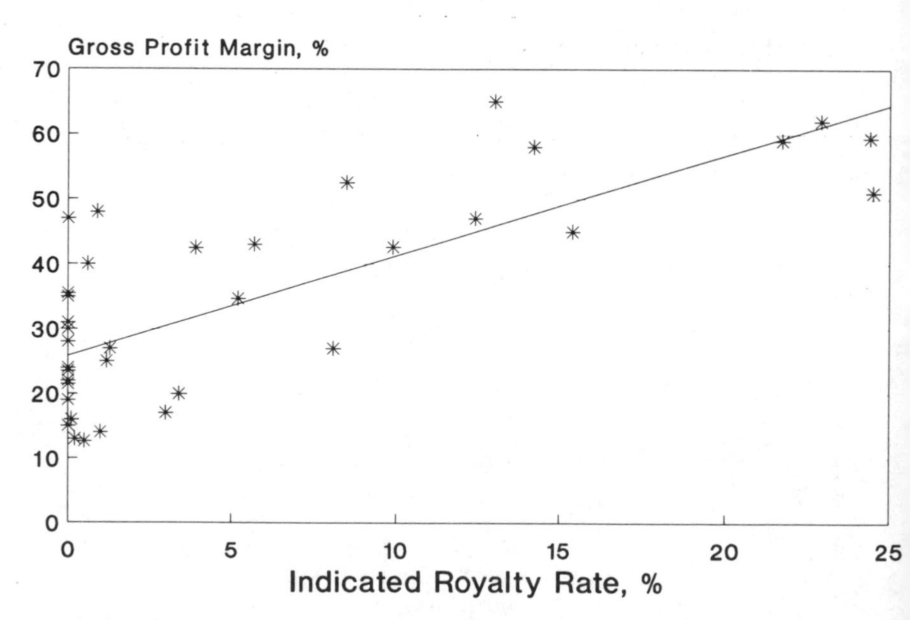

Figure 5.6 Electronics Industry: Excess Returns and Gross Profits

In general, high royalties are not easily supported in the electronics industry because:

- substantial fixed plant investments are required,
- extensive amounts of competition exist,
- new products are expensive to develop,
- new products become obsolete in this industry faster than any other.

FOOD PRODUCTS INDUSTRY ECONOMIC ROYALTY RATES

We studied 22 companies that make food products and sell them under keystone trademarks. All but three enjoyed intangible returns that are available for royalties. Where intangible returns are found to exist, they are primarily attributed to the trademarks of these companies. For the most part, the products of these companies are at parity. In many cases, they are almost commodities. It is the existence of the well-known trademarks that gains shelf space, customer loyalty, and premium prices for their owners.

Companies

The companies in this study include:

Seneca
Tasty Baking
MEI Diversified
Dean Foods
J&J Snack Foods
McCormick

Sara Lee
Quaker Oats
Campbell Soup
Ralston Purina
Cadburry Schweppes
Hershey Foods
Gerber Products
Kellogg
Lance
PepsiCo
Wrigley
Tootsie Roll
A&W Brands
Coca Cola

Products

Typical products made by companies in this industry include apple juice, snack foods, baked goods, cereals, soft drinks, candy, gum, prepared foods, and soups.

Industry Conditions

Growth in this mature industry is fueled by population growth, demographics, and the purchase of new value-added products. Major companies dominate this industry, and successful start-ups are rare. Without belittling the research that is conducted in this industry, advertising expenses that promote and nurture trademarks are the fundamental driving force behind intellectual property in this industry.

Intangible Earnings Analysis

A correlation exists for the companies studied between intangible returns and debt-free net income. Reference to Figure 5.7 provides an indication of the magnitude of a fair royalty rate if the net debt-free profit margin is known or can be estimated. As an example, if utilization of a licensed trademark is expected to generate a debt-free net income profit margin of 10%, then a pretax royalty of 8% on sales is indicated. If the debt-free net profit margin is anticipated to be 5%, then a royalty rate of approximately 2% is indicated.

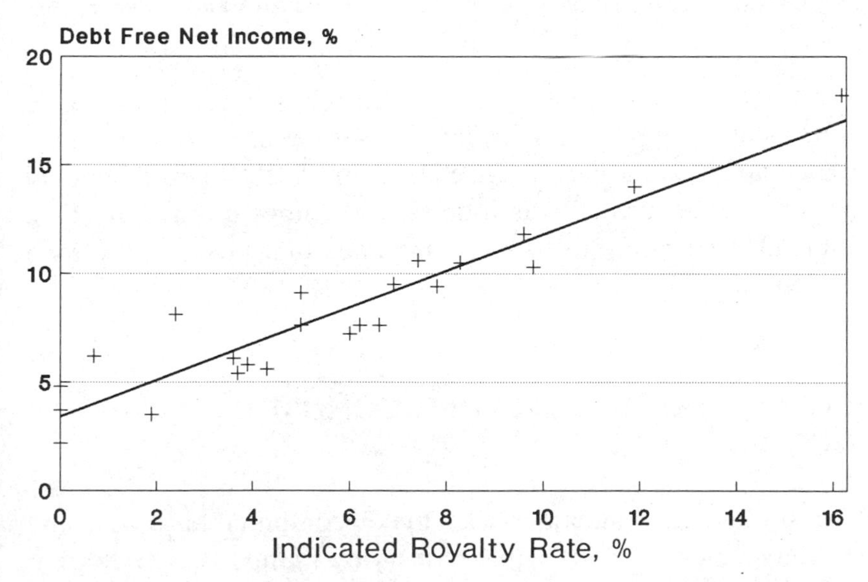

Figure 5.7 Food Products Industry: Excess Return and Debt-Free Net Income

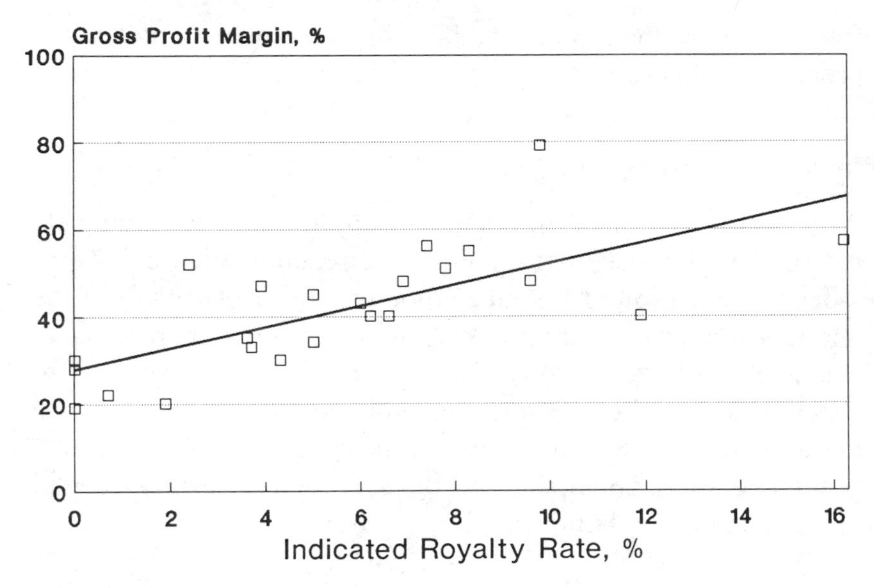

Figure 5.8 Food Products Industry: Excess Return and Gross Profits

Figure 5.8 presents a similar correlation using intangible returns and gross profit margins. If a 40% gross profit margin is anticipated from using a licensed trademark, then approximately 5% of sales is available as intangible earnings to pay royalties. Intangible earnings go to the companies that possess keystone trademarks.

COMPUTER HARDWARE ECONOMIC ROYALTY RATES

We studied 21 companies that make computer hardware and peripherals. Where intangible returns are found to exist, they are primarily attributed to the proprietary technology of the companies. High royalty rate levels, as a percentage of sales, are not common.

Companies

The companies in this study include:

- Adaptec Inc.
- Alpha Microsystems
- Archive Corp.
- AST Research Inc.
- C Cor Electronics Inc.
- Chips & Technologies Inc.
- Convex Computer Corp.
- Cray Research Inc.
- Data Switch Corp.
- Dataflex Corp.
- DH Technology Inc.
- EKCO Group Inc.
- Elbit Computers Ltd.
- Emulex Corp.
- Everex Systems Inc.
- Filenet Corp.
- Fingermatrix Inc.
- Genus Inc.
- Griffin Technology Inc.
- Hutchinson Technology Inc.
- Infotron Corp.
- Intermec Corp.
- Interphase Corp.

Key Tronic Corp.

LDI Corp.

Products

Products made by computers in this industry include magnetic storage devices, cathode ray tubes, disk drives, computer terminals, tape storage units, computer auxiliary storage units, bar code printers, optical scanning devices, magnetic ink, readers, sorters, inscribers, microcomputers, mainframe computers, and keyboards.

Industry Conditions

Circumstances within the computer peripherals industry are not encouraging. The general economic recession has greatly reduced the general level of domestic demand, which is further exacerbated by cutbacks in the defense budget. The amount of demand that still exists is subject to intense competitive pricing pressures.

This research-intense industry is besieged by an enormous number of competitors. The combination of competitive pricing and high research costs is likely to force a consolidation of industry participants in the near future.

The *1990 Business Week's R&D Scoreboard* issue reported that R&D expenses for a sample of 94 computer systems and peripheral companies reached $13.4 billion in 1989, representing 8.4% of revenues. This is more than twice the 3.4% of revenues spent on R&D for all industries.

Low profit margins and high research expenses are not an ideal combination for realizing high levels of royalty income. When these circumstances are coupled with the huge investments required in plant facilities, then low royalty rates in the industry are not surprising.

Intangible Earnings Analysis

Our analysis isolates the earnings that are attributed to intellectual property, and expresses them as a percentage of sales representing an indication of the amounts that are available for royalties. The study shows that a high correlation exists between intangible earnings and a nontraditional measure of return on investment, where the investment equals the book value of working capital plus an estimate of fair market value for fixed assets (see Figure 5.9). Also, a weak correlation exists between intangible returns and gross profit margins (see Figure 5.10).

A correlation exists for the companies studied between intangible returns and investment returns on the combined amount of net working capital and fixed assets. The amount of return is defined as debt-free net income as represented by the after-tax earnings of the company after reversing debt expenses. The in-

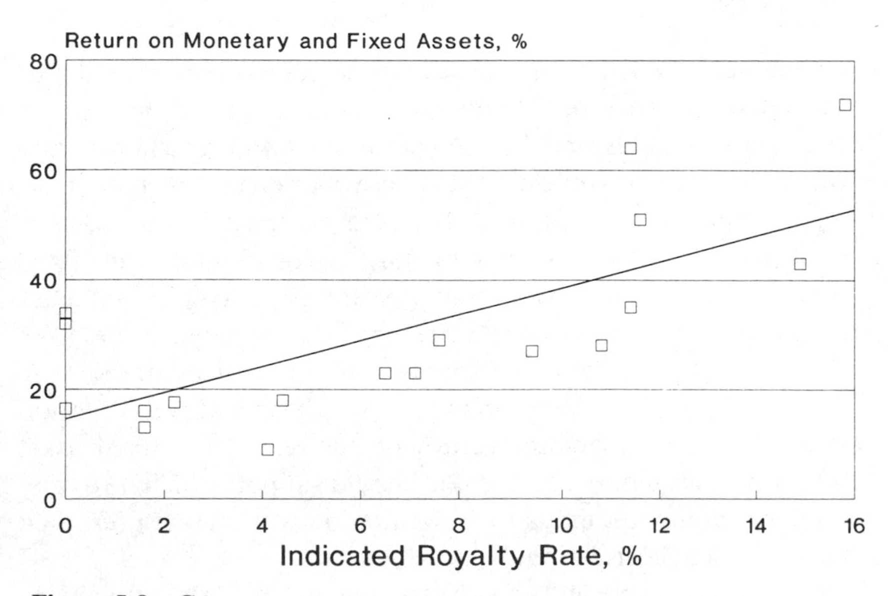

Figure 5.9 Computer Peripherals Industry: Intangible Returns Versus Fixed Return

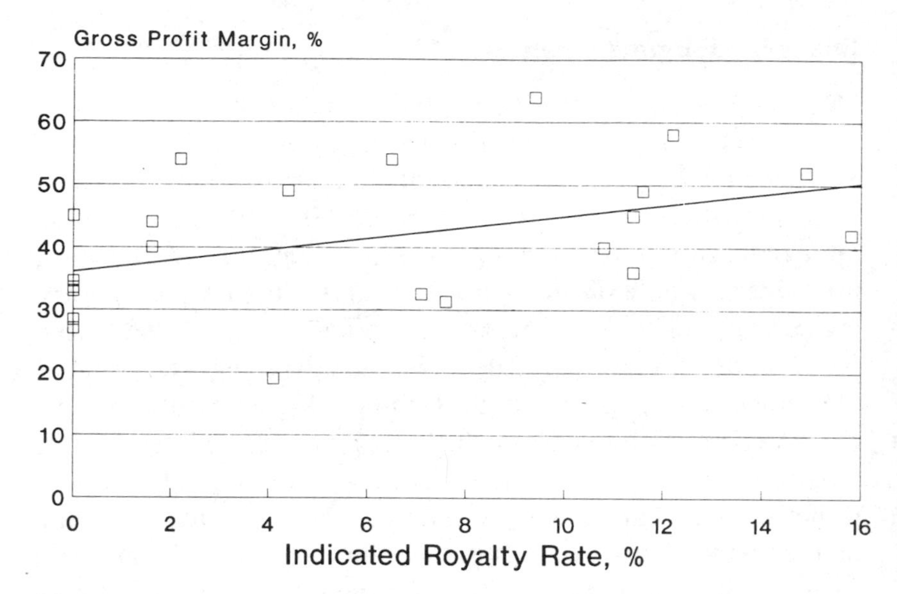

Figure 5.10 Computer Peripherals Industry: Intangible Returns and Gross Profit

vestment is defined as the book value of net working capital plus the adjusted gross book value for fixed assets. Reference to Figure 5.9 provides an indication of the magnitude of a fair royalty rate if the return on investment is known or can be estimated. As an example, if utilization of licensed computer technology is expected to generate an investment return on monetary and fixed assets of 20%, after taxes, then a pretax royalty of 2% on sales is indicated. If the investment return is anticipated to be 40%, then a royalty rate of approximately 11% is indicated.

Intuitively, this relationship makes perfect sense. Technology that allows a greater return on monetary and fixed asset investments is more valuable and should support a higher royalty rate. The computer industry is the first, however, that presented such a strong correlation.

Figure 5.10 presents a similar, but weaker, correlation using intangible returns and gross profit margins. If a 40% gross profit margin is anticipated from using licensed computer technology, then approximately 5% of sales is available as intangible earnings to pay royalties.

COMPUTER SOFTWARE ECONOMIC ROYALTY RATES

We studied 22 companies that sell different types of computer software for use with microcomputers, minis, and mainframes. Our study shows that a high correlation exists between intangible earnings and debt-free net profits. A slightly weaker correlation was also found between intangible earnings and a nontraditional measure of return on investment, where the investment equals the book value of working capital plus an estimate of the fair market value of fixed assets.

Companies

The companies in this study include:

Acxiom
Adobe
Aldus
Anacomp
Analytical Technologies
Ask Computer
Autodesk
Autoinfo
Compumat
Computer Associates

Comshare
Convergent
Cybertek
DST Systems
Hogan
NCR Corporation
Oracle
Perfectdata
Sandata
Saztec
Sterling Software
Systems Software
Weitek

Products

The types of products that these companies produce include accounting software, manufacturing controls, personal computer database programs, word processing software, networking software, utility software tools, integrated retail software, insurance industry software, integrated hotel industry software, and banking software.

Industry Conditions

The world market for packaged software reached $43 billion in 1990. The United States is the world leader in supplying computer programs, having 1990 sales of $29 billion. Sales growth has been and is expected to continue at the annual rate of 20%.

High royalties for software are supported by the relatively

low investment requirements in manufacturing equipment. Once the software is designed and perfected, the cost to reproduce and package the product is far below typical manufacturing costs. If selling prices can be maintained, then profits are directly enhanced, and the software intellectual property is the source of the enhancement. Less complementary working capital and fixed assets are needed.

In contrast, computer hardware makers have substantially more invested in manufacturing facilities. Costs are higher. Profits are proportionately reduced, and the amount of return required on fixed investment is much higher for hardware companies. This leaves less profit available for attribution to the hardware intellectual property. Product uniqueness also accounts for the difference is selling costs. Computer hardware products are approaching technological parity, and in some respects have become a commodity product. Software products possess infinitely more custom characteristics, and thus require more selling effort.

Software royalties are higher simply because they have much less invested in complementary assets. More return is therefore being generated by the software intellectual property.

Software sales, however, are not entirely free of expenses. The amounts spent by companies on marketing and administrative overhead are far greater than computer hardware companies. Possibly, this represents the unique nature of software products and the added effort that is needed to sell a program. Profits are also held in check by strong competitive forces and the constant need to create and improve software products.

Intangible Returns Analysis

Where intangible returns are found to exist, they are attributed to proprietary software programs. Three of the companies studied did not earn enough return to provide for a fair return on their working capital and fixed property investment. Only six generated intangible returns of less than 5% of sales. The majority, 86%, delivered intangible returns over 5% of sales, with 50% of the companies generating over 12% in intangible returns.

Figure 5.11 presents a correlation using intangible returns and debt-free net profit margins. If a 20% debt-free net profit margin is anticipated from using licensed software, then approximately 15% of sales is available as intangible earnings to pay royalties on a pretax basis. If profits are 30%, then a royalty of over 20% was found to be appropriate.

A correlation exists for the companies studied between intangible returns and fixed investment return. An intangible return is defined as the total amount available for royalty rates after adequate earnings are allocated to other operating assets of the company. Fixed investment returns are measured on the combined amount of net working capital and fixed assets. The amount of return is defined as debt-free net income, and it represents the

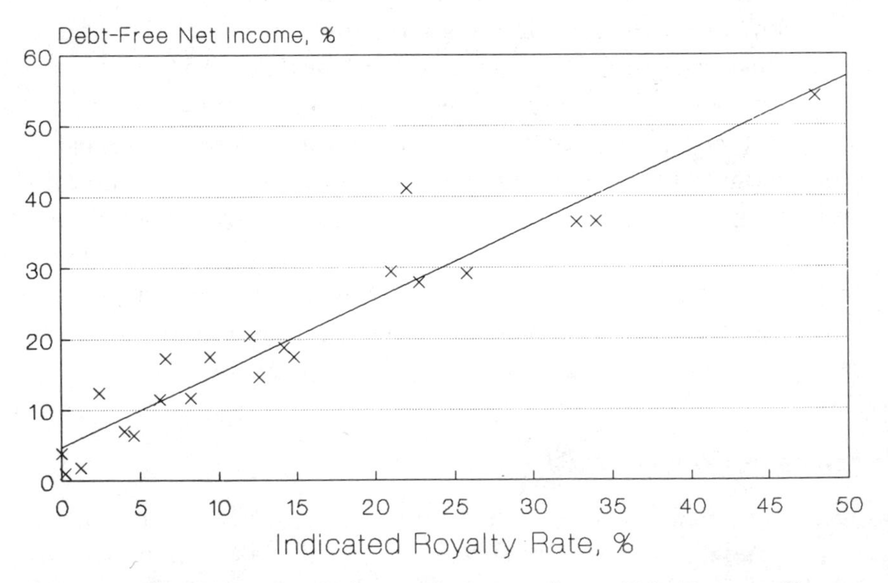

Figure 5.11 Computer Software Industry: Intangible Returns Versus Debt-Free Profits

after-tax earnings of the company after reversing debt expenses. The fixed investment is defined as the book value of the net working capital plus the adjusted gross book values for fixed assets. Reference to Figure 5.12 provides an indication of the magnitude of a fair royalty rate if the return on fixed investment is known or can be estimated. As an example, if utilization of licensed computer software is expected to generate an investment return on monetary and fixed assets of 30%, after taxes, then a pretax royalty of approximately 12% on sales is indicated. If the investment return is anticipated to be 40%, then a royalty rate of approximately 17% is indicated.

Intuitively, this relationship makes perfect sense. Technology that allows a greater return on monetary and fixed asset investments is more valuable, and should support a higher royalty rate.

Figure 5.12 Computer Software Industry: Intangible Returns Versus Fixed Return

HOSPITAL INSTRUMENTS AND MEDICAL PRODUCTS ECONOMIC ROYALTY RATES

We studied 31 companies that make different types of medical and hospital instruments. A substantial amount of intellectual property resides in this industry, and substantial royalties can be supported.

Companies

The companies in this study included:

Biomet Inc.

Cabot Medical Corp.

Circadian Inc.

Coherent Corp.

Diasonics, Inc.

Elscint Ltd.

Gelman Sciences, Inc.

Gendex Inc.

Healthdyne, Inc.

Imatron Corp.

Lectec Corp.

MDT Corp.

Medical Graphics Corp.

Medtronic, Inc.

Micron Products, Inc.

Modern Controls, Inc.

Staodynamics, Inc.

Stryker Corp.

Survival Technologies, Inc.

Waters Instruments

Products

The types of products that these companies produce include orthopedic appliances, endoscopic equipment, electrocardiagraphs, scanning devices, IV transfusion apparatus, transcutaneous electrical nerve stimulators, surgical equipment, hemodialysis apparatus, implants, ultrasonic medical cleaning equipment, pacemakers, sterilizers, and computerized axial tomography equipment.

Industry Conditions

Total expenditures for health care services in the U.S. are annually over half a trillion dollars. Medical instruments are vital for delivering these services. The medical instruments industry has annual sales of about $25 billion. Hospitals account for over 50% of the annual sales of medical equipment. While the industry has continued to grow at double-digit growth rates, cost containment pressures are becoming extreme as the U.S. Government and third-party payers try to curtail spiraling health care expenditures.

The use of high-quality medical devices that can reduce or eliminate the need for surgery and long hospital stays is fundamental to the cost control efforts. Demand by hospitals for these devices is therefore growing. Additional growth for the industry is fueled by the aging U.S. population. The proportion of the population that is age 65 and older is expected to become 13% of the total U.S. population by the year 2000. In 1970, the elderly represented only 9.8% of the population.

Competitive barriers for established medical devices include patent protection reinforced by Federal regulations. Huge investments in research and development, along with huge investments to meet regulatory requirements, protect medical device manufacturers and indirectly support strong levels of profitability within this industry.

All of these factors go towards supporting strong sales, strong growth, high profits, and the ability to pay substantial royalties for proven technology.

Intangible Returns Analysis

Where intangible returns are found to exist, they are primarily attributed to proprietary technology. Our study shows that a high correlation exists between intangible earnings and a nontraditional measure of return on investment, where the investment equates to the book value of the working capital plus an estimate of the fair market value for fixed assets (see Figure 5.13). An even stronger correlation was found between intangible returns and debt-free net income profit margins (see Figure 5.14).

A correlation exists for the companies studied between intangible returns and fixed investment return. An intangible return is defined as the total amount available for royalty rates after adequate earnings are allocated to other operating assets of the company. Fixed investment returns are measured on the combined amount of net working capital and fixed assets. The amount of return is defined as debt-free net income, and it represents the after-tax earnings of the company after reversing debt expenses. The fixed investment is defined as the book value of net working capital plus adjusted gross book values for fixed assets. Figure 5.13 shows the magnitude of a fair royalty rate if the return on fixed investment is known or can be estimated. As an example, if utilization of licensed medical products technology is expected to generate an investment return on monetary and fixed assets of

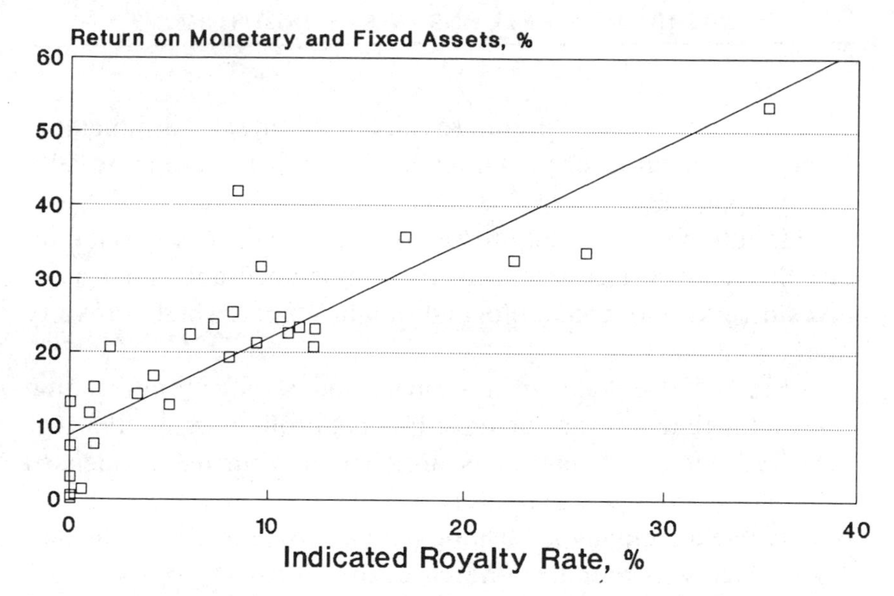

Figure 5.13 Hospital Instrument Industry: Intangible Return Versus Fixed Return

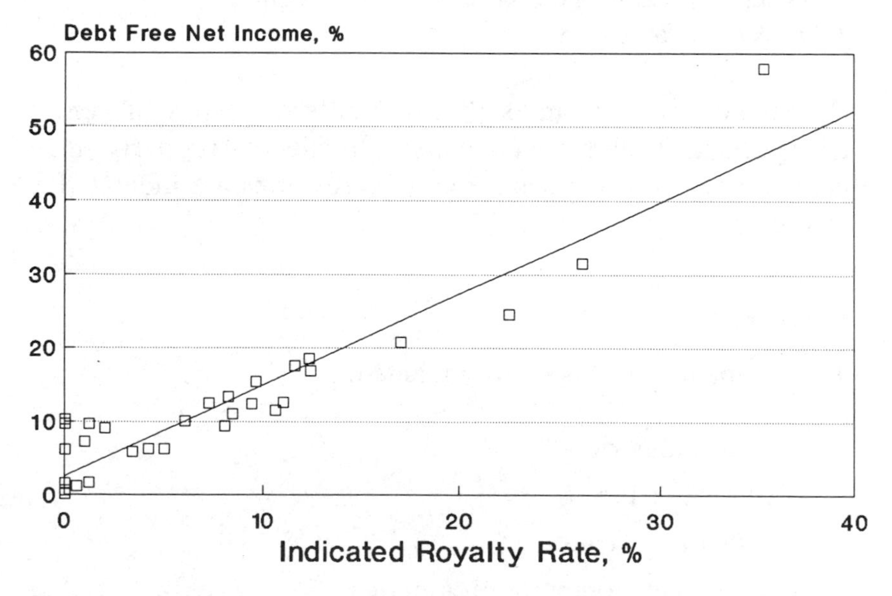

Figure 5.14 Hospital Instrument Industry: Intangible Return Versus Debt-Free Profits

20%, after taxes, then a pretax royalty of 9% on sales is indicated. If the investment return is anticipated to be 40%, then a royalty rate of approximately 24% is indicated.

Intuitively, this relationship makes perfect sense. Technology that allows a greater return on monetary and fixed asset investments is more valuable, and should support a higher royalty rate.

Figure 5.14 presents a similar, and stronger, correlation using intangible returns and debt-free net profit margins. If a 10% debt-free net profit margin is anticipated from using licensed technology, then approximately 5% of sales, on a pretax basis, is available as intangible earnings to pay royalties. If profits are 30%, which was found in one case, then a royalty of over 20% was found to be appropriate.

INDUSTRIAL MACHINERY ECONOMIC ROYALTY RATES

We studied 31 companies that sell different types of general and specialized industrial machinery. Intellectual property values cannot be easily supported, and slim royalties are indicated by this analysis.

Companies

The companies in this study included:

Astec Industries

Automatix Inc.

Critica Industries

Equipment Company of America

Executone
Gencor
Gould Pump
Helix Technology
Helm Resources
Hurco Companies
Ingersoll-Rand
Ionics
Machine Technology
Manitowoc
Morehouse
Mueller
Osmonics
Parker-Hannifin
Possis
Quipp
Reece
Ross Industries
Rule Industries
Selas Corporation of America
Silicon Valley Group
SSMC
Thermo Process
Trinova
Trion Inc.
Union Corp.

Van Dorn
Veloblind

Products

The types of products that these companies produce include asphalt plant equipment, gravel production equipment, asbestos removal equipment, vacuum pumps, refrigeration equipment, water purification devices, industrial sewing machines, water treatment systems, filtering equipment industrial furnaces, process ovens, and flow instrumentation.

Industry Conditions

The current recession in the United States, coupled with the competitive products offered by foreign corporations, has significantly hurt the growth potential and profitability of industrial machinery makers. All categories of industrial machinery are hurt by these factors, including machine tools, construction equipment, and process equipment.

Technological advances for industrial machinery are typically not huge events either. They are better characterized as incremental improvements. As such, the value of technology is low, and royalties for such technology are not supported by high amounts.

Intangible Earnings Analysis

Over half of the companies in this industry analysis could not justify their investment in working capital and fixed property. Sixteen of the companies did not generate any intangible returns. Only a few of the remaining companies showed reasonable levels of intangible returns.

Where intangible returns are found to exist, they are attributed to proprietary technology. The study shows that a high correlation exists between intangible earnings and debt-free net profits (see Figure 5.16). A weaker correlation was found between intangible earnings and gross profit margins (see Figure 5.15).

Figure 5.15 presents a correlation using intangible returns and gross profit margins. If a 30% gross profit margin is anticipated from using licensed industrial machinery technology, then less than 4% of sales is available as intangible earnings to pay royalties. If profits are expected to reach 40%, the graph indicates a royalty of over 10%, but very little actual data points exist to support a royalty rate of such a magnitude. Very few of the companies in our study achieved gross profit margins above 35%.

A correlation exists for the companies studied between intangible returns and debt-free net income. Reference to Figure

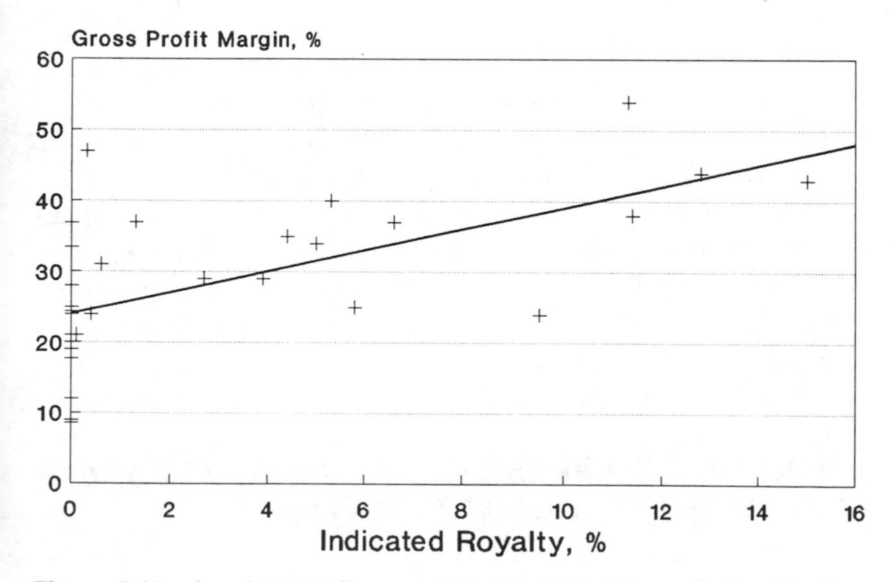

Figure 5.15 Special and General Industrial Machinery: Intangible Returns Versus Gross Profits

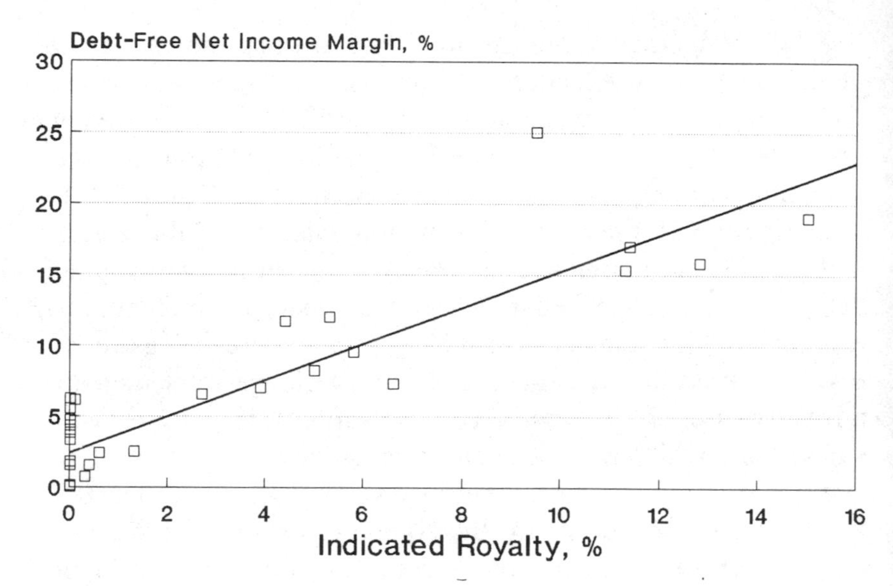

Figure 5.16 Special and General Industrial Machinery: Intangible Returns Versus Debt-Free Profits

5.16 provides an indication of the magnitude of a fair royalty rate if the debt-free net income can be estimated. As an example, if utilization of a licensed machinery patent is expected to generate debt-free profits of 5%, then a pretax royalty of less than 2% is indicated by the trend analysis. Close inspection of the figure shows that many of the companies in our study could not support a technology royalty, even when debt-free profit margins of 6% were achieved. If the debt-free net income reaches 10% of sales, then a 6% royalty is indicated.

COSMETIC AND PERSONAL HYGIENE PRODUCTS AND ECONOMIC ROYALTY RATES

Companies that manufacture and sell cosmetics, personal hygiene products, and grooming aids are the subject of our royalty economics analysis this month. Key intellectual property for this industry is primarily represented by well-established trademarks. The earnings that are attributed to the trademark assets of this industry have been isolated as a percentage of sales, and are considered to represent a point at which to begin royalty rate negotiations. Where intangible returns are found to exist, they are attributed to trademarks. The product characteristics in this industry approach parity among competitors. The major point of differentiation is considered to be trademarks.

Companies

We studied 18 companies that sell different types of cosmetics and grooming aids. The companies included:

Alberto-Culver Co.

Alfin Inc.

Aloette Cosmetics, Inc.

Avon Products, Inc.

Beauticontrol, Inc.

Beauty Labs, Inc.

CGA, Inc.

Cascade International, Inc.

Del Labs, Inc.

DEP Corp.

Gillette Co.

Goody Products, Inc.

Guest Supply, Inc.

Helene Curtiss, Inc.

Johnson Products Co., Inc.

MEM Co., Inc.
Neutrogena Corp.
Ross Cosmetics

Products

The types of products that these companies produce include natural perfumes, synthetic perfumes, toilet preparations, hair preparations, shampoo, grooming products, lipsticks, manicure preparations, shaving razors, shaving blades, personal scissors, combs, face creams, lotions, and hair conditioners.

Industry Conditions

The sale of fragrances, shaving products, hair preparations, dentrifices, and cosmetics have been estimated at 1990 levels to have reached $18.5 billion. The business is highly competitive and is maturing as the population growth stabilizes. Most of the new product introduction from this industry includes only incremental improvements. Technological breakthroughs are few and far between. New products typically focus on milder formulations, natural ingredients, and environmentally safer packaging. Cosmetic products are mostly commodities, only differentiated by the cache that is fueled by creative and sometimes strange advertising campaigns. Most new products are estimated to have only a five-year economic life. Further profit pressures are brought about by the costs associated with launching a new product, such as a fragrance. A major new fragrance costs $50 million to introduce.

Intangible returns are still quite obtainable because fixed asset investment requirements in manufacturing equipment are more stable. The equipment used to mix and package fragrances and other cosmetics will likely be efficient equipment for the same purpose ten years into the future. While many industries must replace obsolete manufacturing equipment, often the cosmetics industry is less affected by this problem.

Intangible Returns Analysis

Our study shows that a high correlation exists between intangible earnings and fixed asset returns for the 18 companies studied (see Figure 5.17). Also, a high correlation was found between intangible earnings and debt-free net profits (see Figure 5.18). The results of our analysis are presented in the accompanying figures, and indicate that a significant amount of earnings is associated with intellectual property in the cosmetics and personal hygiene industry. We attribute these earnings to the associated trademarks.

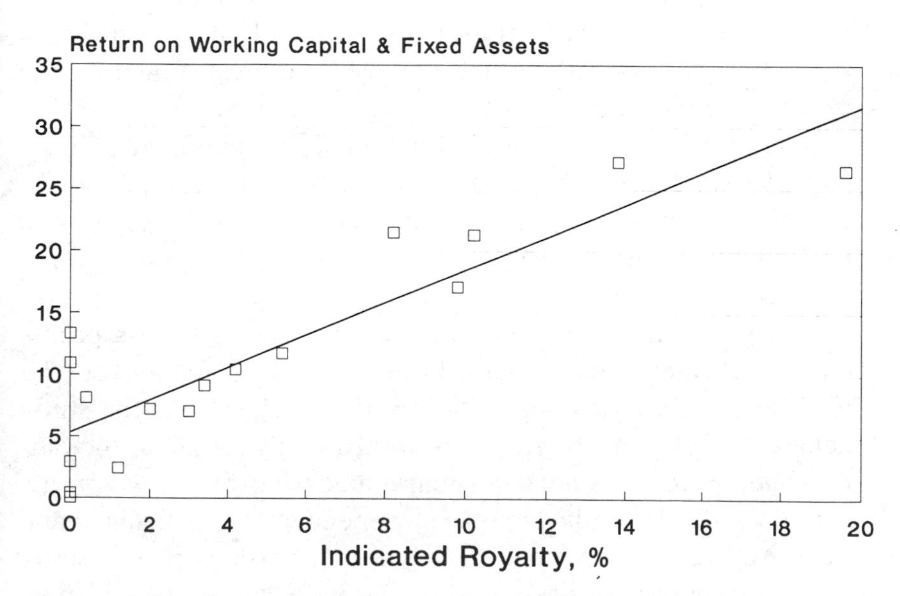

Figure 5.17 Cosmetics Industry: Intangible Returns Versus Fixed Return

A majority of companies in the study earned more than enough to provide for a fair rate of return on their basic investment in working capital and tangible assets. Of the 18 companies that were studied, only five failed to have any earnings that could be attributed to trademark assets. The remaining 72% of the companies achieved intangible earnings.

Figure 5.17 presents a correlation between intangible returns and fixed returns. Fixed return was measured as the amount of debt-free net income that was earned on the total value of tangible equipment and working capital investments. If the profit margin on fixed investment is anticipated to reach 20% from using licensed cosmetic trademarks, then a royalty of approximately 11% of sales, on a pretax basis, is available as intangible earnings to pay royalties. If profits are expected to reach 25%, the graph indicates a royalty of over 15%.

A good correlation also exists for the companies studied between intangible returns and debt-free net income. Debt-free net income is the amount of profits earned without consideration as to how the operations are financed. Interest expenses are reversed in the calculations.

Figure 5.18 provides an indication of the magnitude of a fair royalty rate if the debt-free net income can be estimated. As an example, if utilization of a licensed cosmetic trademark is expected to generate debt-free profits of 10%, then a pretax royalty of about 10% is indicated by the trend analysis.

A correlation between intangible returns and gross profits was not evident, even though the industry is categorized by high levels of gross profits. Most of the companies in the study achieved high levels of gross profits. Bringing profits to the bottom line, however, is not at all guaranteed when high gross profits are achieved. The industry is very dependent on advertising and other selling/distribution costs. Some companies in the study showed high gross profit margins, but were still unable to show

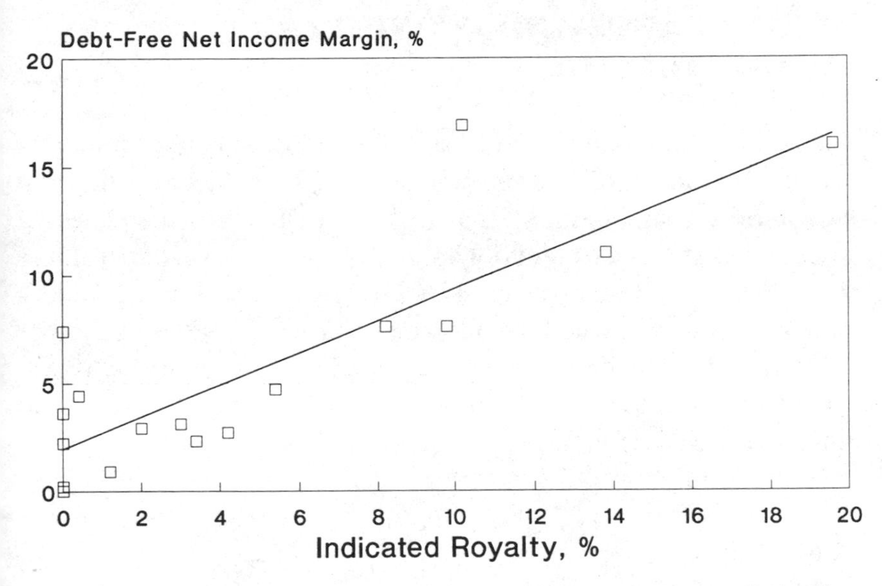

Figure 5.18 Cosmetics Industry: Intangible Returns Versus Debt-Free Profits

any intangible returns. The contribution of the trademarks is not evident until the selling and distribution expenses are taken into account. In the cosmetics industry, royalty rate negotiations should not be guided by gross profit margins.

Companies that possess well-known trademarks, like Gillette, Neutrogena, Cascade, and Avon, achieved the highest amounts of intangible returns. Commodity companies that do not have keystone trademarks, like Goody Products, failed to achieve any intangible returns. It might be argued that all cosmetic products are commodity-like. When a big name like Avon is associated with common products like lipsticks, then intangible earnings are achieved. When a lesser-known name like Goody Products is put on a common product like combs, then intangible earnings are elusive.

MEGA-BRANDS AND ECONOMIC ROYALTY RATES

Companies that manufacture and sell various consumer products under a world-renowned brand name are the subject of this final section. Our study shows that the particular industry in which the brand name is used did not limit the potential level of royalties.

These companies were selected because each has a collection of world-renowned brand names that are used on consumer products. We excluded service companies, auto makers, retailers, and communication companies so that our analysis could focus on quasi-commodity consumer products.

Companies

We studied 14 companies that sell different types of consumer products. The companies were selected from a list entitled, "Top 200 Mega-Brands by First-Quarter Ad Spending," which appeared in the August 19, 1991 issue of *Advertising Age*. The study included:

Campbell
Clorox
Colgate-Palmolive
Gillette
Johnson & Johnson
Kellogg
Kimberly-Clark
Neutrogena
Nike
PepsiCo

Philip Morris
Reebok
Seagram
Wrigley

Products

The diverse product offerings include food, bleach, soap, shavers, medical remedies, cereal, paper products, hair shampoo, sportswear, beverages, cigarettes, and chewing gum. The quasi-commodity nature of these typical products means that above-average profits are strongly related to a keystone brand name.

Industry Conditions

The industries covered by this sample of companies cover a broad range of industries, but all sell directly to consumers, and all possess keystone internationally known brands. All of the companies must spend huge amounts annually on advertising, and all of them must develop and maintain distribution networks. Regardless of competition, economic downturns, and changing demographics, the brand names owned by these companies give the owners an advantageous position from which to launch competitive strategies.

Intangible Earnings Analysis

All of the companies in the study earned enough to provide for a fair rate of return on their basic investment in working capital and tangible assets. All of the companies also earned intangible returns. Only three of the 14 companies indicated royalties of less than 9% of sales. The results of our analysis are presented in three graphs. In almost all cases, a significant amount of earnings is attributed to the brands.

Figure 5.19 presents a correlation using intangible returns and gross profit margins. If a 40% gross profit margin is anticipated from using licensed brands, less than 5% of sales is available as intangible earnings to pay royalties. A 50% gross profit margin indicates a royalty rate of over 12% of sales. The flat slope of the line in Figure 5.19 shows that most of the data points fell between 40 and 50% gross profit margins. Indicated royalties ranged between 6 and 15%. Clearly, reliance on gross profit margins for determining brand name royalty rates cannot provide very much precision. The value of brands and the level of royalty that individual names deserve require analysis that goes beyond the gross profit margin. Other significant expenses such as selling, advertising, promotion, and overhead must be considered. Brands that require lower amounts of overhead support are more valuable and deserve higher royalties.

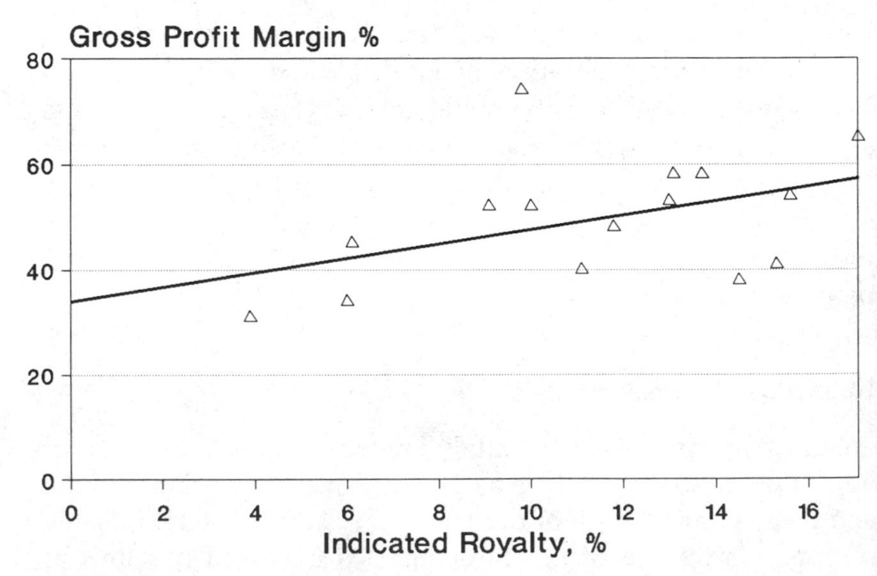

Figure 5.19 Mega-Brands: Intangible Returns Versus Gross Profits

An excellent correlation exists for the companies studied between intangible returns and debt-free net income. Figure 5.20 provides an indication of the magnitude of a fair royalty rate if the debt-free net income can be estimated. As an example, if utilization of a licensed brand is expected to generate debt-free profits of 4%, then a pretax royalty of 4% is indicated by the trend analysis. If the debt-free net income reaches 10% of sales, then a royalty of almost 9% is indicated.

Figure 5.21 shows a strong correlation between intangible returns and the rate of return earned on monetary and fixed assets. If the use of a licensed brand is expected to provide a 20% return on the investment in working capital and fixed assets, then almost 9% of sales is available for brand royalties. The return on monetary assets (working capital) and fixed assets represents the amount of debt-free net income that is earned from the amount invested in these *hard* assets.

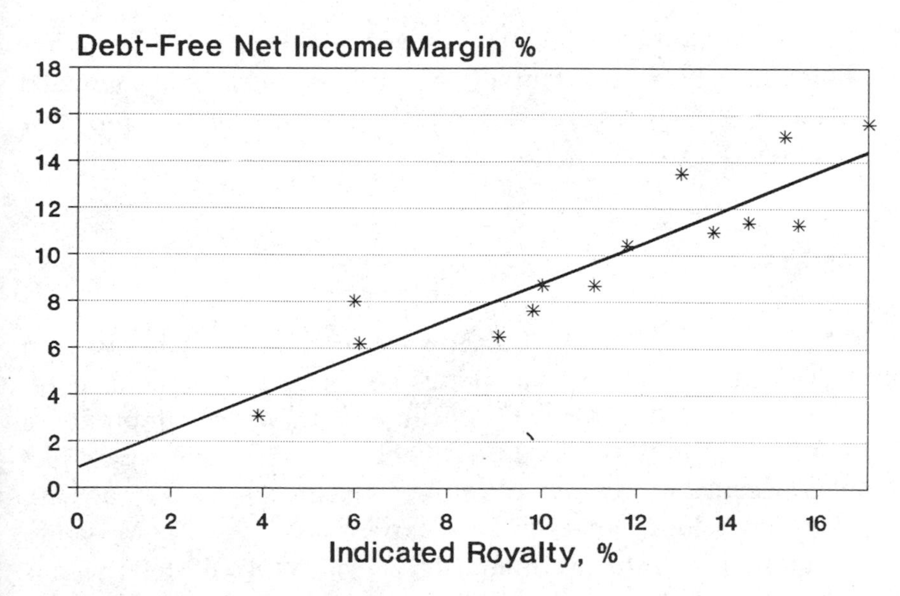

Figure 5.20 Mega-Brands: Intangible Returns Versus Debt-Free Profits

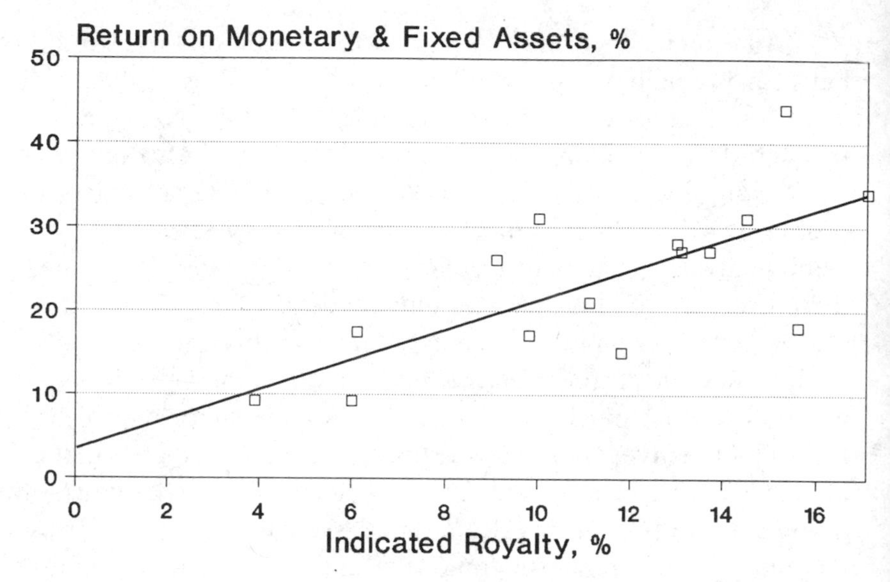

Figure 5.21 Mega-Brands: Intangible Returns Versus Fixed Returns

Regardless of the industry, a well-known brand name contributes directly and substantially to earnings, and should command some of the highest royalty rates among intellectual property licenses.

SUMMARY

The analyses just presented show that each industry has its own capacity for royalties. Some industries, such as industrial equipment and electronics, have difficulties earning enough profits to justify their fixed assets investments. In other industries, like pharmaceuticals, almost all of the companies have the capacity to pay royalties, sometimes at extraordinary levels. Most important is that within each industry, a wide range of royalty rates can be justified because specific intellectual property introduces different economic characteristics to a license or joint venture.

SUMMARY

Industry standards and rules-of-thumb are dangerous to use when structuring licenses and joint venture. The graphs show that reasonable royalties cover a broad range within most of the industries studied. Rule-of-thumb royalty rates, which tend to be fixed percentages of sales, do not correlate with any of the studies conducted.

The industry graphs presented in this chapter can be useful for intellectual property strategies. They provide a reasonable indication of where to begin negotiations for joint venture profit splits or license royalty rates. Most often, the best correlation existed between intangible earnings and debt-free net income levels. This analysis correlated the earnings generated by intellectual property with a profitability measure that accounted for selling and support expenses. It presented a correlation between intellectual property contributions and bottom-line profitability.

Gross profit correlations sometimes showed good correlations with intangible returns, but too often failed to be useful. Commercializing intellectual property requires more than manufacturing efforts. Selling, marketing, and support efforts are required to different degrees by various intellectual property products. Only after these additional expenses are considered is the indicated royalty rate information dependable.

Another regression analysis tried to show the relationship between royalty rates and the return on operating investment, defined as net working capital and the original cost of plant, property, and equipment. Technology which allows a high rate of return from fixed plant investment should indeed command higher royalties, but unfortunately, this type of relationship was not consistently found.

Reference to these graphs is a better alternative to using industry standards or rules-of-thumb. Even better is application of the methods described in Chapter 5 directly to specific circumstances.

6

RISKS OF EXPLOITATION

In Chapters 4 and 5, we presented analysis techniques for estimating the economic contribution of intellectual property, or the *income* ingredient needed to evaluate exploitation schemes. In this chapter, we will examine the other two essential factors—elements of risk and economic life. In a previous section, we introduced the concept that if one can develop an opinion about the amount of income attributable to intellectual property, the risk of obtaining that income, and the duration of the income, one can calculate the present value of an exploitation possibility.

Even if one is not evaluating alternative exploitation possibilities, it is essential to be able to form an opinion about the relative risk associated with a licensor's or licensee's operation, or those of potential joint venture partners.

We will not, in this chapter, include a discussion of those elements of risk that may be peculiar to international transactions, as they will be covered in a later chapter.

ELEMENTS OF RISK

An investment is the act of reaching into one's pocket for cash and exchanging it for some object or right in the expectation of gain. The gain may be smaller or larger than expected, come earlier or later, or not come at all. Every investment decision, even the decision *not* to invest, is therefore an evaluation of risk. As Mark Twain is said to have said:

> There are two times in a man's life when he should not speculate: when he can't afford it, and when he can.

Speculation is, however, in the eye of the beholder. One person's speculation is another's "sure thing." That is what makes horse races and, we suspect, business as well. That is why we will concentrate on the risk of business investing. There is a myriad of other investment opportunities that we will ignore. Should I lend my brother-in-law $1500? Probably not, but that question will have to be answered somewhere else; it will not be dealt with here.

Enterprise Risks

When one invests in a business enterprise, several forms of risk must be considered. The primary forms are *business risk* and *financial risk*. Additionally are the risks associated with changes in *purchasing power* and *interest rates*, and *marketability*.

In the world of business and investment, risk is best quantified by volatility (or the degree of predictability) of income and the probability of default. A classic high-risk investment is taking a quarter from my pocket and inserting it into a slot machine. The volatility of income is extreme—from zero to perhaps $1 million. The probability of default (losing the quarter) is also very high. At the other extreme, using these measures, would be the purchase of a U.S. E Bond. In between are all of the other business investment possibilities, and we will discuss their characteristics.

Business Risk

A business enterprise does not exist in a vacuum. It has connections with a myriad of outside entities such as government, customers, suppliers, employees, and banks. The character of those relationships has a great impact on the risk of the enterprise. Other business elements are important as well.

Size

Generally speaking, the smaller the enterprise, the higher is the risk. A small enterprise has more difficulty weathering the normal up and down cycles. It also cannot take advantage of economies of scale, command the best prices for goods and services, and advertise nationally because it cannot assemble a "critical mass" to do so.

Geodiversity

A business operating in many locations is one of lower risk than otherwise. The risk of owning a single fast food store is much greater than owning several because the single operation is dependent on a very small (neighborhood) economy or a particular location, either of which can change rapidly.

Customer Diversity

An enterprise serving a multiplicity of customer types has less risk. All else being equal, the pocket comb business ought to be steadier than making curling irons. Risk is reduced by serving customers in unrelated industries that are not affected by the same economic conditions.

Product Diversity

A large portfolio of products or a business built on technology that has wide application tends to be less risky. It is unlikely that everything will go poorly (or well) at the same time, making earnings more predictable.

Technology

An enterprise dependent on high technology is more risky. It is faced with keeping its products or services current at an accelerating pace. It is also likely to have heavy competition. The high profitability of high-tech products attracts others into the market.

Assets

A heavy investment in physical assets tends to increase risk, and if those assets are highly specialized, risk is increased even more. Large physical assets take time to assemble, and the business climate can change while that is going on. Classic examples are electric utilities that constructed nuclear generating facilities. These plants required massive amounts of money to build, took years to complete, and while this was happening, regulatory, environmental, and technological changes took place, and the demand for power fell. Many of these investments turned traditionally low-risk enterprises into high-risk operations—some into bankrupt ones!

The same can result if the assets are not tangible. Research or development that is going to require heavy investment and which will take a long time before any milestones are reached carries with it the same high risk that, by the time the money is spent, conditions have changed and the result is no longer of value.

A smaller investment in assets, especially general-purpose ones, allows the business much more flexibility to redeploy them if the needs of the business change.

Environmental

While it becomes difficult to imagine a business that is not subject to some environmental concern, those with less potential involvement would have less risk. Environmental standards are continually changing as we discover more about our surroundings and as constituencies shift. We once thought computer monitors and keyboards were pretty innocuous.

Governmental

In general, less involvement with government results in less business risk. One reason is relative cost. Heavy regulation, such as FDA approval for a drug, results in high costs. This is not a political statement, but a fact of life. Others can argue about the necessity of regulatory activities. Another result of regulatory involvement is increased development time which, as we noted above, increases risk. Government involvement also results in change. Elected officials of today will likely not be there tomorrow, and those who are may be responding to a different constituency. An enterprise can, therefore, be faced with the challenge of attempting to satisfy a moving regulatory target.

Inventory

When a business must maintain a large inventory of raw materials and/or finished goods, risk is increased because the enterprise will have more exposure to fluctuations in the marketplace. Falling raw material prices will cause the business to have high priced goods versus competitors. Falling retail prices can erode profits, and changes in market needs can cause inventory to be unsaleable.

Marketing

When a business is built around products or services that require heavy sales and marketing expenditures, it would be more risky than otherwise. Such an enterprise is often in a highly competitive, commodity-like market where wide swings in marketplace needs and desires are possible, or in a situation in which massive sales are necessary to support heavy product research and development (computers or pharmaceuticals).

Management

While very difficult to assess, management ability is an important component of business risk. It can be critical in the exploitation of intellectual property, however. Imagine a joint venture between a tire manufacturer and an insurance company to produce and sell toys. Where would the joint venture management come from? Or consider a joint venture with Japanese and English partners where the business culture is so dissimilar. Would one be eager to license biotechnology into a bank subsidiary? One can hardly expect a successful outcome if an insurmountable obstacle is placed before even very skilled managers.

Financial Risk

We noted in a previous chapter the fact that an investment in a business enterprise, in the form of common stock, introduces a layer of control between the investor and the property invested in. We noted that in some cases, such as the ownership of a minority stock interest, the risk could be substantially greater. Even with respect to the entire business enterprise, however, there are elements of risk introduced by other financial factors.

Leverage

This is the most commonly referred to element of financial risk. Called "gearing" by the English, this refers to the amount of risk that results from management's choice of capital structure. It should be the objective of management to balance business and financial risk in a complementary fashion. When business risk is great, financial risk should be small, and vice versa.

An appropriate capital structure may, in a sense, be forced on management no matter what its views are. Investors make a judgment as to business risk, and simply will not commit capital in a mix that they judge to be improper.

A large amount of debt capital increases the financial risk of the enterprise. In order to prudently support heavy debt, a business must have assured and steady earnings. We liken this to an airplane flying a few feet above the ground. It only takes a slight engine misfire to crash. This has been vividly illustrated in the recent bankruptcies of large, even multinational corporations. They took on staggering debt loads, perhaps with the expectation that the value of their real estate developments would continue to rise without end, or perhaps to finance an acquisition, or to turn away an ardent, but unwanted suitor. A downturn in the overall economy put them under.

Financial risk may not be a common consideration in the exploitation of intellectual property, but it is a factor to consider. While a joint venture is rarely financed with debt capital, one or another of the partners could be, and could be overleveraged. It could become a factor in the ability of that partner to contribute additional capital to the joint venture or to fulfill other obligations necessary to its success.

The financial stability of a licensee or licensor should be important to both parties. Without this, royalties may not be paid, exploitation may be laggard, infringements may not be challenged, or continued development of the intellectual property may be in jeopardy.

The parties to any form of intellectual property exploitation should examine one another in much the same way that a banker scrutinizes our home equity loan.

Accounting

Bernstein[1] describes accounting-related risk in terms of an investor relying on accounting information to evaluate a business. In intellectual property exploitation, we would expand that to include relying on accounting information supplied by an exploitation partner. A license or joint venture arrangement must be structured in such a way that the participants have confidence in the information they receive. If that confidence cannot be reasonably assured at the outset, then the venture must be judged as having more risk. This may be more applicable to international transactions because of differing customs and accounting standards. In any locale, however, closely held businesses have con-

[1] Leopold A. Bernstein, *Financial Statement Analysis* (Homewood, IL: Richard D. Irwin, Inc., 1978).

siderably more latitude in keeping their books than publicly traded entities.

Perspective on Financial Risk

To place financial risk measurement in some perspective, we can observe the financial structure of a large group of industrial companies, as well as that of selected industry groups. The information, taken from VALUE LINE,[2] can provide some broad benchmarks.

VALUE LINE'S Industrial Composite comprises approximately 825 industrial, retail, and transportation companies. As of their 1991 fiscal year, the composite capital structure of the group was:

Long-term debt	39%
Preferred stock	3%
Common stock	58%

One can conclude from this that the business risk associated with a large cross section of U.S. industry is such that a capital structure of 40% fixed capital and 60% common equity capital is appropriate. When one looks at industry groups, there begins to be a range, reflecting investors' perceptions of relative business risk. In analyzing the following table, the reader should recognize that sometimes capital structure may be forced on management. When earnings fall and losses are incurred, the book value of common equity falls as well. This produces an unexpected, and really uncontrollable, increase in the percentage of debt capital. We leave it to the reader to detect which cases are planned and which are not:

[2] "The Value Line Investment Survey," August 7, 1992, Value Line Publishing, Inc., New York, NY.

Industry	Capital Structure %	
	Debt	Equity
Computer Software, Data Processing	9	91
Drug Manufacturers	9	91
Rare Metals Mining	17	83
Oil, Gas Exploration	23	77
Medical Instruments & Supplies	23	77
Contractors, General	23	77
South Atlantic Banks	23	77
Computers, Subsystems, Peripherals	23	77
Electronic Equipment Manufacturers	23	77
Aerospace Components	29	71
Machine Tools	29	71
Chemicals, Synthetics	33	67
Iron, Steel Mills	38	63
Grain Mill Products	38	63
Communications	41	59
Paper Products	44	56
Newspapers	44	56
Railroads	47	53
Waste Management	47	53
Lumber, Wood Products	50	50
Farm Products	52	48
Soft Drinks	52	48
Retail Department Stores	55	45
Airlines	55	45
Electric Utilities	55	45
Restaurants	57	43
Water Utilities	58	42
Automobile Manufacturers	63	37
Investment Brokers/Bankers	66	34
New England Banks	68	32

Fitch Investors Service, Inc.[3] is a rating agency that analyzes companies and governments and publishes ratings of their debt capital for the use of investors. In a recent special report entitled, "Rating Intangible Assets," this firm recognized the importance of intangible asset value in the rating of public and private debt of major companies. It cites the importance of intangible assets, even though they rarely appear on the balance sheet. The firm has developed a system to reflect this reality in its debt ratings. This is the first such recognition of which we are aware.

Purchasing Power Risk

Even if the expected stream of economic benefits from an investment could be determined with absolute certainty, risk still exists with regard to the purchasing power of the future dollars that are expected to be received. There always exists the risk that inflation will intensify and consume any gains that may be realized from investment performance.

The Consumer Price Index shows that between 1946 and 1989, inflation averaged 4.4%. If this rate could be expected to continue in the future at this same level, then investment planning could include an element in the rate of return requirements to assure that this amount of inflation was incorporated into the contemplated investment returns. In a sense, the purchasing power risk would be eliminated.

Unfortunately, there are periods within the 43-year span between 1946 and 1989 which provided the economic environment with wide and unanticipated swings of inflation. It is the unanticipated changes that introduce investment risk. The following table provides a sample of the level of inflation during selected time periods.

[3] Fitch Investors Service, Inc., One State Street Plaza, New York, NY.

Selected Inflationary Periods

Period	Inflation Rate
1946–1989	4.4%
1950–1959	2.2%
1960–1969	2.4%
1970–1979	7.2%
1980–1989	5.1%
1989–1990	5.4%
1990–1991	4.2%

Even though inflation has averaged 4.4% since World War II, investment rate of return requirements that were based upon this average were never quite correct during the selected periods.

Unanticipated events, such as inflation, greatly affect the amount of investment returns that are actually achieved. This represents risk, and a portion of investment rates of return on all types of investment properties must include an element that compensates for this risk component.

Interest Rate Risk

This element of financial risk presents uncertainty similar to purchasing power risk. Alternate forms of investment such as corporate bonds, treasury securities, and municipal debt provide another investment opportunity with which an intellectual property investment must compete. If the future brings with it higher returns that are available from investments of lesser risk, then the value of the intellectual property investment may be diminished.

Market Risk

A unique and often unkind element of risk is, in large part, associated with "market psychology." Irrespective of any fundamental changes in the expected performance of an investment, market risk reflects the fluctuation in the demand for a specific type of investment. On October 19, 1987, the stock market plunged in value by over 500 points as measured by the Dow Jones Industrial Average. There was neither a fundamental change in economic outlooks nor a cataclysmic event such as the declaration of a world war. Yet, the value of all investments plunged. This is indeed an example of the risk that is classified as market risk.

An additional component of market risk is the risk associated with investment marketability. An investment for which an active market exists is more valuable, all else being equal, than an investment for which no active market exists.

While the purchasing power, interest rate, and business risk elements are easy to conceptualize, the marketability risk is a little less obvious. Several studies have been conducted to identify and measure the discount to investment value that the market places on investments which lack liquidity. This is discussed more fully in the section of Chapter 2 entitled, "Market Risk and the Discount for Lack of Marketability." While the studies presented centered upon common stock, the same risk element is present for all types of investments, including those in intellectual property.

RISK AND ROYALTIES

One can, without a formal analysis, intuitively sense the relationship between the amount of royalty and these elements of risk. But for those who feel more comfortable with some numerical support, we offer the following.

Investment risk is directly related to the amount of royalty that a licensee can afford to pay. Investment risk is an important factor that hypothetical licensing partners would consider in an arm's length negotiation. More risk translates to lower royalties, everything else being equal. Calculations are presented that show how higher investment risk translates into lower royalty rates.

Consider a manufacturer planning to enter a new industrial market using licensed technology. Figure 6.1 presents the expected cash flows of the contemplated project. The product will be manufactured and marketed by the licensee. Manufacturing expertise and marketing know-how are assumed to be possessed by the licensee. But the licensee needs an exclusive license of the product technology so that it can capture the market and get the sales that are shown in the ten-year forecast.

Notes for Figure 6.1:

EBDIT&R = Earnings before depreciation, interest, taxes, and royalty payments.

EBIT&R = Earnings before interest, taxes, and royalty payments.

EBIT = Earnings before interest and taxes.

Capex = Capital expenditures.

The starting point of the analysis is to consider the investment value of the project assuming that no royalty must be paid. The cash flows show an initial investment of $3,000 by the licensee for:

- the purchase of capital equipment,
- the contributed value of a well-established marketing department,
- the contributed value of the company's well-known trademark.

The initial investment of $3,000 represents the contribution of value to the new venture by the licensee. A portion of the

New Project Cash Flows

Year	0	1	2	3	4	5	6	7	8	9	10
Sales		1,000	2,000	4,000	8,000	10,000	12,000	14,000	16,000	17,600	18,480
EBDIT&R		200	400	800	2,000	2,500	3,000	3,500	4,000	4,400	4,620
Depreciation		50	200	300	600	285	285	285	285	285	126
EBIT&R		150	200	500	1,400	2,215	2,715	3,215	3,715	4,115	4,494
Royalty	0.0%	0	0	0	0	0	0	0	0	0	0
EBIT		150	200	500	1,400	2,215	2,715	3,215	3,715	4,115	4,494
Taxes	40.0%	60	80	200	560	886	1,086	1,286	1,486	1,646	1,798
Debt-free Net Income		90	120	300	840	1,329	1,629	1,929	2,229	2,469	2,696
add: Depreciation		50	200	300	600	285	285	285	285	285	126
less: Working Capital		20	100	200	400	200	200	200	200	160	88
less:Capex		3,000	100	200	400	200	200	200	200	160	126
Net Cash Flow		(2,880)	120	200	640	1,214	1,514	1,814	2,114	2,434	2,608
Discount Rate	15.0%	0.9333	0.8115	0.7057	0.6136	0.5336	0.4640	0.4035	0.3508	0.3051	2.4718
Present Value		(2,688)	97	141	393	648	702	732	742	743	6,448
Total Present Value		7,957									

Figure 6.1 New Project Cash Flows

forecasted cash flows is generated by the initial investment of the manufacturer, and a portion of the expected cash flows is from the licensed technology. By showing the $3,000 contribution of the manufacturer, the residual present value of the cash flows is attributed to the licensed technology.

Figure 6.1 shows the present value of the new project division by discounting the cash flows, with 0% of sales as a royalty, at a required rate of return of 15%. The present value of the project is $7,957. This shows that not only will the licensee earn 15% on its investment, but it has created excess value. The licensee will earn its required rate of investment return of 15% plus $7,957. But some or all of the excess value should be considered as contributed by the technology and should be paid to the licensor as royalty. How much royalty can the licensee give to the licensor and still make this investment project a good deal?

If we insert a 2% royalty into the model, the present value of the cash flows equals $6,955. The licensee has earned the required 15% plus the created excess value of $6,955. At a 4% royalty, the present value equals $5,593. See the table below.

Present Value of New Project Cash Flows Using Different Royalty Rates Discounted at 15%

Royalty Rate	Value Created
0%	$7,957
2%	$6,955
4%	$5,953
6%	$4,951
8%	$3,949
10%	$2,947
12%	$1,932
14%	$900
16%	($141)

At a royalty rate of 16%, the discounted cash flow model shows a present value that turns negative. When the present value is negative, the investment is not earning the 15% required rate of return. Too much royalty is being given to the licensor at this point.

Figure 6.2 graphs the different values of the business enterprise for the different royalty rates. The graph shows that a royalty rate of approximately 15.7% can be paid to the licensor and yield a net present for the cash flows at $0. This level of royalty allows the licensor to earn the 15% required rate of return on the new project investment, but no more. It represents the highest level of royalty that the licensee can afford to pay while

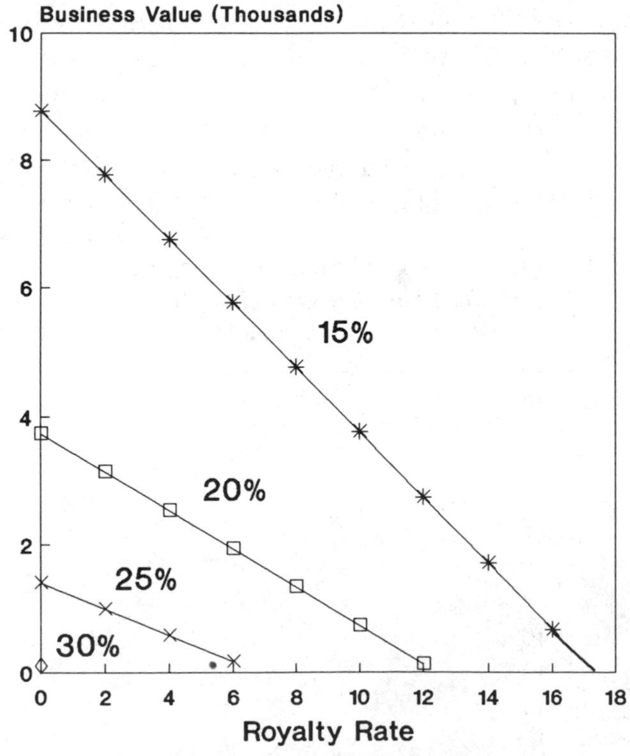

Figure 6.2 Business Risk and Royalties

still earning the required rate of return. If a royalty rate of something less than 15.7% can be negotiated, all the better—but a royalty rate greater than 15.7% would not allow the licensor to earn a fair return on the investment.

All of this assumes that 15% is the proper rate of return for the new project investment. A business in a mature industry with a steady market share and relatively predictable profits might be happy with a 15% rate of return from operations within its core business. But new investments into ancillary or new industries represent added investment risks. If the new project is considered riskier than 15%, then a 15.7% royalty rate would have disastrous consequences on the value of the new project enterprise.

Let us look at the present value of cash flows, using the same range of royalty rates, but a higher rate of return requirement of 20%.

Present Value of New Project Cash Flows Using Different Royalty Rates Discounted at 20%

Royalty Rate	Value Created
0%	$3,436
2%	$2,836
4%	$2,235
6%	$1,635
8%	$1,035
10%	$434
11%	$0

If the new project investment is actually riskier than 15%, then a royalty rate at 15.7% of sales would yield a negative present value for the licensor. The highest royalty rate that the licensee can afford to pay at the 20% rate of return requirement level is 11%. At this lower royalty, the licensor has earned its required investment return on the higher rate of 20%. If a lower royalty rate can be negotiated, great. But at this higher level of risk perception, a royalty rate of 15.7% is a disaster.

Figure 6.2 shows a third line that plots the present value of cash flows for different royalty rates using a rate of return requirement of 25%. The highest amount of royalty the licensor can afford to pay at this higher rate of return requirement is less than 7%. Also shown in Figure 6.2 is a very short line that represents the new project investment value discounted at a 30%. If no royalties are required, then an excess value of 287 is created. Royalty payments of 2% of sales or more would make the investment a loser. If the new project investment is truly considered to be so risky as to require a 30% rate of return, and if the cash flows accurately reflect the potential for the technology, no more than 2% of sales can be paid as a royalty.

The investment risk of the industry into which the licensed property is being introduced is an important consideration when determining the proper amount of royalty to be paid. When negotiating a royalty rate, the licensor and licensee must consider many different factors. They must agree, or at least independently come to the same conclusions, on:

- sales potential,
- profit margins,
- up-front investment requirements,
- market penetration time frames,
- and . . . .

They must also understand and agree on the amount of investment risk associated with the new project.

INTELLECTUAL PROPERTY ECONOMIC LIFE

Economic life could be described as the period during which it is profitable to use an asset. Economic life ends when it is no longer profitable to use an asset (the future benefits are used up), or when it is more profitable to use another asset. This is quite different from the *service life* of an asset, which is the period from its installation to the date of its retirement, *irrespective* of its earning capability along the way.

Measuring Economic Life

Legal/Contractual Life

The economic life of tangible assets is commonly not affected by legal or contract terms. These assets belong to the business, and they remain in place as long as management decides.

Many forms of intellectual property, however, do have a recognized legal or contractual life. These include:

1) patents,
2) copyrights,
3) trademarks.

Indefinite Economic Life

Most intellectual property will be found to have an economic life undefined by law or contractual terms. These assets must, therefore, first be analyzed in order to determine whether the legal or contract terms will be controlling with respect to remaining economic life. In many cases, *economic life* is shorter than *legal life*. The effectiveness of a patent may be ended before its 17-year legal life because of, as an example, advancing technology, or because the product in which it is used has lost its place in the market.

In our experience, the legal or contractual life is most often *not* controlling with respect to the economic life of intellectual property. The economic life of these assets depends upon their response to a host of outside forces that either must be measured by their influence in the overall, or by analyzing the individual forces.

Subjective Analysis

Correlative Data

There are situations in which one must combine the data from more than one source in order to form a conclusion. We were engaged to estimate the economic life of the relationship between the depositors and their bank. One group of these was comprised of customers holding certificates of deposit. In analyzing their turnover, we observed that the holders of short-term CDs nearly always rolled them over at maturity. This caused us to look further, and we discovered that nearly all of these customers also had checking accounts into which the interest from the CDs was being deposited. We had already made a study of the remaining life of checking account holders, and therefore could use these data to forecast the probable remaining life of the CD accounts after maturity.

In other examples, data relative to the failure rate for small businesses could be utilized in estimating the life of newspaper advertisers in a suburban area, or the population turnover and home mortgage life experience could be used to augment sparse data on the turnover in the newspaper's subscriber base.

It is common to relate the economic remaining life of a group of patents with varying legal lives to the last one to be in effect. It may well be that the economic remaining life of a family of patents is defined by the economic remaining life of the product line in which they are utilized.

Change is Everywhere

One would think that the recipe for a food product or the formula for a paint pigment or metal alloy would be long-lived information. In actuality, formulas such as these are constantly changing due to:

1) The varying availability of raw materials.
2) Changes in the quality or specifications of raw materials.
3) Changes in taste and preference (e.g., low-sodium, low-fat, low-sugar foods).
4) Efforts to obtain less costly materials or reduce energy requirements.
5) Environmental concerns (e.g., lead and petroleum distillates in paint products or toxic effluent in the manufacturing process).
6) Changes in marketing (e.g., longer shelf life required or less expensive packaging available).
7) Changes in governmental regulations or industry standards.

The result is that a formula for white paint or a recipe for cupcakes may have to be modified many times, even though the product line will be in existence for many years. Computer software is a classic example of this situation. Almost every business has a computer program for processing the payroll, and has had one for several years. Is it the same software today that it was five years ago? Almost certainly not. Small, but continual modifications have been made; it has been modified for new hardware, and to conform to changing income and benefit laws. It is logical to assume that this process will continue into the future, and may even accelerate.

Higher and Higher Tech

One of the most difficult estimates of economic life to make is in connection with assets that are related to new technology. An example might be the tangible and intangible assets in an enterprise that began two years ago to develop a product which is, at the time of the appraisal, six months from being introduced to the market.

Millions of dollars may have been spent during the development period, and one must decide how many of them now constitute assets of material value, *and* what is their economic remaining life.

Here, specific history is nonexistent, and the future is uncertain. In this situation, one must ask questions such as:

1) What is the potential market?
2) Who are the competitors?
3) What will the further development costs be?
4) What product or service is being replaced?
5) Are financial resources present to see the project through?
6) What is the level of protection (patents, trade secrets, a "head start")?
7) What is the cost of market entry?

Generation Gap

One of the tools we have used is to trace the development of a product or service through its "generations" to detect whether there is a constant progression or, more typically, an increasingly shorter generation life span.

A good example is computer hardware, which has moved through several generations, from vacuum tubes and unit record (punched card) peripherals to transistors, to chips and magnetic tape, to large disks, to floppy disks, and to optical disks. Another example is the well-documented progression in communications equipment from manual switchboards to digital switches. Medical diagnostic equipment has undergone similar "generational" changes that can be tracked.

This type of analysis provides an overview of how fast technological advances are taking place in the subject industry. It also gives some insight as to whether these advances come in evolutionary fashion or in "breakthroughs."

Outside Influences

It seems to us that forces external to a business are exerting an ever-increasing influence over managers and the business assets that they use. The value and economic life of a loan or mortgage portfolio held by a financial institution can vary substantially with the vagaries of the interest rate. The value of an inventory fluctuates with the trading value of currency. A chemical process or material that is a basic product building block today is restricted in the marketplace tomorrow. Employee turnover may be significantly changed as a result of legislation. Changes in health or safety standards can render a process, product, or service too costly to compete. The impact of product liability litigation is well known.

Product/Service Life

It must be remembered that this entire discussion concerns intellectual property that is part of a business enterprise. It is therefore capable of producing income to that enterprise, and its worth is commensurate with that capability. Its economic life is also commensurate with that capability. Therefore, whatever the intellectual property is, we must look towards some product or service with which it is associated. It is that product or service, converted into money in the marketplace, that is the source of the economic benefits by which the value and economic life of underlying assets can be measured. It is therefore necessary to link the particular assets under study with a product or service, either existing or contemplated. If no such linkage exists, the asset is likely to have no value and no economic life.

We therefore must be attentive to the life of products and services in this analysis. A typical product life cycle is illustrated in Figure 6.3.

In the following paragraphs, we will highlight considerations which, in our experience, have proved helpful in studying the economic life of intellectual property.

In general, the process of estimating economic life is one of identifying all of the factors that bear on economic life in a given situation, and then making a judgment as to which of them indicates the shortest life.

Economic Life Factors

Patents

The path from patent to product can be tenuous. An example is a patent that protects a process for the efficient production of a chemical compound. That compound may find its way into virtually millions of end-use products. If these products represent a broad spectrum of markets, the patent, based on this consideration alone, ought to be quite valuable, and its economic life ought to be long (perhaps equal to its legal life) because the diversity of products acts as a shield against an overall downturn in sales. If the patent protects the chemical compound itself, it may be even more valuable and long-lived, again because of the potentially broad applications.

Looking through to the economic life of the end product can provide an indication of the high end of the range of economic

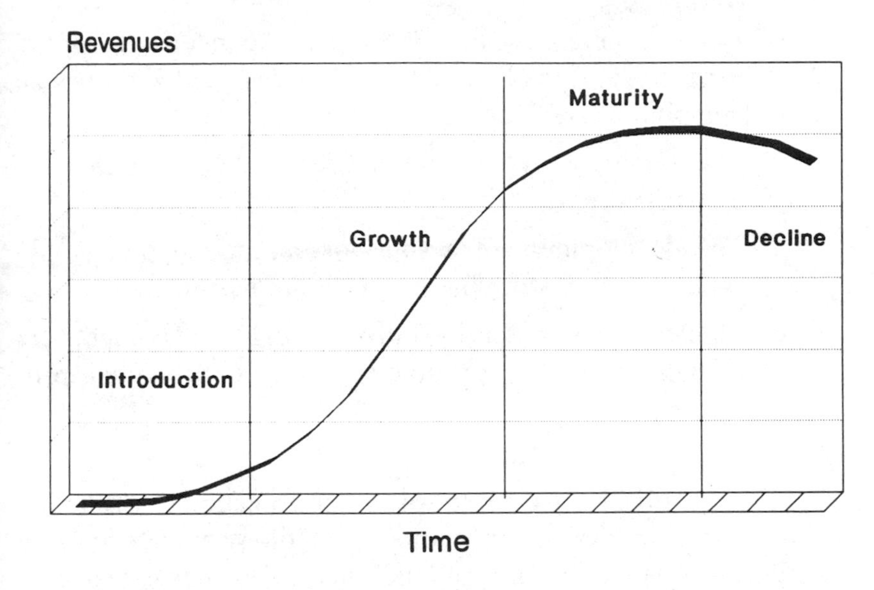

Figure 6.3 Typical Product Life Cycle

Source: Gordon V. Smith and Russell L. Parr, *Valuation of Intellectual Property and Intangible Assets* (New York: John Wiley & Sons, 1989), p. 270. Reprinted by permission of John Wiley & Sons, Inc.

life for a patent or series of patents that support it. Stated another way, the economic life of intellectual property cannot exceed the period during which it or the products it supports find favor in the market.

From this upper range, one should then consider the factors not related to the product marketplace that can also have an effect on the its economic life. Continuing to use the example of the process patent cited above, these would include:

1) Loss of supply or price escalation in a raw material that could render the process uneconomic.
2) An increase in energy costs that would render the process uneconomic.

3) Legislation relative to environmental concerns about the use of feedstock, handling of process effluent, or the compound itself.
4) The possibility of a competitor designing around the protected process.
5) The development of a superior compound that would replace the existing one in the same markets.
6) Challenges of patent validity brought by competitors motivated by the profitability of the protected process.

The most difficult patents for which to estimate economic life are those involving embryonic technology which may be emerging well ahead of any practical use, and those related to "faddish" consumer products such as toys. An educated guess may have to do, knowing that the margin for error may be considerable.

Trade Secrets and Know-How

Most of the patent considerations noted above apply here, with the exception that there is no statutory limit to trade secret protection. End-product economic life also applies to trade secrets as an upper limit to the range of economic life. Additional unique considerations include:

1) The transferability of the trade secrets or know-how. An extreme example might be the skills of a master violin maker. Without an apprentice system that ensures a very long training period, these might have an economic life equal to that of an individual. Another consideration here

is the extent to which such information has been reduced to writing or another transferable form. The skills of a writer, musician, test pilot, or surgeon can be extremely valuable know-how, but largely untransferable.

2) The care with which the confidentiality of the information is protected. To borrow a slogan from the World Wars, "Loose lips sink ships."
3) The versatility of the know-how enhances its economic life. This is always true in that it can be redeployed if there is a change in the market. Grumman Corporation, as an example, extended its know-how in sheet aluminum fabrication of aircraft to the manufacture of vehicle bodies and canoes.

Trademarks

Conventional wisdom would have us accept the notion that trademark rights have no discernible economic life since they exist as long as they are used, maintained, and not proved to be generic. We have grappled with this idea, primarily because it is difficult to agree with the concept that *any* business assets have a perpetual life.

We also question the conventional wisdom because it is clear that even the best, most well-recognized trademarks must be continually maintained by advertising and by being associated with a product or products that continue to find favor with the buying public. This requires continued investment of labor and capital.

Trademarks can die with a product if they are so closely identified with it that they cannot be redeployed. They certainly can be misused by unwise extension to inappropriate or poor quality products, and their value degraded thereby. It is clear to us, therefore, that they are not, by their nature, eternal.

No one disputes the fact that a piece of machinery wears out, becomes obsolete, and eventually is scrapped. During its life, an investment of labor and capital is made to repair and maintain it in order to slow the aging process. As a practical matter, however, it can never be maintained in "100%" condition.

A trademark (or customer base) *can* be maintained in "100%" condition, or even *improved*. That is, all the forces of depreciation can be held at bay by astute management and the investment of capital. Should this fact, however, cause us to believe that a trademark is eternal? We think not.

We offer for further consideration the idea that a trademark is, at any specific moment, the product of investments of the past. If all future investments were to cease, the mark would die, that is clear. Even without this extreme assumption, we submit that the future investments can *replace* those made in the past, and therefore the value of a trademark at a specific time will diminish, its place to be taken by new investment.

Trademarks do change, as an example. Our perception is that very few trademarks have existed unchanged for very long, especially those associated with consumer products. Even the venerable "BETTY CROCKER" and the "CAMPBELL KIDS" (created in 1904) have changed over the years. Even this change is costly, with design firms retained, and their staffs interacting with top management over a long design and approval period. When the approval process is complete, an advertising campaign is mounted. These expenditures are replacing those of previous years. Styles and tastes change, and so do trademarks.

Relative to trademark exploitation, we suggest that it is not proper to assume that, once a deal is made, the benefits will continue indefinitely. We would certainly emphasize that those benefits will not continue without further investment. I once asked the pilot of a corporate jet whether it required much maintenance. He replied that it only required a "rubdown with $100 bills each morning." Trademarks are like that.

Copyrights

According to statute, copyrights have a very long economic life. In our experience, however, copyrighted works enjoy economic benefits for a much shorter period than their legal life, and most often they are not distributed evenly over that shorter life. There is such a variety of copyrighted works that it is impossible to make statements that will apply across the board. Economic life is dependent on the type of work and the manner in which it can be exploited.

Our experience with copyrights of reference books has indicated that sales reach their height about one to two years after publication, and decline thereafter in a pattern similar to that illustrated in Figure 6.4.

This is the product life cycle pattern referred to earlier, with a sharper growth period, a short peak, and a gradual decline. A literary work can also remain in relative obscurity for some period, be "discovered," and enjoy a rapid rise to popularity. The same can occur with musical works.

We were once involved in valuing a large library of copyrighted musical works. In it were "standards" that were 40 years old, and still returning a steady stream of royalties to their owners. Other songs had enjoyed a brief, and sometimes meteoric, popularity, and were earning very small royalty income. One song had been part of a motion picture score, and had enjoyed some popularity when the motion picture was playing in theaters. It had fallen to a low earnings level when it was selected to be the background music in a radio and television commercial. The product advertised has been very successful for over 20 years, and the copyright royalties are still pouring in! Currently, "rock

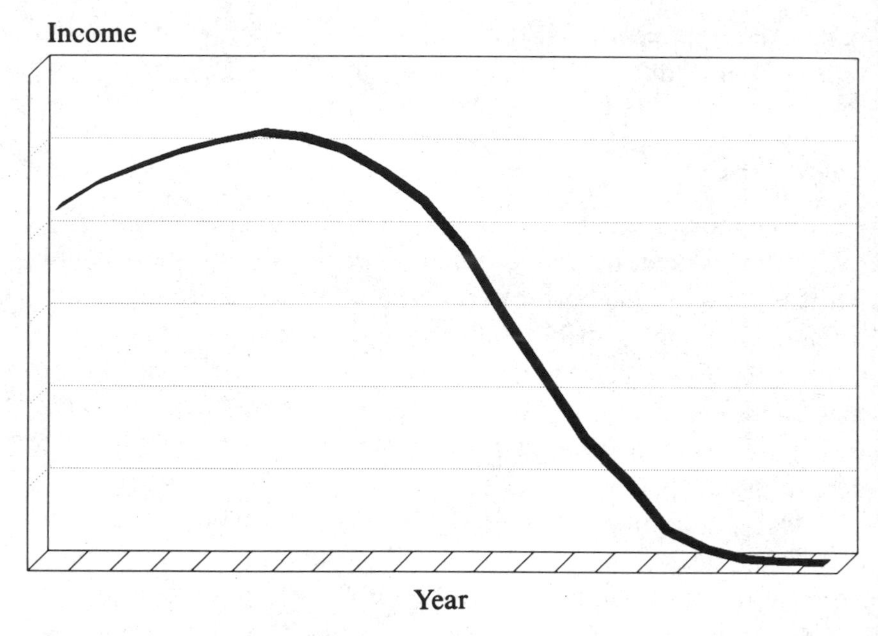

Figure 6.4 Copyright Value

Source: Gordon V. Smith and Russell L. Parr, *Valuation of Intellectual Property and Intangible Assets* (New York: John Wiley & Sons, 1989), p. 319. Reprinted by permission of John Wiley & Sons, Inc.

and roll'' songs and performers of the 50s are enjoying new popularity, and there has been a resurgence of the big band music of the 40s.

These events are impossible to predict, of course, but there are a number of considerations that have merit in estimating the potential economic life of copyrighted works:

1) The breadth of exploitation is important. Cartoon characters, as an example, have been widely exploited in greeting cards, on toys, as dolls, on clothing, and so on. It is common today for a story and characters in a book to be

exploited in a wide variety of media, as well as ancillary products.

2) As with other intellectual property, versatility is very important, broadening the opportunities for exploitation.
3) "Timelessness" is important. The motion pictures of Walt Disney are always playing to a new generation of delighted children. Colorized versions of *Gone with the Wind* and *Casablanca* are again playing to a new (as well as old) generation of delighted adults.

Computer Software

If the software in question is itself a product, then some of the considerations discussed above are applicable. One must look through to the end purchaser/user and ask a number of questions:

1) Is the application somewhat narrow (i.e., an accounting system for a dental practice), or is it broad, such as a "spreadsheet" or word processing system? (Versatility and a diverse market again.)
2) Is the system tied to a particular brand of hardware? This is especially important in the personal computer market.
3) Who is the competition? What is their size and expertise?
4) Have there been "generations" of this type of software that have been on the market and are gone?
5) What changes are going on in the business of the end users?
6) Is the software dependent on a particular operating system? If so, what is its degree of obsolescence?

For software that is in use within a business and may have been designed especially for it, some of the above questions apply, in addition to others:

1) Are the end users (operating departments within the company in this case) satisfied with what the software produces?
2) How old is the system? Was it designed for some prior hardware and operating in an "emulation" mode?
3) Is the software efficient to use in terms of processing speed and effective use of storage and ease of data input?

These are really directed at measuring the degree of functional obsolescence in the software. The more functional obsolescence that is present, the shorter is the economic life.

Software for specific, ad hoc projects can have a life as short as one year, while "core" tasks can be addressed by software that lasts 10 or 12 years, with very little change.

Right of Publicity

Can there be any quantifiable economic life associated with the right of publicity? Yes, but it is difficult to measure. First, everyone has the right of publicity, but it only has value in rare cases. Of some assistance in the estimation of economic life is the fact that there must be some economic substance to the right. That is, the right must be exploitable. What are the factors to consider in estimating economic life?

1) The expected life span of the personality is a factor. This is not completely limiting, but the economic benefits of exploitation diminish after death.
2) The lifestyle of the personality. Very well-known people have become reclusive, thus diminishing, by their own choice, the potential for exploitation.
3) The arena in which the personality achieved fame or notoriety may be a factor in its longevity. Careers and

recognition periods vary in show business, politics, sports, being involved in a noteworthy event, and even in criminality.

SUMMARY

In Chapter 3, we introduced the basic economic theories that apply to the exploitation of intellectual property. We illustrated the need to quantify the income that intellectual property can produce, the duration of that income, and the risks associated with its realization. In Chapters 4 and 5, we elaborated on ways to quantify the income-producing capability of intellectual property. In this chapter, we examined the risks of intellectual property exploitation and ways to quantify its economic life.

Armed with this understanding, we now turn to specific applications in licensing and joint venture activities.

7

Licensing Economics and Royalty Rates

An intellectual property license is a contractual agreement between two parties, one of whom has title to the complete bundle of rights to the property, and another who has acquired the use of some of those rights. Because the owner has the legal right to prevent the use of the property by others, the license is essentially an agreement by the owner not to prosecute the licensee. It could be called a granting of the right to infringe.

There is an infinite variety of possibilities as to how those rights can be allocated between the parties and as to how compensation will flow from one to the other. Robert Goldscheider, a noted expert in the field, likens the process of designing a license agreement to sitting down at a "mighty Wurlitzer" organ to use the vast array of keys, pedals, and stops to produce the particular music that is agreeable to both licensor and licensee.

We would add another analogy from the world of real estate. Nearly everyone, at one time or another, has rented real property, even if only a cabin in the mountains or an apartment at the shore for a two-week vacation. When we have found the suitable property and sit down to execute the lease, the landlord or agent pulls out "Onerous Lease No.1" from the shelf and pushes it forward for us to sign. If we trouble to read it, as we should, we would find that it puts the entire responsibility of property ownership on us, and that the owner is relieved of all obligations, potential liabilities, and possible expenses. We find that we must give one-year's notice before leaving, we must paint the walls and refinish the floors when we vacate, and that all of our guests must sign a release absolving the owner of every conceivable liability. Then the negotiation begins. We and the landlord agree to strike out clauses, remove or add a word here and there, perhaps the rent or deposit goes up a bit, but when it is all over, we have an agreement both can live with. This is the licensing process, and no wonder, for what is a license but an agreement to rent property rights in return for some compensation?

Let us, however, think about what is really happening in this process. Our first reaction to "Onerous Lease No. 1" is that it requires too much compensation for the rights we are to receive. How do we make that judgment? Our thought process might be as follows:

> "I have never seen such stringent requirements before; it's not what other agents (the market) ask for."
>
> "The rent is already at the high end of the range for this apartment at this season. What more do they want?"
>
> "I can't afford to paint the walls and refinish the floor."
>
> "I've never had to sign a release for anyone I visited. This is really strange."
>
> "It doesn't sound as if they really want to rent this property, but it's a really nice place and I'd like to spend my vacation here."
>
> "I can't see any way that I will enjoy staying in this property enough to justify the amount of rent they are asking."

We tend to evaluate the deal in terms of what is *customary* (what others in the market ask for) and in terms of *dollars*. This framework is quite reliable for evaluating real estate transactions, but cannot meaningfully be applied to what is customary in the marketplace for intellectual property. There are too many markets, and conditions change too rapidly. This is the reason why we remain very skeptical about reliance on "market evidence" to guide us in license negotiations. We would also advise the reader against relying too much on what might appear to be "customary" in the marketplace. There is little, if any, homogeneity in intellectual property or among potential licensors and licensees. Therefore, we believe that the idea of a "typical" license or a "customary" royalty rate has no place in the licensing process. We are not discussing used automobiles; we are faced with highly individual, "big ticket" decisions, and we do not want to follow someone else's royalty rate footprints into the swamp!

We can, however, present some tools that can be used when it is appropriate to evaluate licenses in terms of dollars.

PRICING THE ALTERNATIVES

In Chapter 3, we examined the economics of intellectual property exploitation, and touched on the economics of licensing as well. We learned that the value of a license is:

> To the Licensor:
> The present value of the compensation to be received (typically cash payments) less the present value of the costs that might be incurred to administer the agreement, or income foregone by electing not to exploit the intellectual property internally.
>
> To the Licensee:
> The present value of the future economic benefits of exploiting the licensed intellectual property less the costs (including payments to the licensor) of doing so.

In every licensing transaction, the parties must decide which tune from the "mighty Wurlitzer" is agreeable. Putting this decision in terms of money, we suggest that, for either party, the one of several licensing alternatives that has the highest present value is the best. This assumes that all of the possible future events have been carefully analyzed. We developed, in Chapter 3, the tool to quantify this present value—the discounted cash flow analysis (DCF).

In the following sections of this chapter, we will apply the discounted cash flow technique to specific licensing provisions. We must recognize, however, that the DCF process starts with an estimate of future cash flows, positive and negative, which arise from a myriad of possible events. This is forecasting in its essence.

We often receive the comment that, while our investment analysis techniques make sense theoretically, they are too difficult to apply because one must make forecasts. An example of early-stage biotechnology licensing is often used as an example. This kind of intellectual property is "foundation technology" that may ultimately find its way into countless commercial applications (or none). How can anyone, trying to license this sort of intellectual property, possibly foresee all of the possibilities? If the licensor is too conservative, he or she "leaves money on the table." If the licensor is too aggressive and optimistic in forecasting, licensees will be driven off. Our answer is this:

> You had better make *some sort* of forecast and "take your best shot"; otherwise, you are absolutely leaving the outcome to chance. Doing something is better than throwing darts at the "royalty board."
>
> You can try to negotiate a license with *financial contingencies* so that you will share in good things if they happen, without putting the licensee in concrete shoes if they do not.

> If you do not apply some financial measures, you may not only forego some "upside" potential, but also incur some hidden liabilities! What could be worse than collecting a 1.5% royalty on what is to the licensee a highly profitable blockbuster product *and* having to fund the defense of infringement litigation aimed at the licensee?

As difficult as it may be, does it make any business sense not to make an effort to provide oneself with the best information possible for deciding on the deployment of valuable business assets?

There is a whole host of other considerations in the licensing process that are often called to our attention as reasons why an analytical approach is not appropriate. Sometimes, there is only one possible licensee for a given intellectual property. One "can analyze this transaction *ad infinitum,* and you will still have to accept what is offered." We agree. At times, "the licensor (or licensee) is in dire financial need, and time is of the essence." "There are good negotiators and bad." We agree again. All of these comments have merit, and we agree that it does not always make sense to make a detailed analysis, but when it does, we assert that it does not make any business sense to ignore it. Some say, "Licensing is an art form" in an attempt to justify a continuation of the "seat of the pants" approach. Painting is art as well, but the best painters carefully study light, color, and practice their execution so that they can accurately render their inner art in tangible form. A master craftsman does not ignore the tools available.

What happens in the real world? The "business people" make a deal with a potential licensee/licensor. They take the deal to their legal advisors (inside or outside the organization) to memorialize it. The legal folks see some serious potential pitfalls and suggest some changes. The business folks go back to the drawing board and the potential licensee/licensor. In response to some new ideas, the licensee/licensor has some new ideas. What seemed like a "done deal" is anything but. At this point, everyone needs some tools to work with, and ones that are flexible and can accept the ever-changing parameters and provide some guidance to both sides of the transaction.

When both parties look at the potential transaction, what do they see? The future. In order for either party to move forward, they must have formed some picture of their economic future, or the economic future of the business element that will be the core of the transaction.

Forecasting

There are excellent references on forecasting and tools for doing it, and we will not attempt to reproduce them here. Winston Churchill, responding to a question about desirable qualities in a politician, replied:

> It is the ability to foretell what is going to happen tomorrow, next week, next month, and next year. And to have the ability afterwards to explain why it didn't happen.

Perhaps these are desirable qualities in a licensing executive as well. We will, however, point out some aspects of the process as they relate to forecasting in the licensing process. What might we need to forecast?

Licensor

Cash inflows—which might include up-front payments, milestone payments, or running royalties, in short, all of the permutations of receiving payment for the use of intellectual property rights granted. In the case of running royalties, we will need to make our own estimate of the future royalty base. This is usually net sales to the licensee of products covered by the license, but it can also take a number of forms.

Cash outflows—which might include the expense of continuing research and development, administering and accounting for the license, audits, possible litigation to protect the intellectual property, and costs to indemnify the licensee.

Licensee

Cash inflows—net income from the sale of products covered by the licensed intellectual property, and net income from synergistic sales of related products. This also is based on forecasts of sales revenue and operating expenses of an ongoing business.

Cash outflows—would include research and development expense, marketing costs to get the licensed intellectual property into products ready for the marketplace, continuing development, expenses connected with future infringement litigation, capital costs of new or additional plant and working capital, and of course, payments to the licensor.

Sales Revenue

Forecasting sales revenue seems to be the first and most difficult hurdle in the process, so we will use sales forecasting as the example in this discussion.

It seems to us that forecasts proceed either from the top down or the bottom up. In the top-down approach, one starts with some global information, such as estimates of world population growth, and winnows from that the implication for the situation at hand. The bottom-up approach starts with some known, perhaps historical data, such as the number of customers one has, and extrapolates those data into future revenue dollars.

Top-Down Approach. This ought to be the predominant

approach for intellectual property exploitation forecasts since, most of the time, we have little to build on. Hughes[1] describes the elements of top-down sales forecasting:

> *Market Capacity.* This is the number of units of a product or service that the market can absorb. It is the estimated total unfilled need of the market. This estimate can be for a segment of the market.
>
> *Market Potential.* This converts the market capacity of an industry or segment into sales dollars by introducing unit prices and market strategies.
>
> *Company Potential.* This is the maximum that a company could sell, at a given price, regardless of its ability to satisfy that estimated market. Consideration must be given to economies of scale, learning ability, transportation, site selection, technology requirements, and production planning.
>
> *Company Forecast.* Superimposes on the above the company's ability to produce and market. Introduces market share.

An advantage of the top-down approach is that it begins with global estimates that are available and can usually be agreed upon by negotiating parties. They have third-party disinterest, and usually can represent an uncontroversial starting point. Examples are population estimates, demographic data, Gross National Product estimates, air passenger-miles, railroad revenue ton-miles, units of new home construction, percentage of the population with a given disease, and the like.

In Appendix B, we provide a list of information sources that

[1] Spyros Makridakis and Steven C. Wheelwright, editors, *The Handbook of Forecasting*. (New York, John Wiley & Sons, 1987, Chapter 2, Sales Forecasting Requirements by G. David Hughes.

we have found to be helpful in this process. In the section entitled "Sources of Sources" are listed references that will lead one to specific industry data. There is a plethora of industry and trade associations that assemble data about their members and make them available. There is a wealth of information available.

The difficult part of a sales revenue forecast is making such global forecasts specific to a company or type of intellectual property. One tool is to extrapolate from known data. If, as an example, I am concerned with the potential market for a new sun-protecting skin cosmetic, I can observe from cosmetic industry statistics what percentage of skin care products sold have this characteristic. I could then look to forecasts of skin care product sales as a starting point for the forecast that I need. In this particular case, I might inject an element of judgment and increase the proportion in the future since there is a growing awareness of the effect of the sun on skin. We learn from the *U.S. Industrial Outlook 1992* that: ". . . The skin care industry is introducing new products with better skin protection, particularly against ultraviolet rays that are present all year. Specialty sun care products, with current sales of $400 million, have been increasing at an estimated 7% per year; this trend is expected to continue . . . Skin care products formulated with sunscreens will become increasingly popular." Every bit of information we can find helps us to progress from the global to the particular.

Another tool we find useful is to reduce a forecast to its "least common denominator." As an example, if we are attempting to forecast the sales revenue that could be generated by exploiting the copyright to a cartoon or movie character, we would make individual forecasts for all of the reasonable exploitation possibilities. We would analyze the markets for video, books, apparel, novelty items, endorsements, sports products, and the like. We feel that a summation of individual forecasts (after an analysis of the individual markets) gives a more precise result than attempting to make one global forecast for all forms of exploitation. This method is especially appealing when the forecast for individual exploitation methods differs, such as when income from the original moving picture is expected to fall rather steeply, while income from ancillary exploitations will decline at a different rate or according to a different pattern. It also appeals when the relative risk of the alternative exploitation possibilities is quite different, and we may want to treat the various cash flows differently in the DCF calculation.

A forecast of product sales becomes a form of an econometric model which expresses the relationship between global data and a specific product or intellectual property. It is very useful to design a sales projection with this in mind, and to include all of the individual elements so that they can be changed to test the sensitivity of the result. An example of this is provided in Figure 7.1.

One must also be cognizant of where, on the typical product life cycle curve, the subject intellectual property is located. A typical life cycle curve appears as shown in Figure 7.2.

One of the ingredients of the sales revenue forecast is price. There is a typical evolution of unit price as well. When a product is introduced, customers are unfamiliar and unit sales are low. Manufacturing has not achieved economies of scale. The product is often considered a luxury item. We remember when power steering was introduced. It was expensive and somewhat unreliable. Nevertheless, there were those who purchased it. This is the classic pricing and marketing of a new product.

As a new product moves into mass production, after the encouraging sales to the "gadgeteers," the unit price begins to come down. One of the authors of this book recently purchased a "notebook computer" at what will probably be remembered as the height of the market. He will be reminded of this as he observes the descending pattern of prices and the ascending pattern of capabilities in the Sunday paper advertisements.

As maturity is reached, almost everyone who wants the

	1990	1992	1995	2000	2005	2010
U.S. Population (mill.)	251.4	254.5	260.1	268.3	275.6	282.6
Female (mill.)	138.7	130.2	133	137.1	140.8	144.3
% Users of Cosmetics	52	52	52	52	52	52
Users of Cosmetics (mill.)	72.1	67.7	69.2	71.3	73.2	75.0
% Sun–Sensitive	21	21	21	21	21	21
Sun–Sensitive (mill.)	15.1	14.2	14.5	15.0	15.4	15.8
Avg. Uses per Year	12	15	18	24	30	30
Total Uses (mill.)	181.8	213.3	261.4	359.3	461.3	472.7
Price per Use	$0.03	$0.04	$0.06	$0.06	$0.06	$0.06
Total Market ($)	$5,452,574	$8,530,704	$15,685,488	$21,558,701	$27,675,648	$28,363,608
%Penetration	10	12	15	15	15	15
Sales Revenue ($)	$545,257	$1,023,684	$2,352,823	$3,233,805	$4,151,347	$4,254,541

Figure 7.1 Sales Revenue Forecast

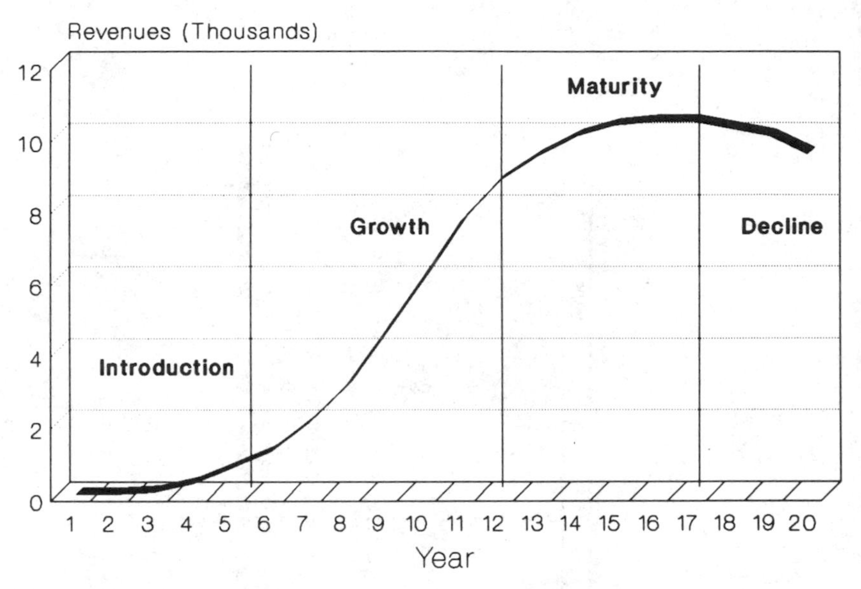

Figure 7.2 Revenue Forecasts: Product Life Cycle

Source: Gordon V. Smith and Russell L. Parr, *Valuation of Intellectual Property and Intangible Assets* (New York: John Wiley & Sons, 1989), p. 270. Reprinted by permission of John Wiley & Sons, Inc.

new product has one, and the early buyers may be purchasing replacements. The effects of competition have been felt, profit margins have been squeezed, and many manufacturers have been forced out of the market.

These factors must be considered when making a forecast of sales revenue. Often, we are well aware of the quantities of products that we expect to sell over the typical life cycle, but we can overlook the unit price changes associated with those sales.

Since the U.S. population data used as a basis for the sales forecast shown in Figure 7.1 are not continuous, we can use trendline techniques to "fill in" the intervening points, so that we have sales revenue for each year in the series. It would appear that the growth is linear (see Figure 7.3).

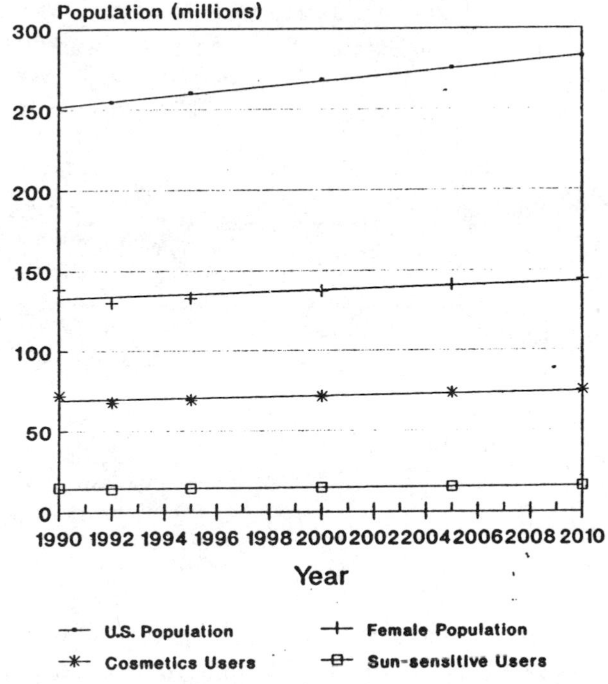

Figure 7.3 Foundation for Sales Revenue Forecast

LICENSING

By using the tools of forecasting and DCF, we can develop a picture of the business opportunity potential of our subject intellectual property. We now will apply those techniques to the evaluation of a license agreement. For the purpose of this discussion, we will assume that we are the *licensor*.

In essence, we will develop a DCF model, but instead of using an income statement as the basis as we did in Chapter 3, we will structure it on the basis of the intended license clauses. Our ultimate objective is to estimate the net present value of the whole transaction, from our point of view. We will include the effect of all of the possible positive and negative cash flows that could reasonably be expected. This can be illustrated as follows:

	Present Value
License Provision #1	$(25,000)
License Provision #2	50,000
License Provision #3	250,000
License Provision #4	(8,000)
	$267,000

If we can find a way to calculate the probable present value of the essential parts of the contemplated license agreement, then we have a valuable tool with which to evaluate different agreements or to support our license negotiations. Even if we find it necessary to express some of the present values in terms of a range (because it is not possible to be precise), the tool is still very useful.

	Present Value
License Provision #1	$(25,000)–(175,000)
License Provision #2	50,000
License Provision #3	250,000
License Provision #4	(8,000)
	$267,000–$117,000

If we are uncomfortable with the magnitude of this range, or the fact that one of the extremes is negative, then we need to examine Provision #1 and see what we can do to limit its potential liability, or turn to Provision #3 and see if we can improve on the "plus side."

Generally speaking, license provisions have the potential of generating either positive or negative cash flow, but not both. Remembering that we, for the purpose of this discussion, are taking the place of the licensor, those provisions that define obligations of the licensor tend to define negative potential cash flows, and those that relate to licensee obligations, positive potential cash flows.

License Provision Characteristics

In one way or another, every provision in a license (or even one that is missing) can have an effect on the present value of the deal. That is why care in the process is so important. We are, however, going to define provisions as Primary or Secondary Economic Drivers. Primary Economic Drivers are those clauses that have a directly measurable effect on present value, such as Consideration (royalty). Secondary Economic Drivers are those that define conditions that, while they are important, are inputs to the Primary Drivers. As an example, a Territory provision puts boundaries on the potential business of the licensee (and therefore royalties), and so its effect on present value can only be measured by reference to other license provisions.

Another structure within which to examine a license is to separate those Primary Economic Drivers which (from the standpoint of the licensor) have positive cash flow attributes from those that can result in negative cash flows. In the remaining sections of this chapter, we will present a model that provides a framework within which to examine and evaluate these cash flows. Readers should not take the money amounts as benchmarks or guidelines for the transactions they are working with. We have tried to make our cost and royalty estimates reasonable, but these are examples only, and should not be taken as "norms."

Royalty Rates

We remind the reader that, in the discussion which follows, we are not presenting a methodology for determining an appropriate royalty rate, but rather a methodology for evaluating alternative licensing scenarios.

The determination of a royalty rate should be made using return on investment techniques. This is explained in our previous book, *Valuation of Intellectual Property and Intangible Assets*. If one were to evaluate licensing scenarios from the licensee's perspective, returns on complementary assets (such as working capital and tangible assets) would have to be considered. The licensee is usually the party who must make these investments in order to exploit the licensed intellectual property, and any analysis of the licensee's position must include these investments in the net cash flows.

In order to simplify what would otherwise be a complex explanation, we have chosen to present these evaluation tools from the standpoint of the licensor who typically is not required to make an investment in either monetary or tangible assets as part of the transaction. The net cash flow realized by the licensor is therefore the product of royalty income and expenses of a current nature.

PRIMARY ECONOMIC DRIVERS

Positive Cash Flow Provisions

These provisions primarily are those which define royalties and those concerning grantbacks and sublicensing. The licensor can receive compensation in the form of cash royalty payments or in the form of the value of enhanced technology developed by the licensee which, under the terms of the license, is shared with the licensor. In the first case, it is cash for the bank; in the second, it is akin to principle, which again must be redeployed. In any case, it represents positive cash flow.

As we noted above, there is an infinite number of ways that compensation can be paid and received. Just like the inventor of the "super putter" in Chapter 3, we must quantify these positive cash flows in their least common denominator, their present value. To illustrate, we will use an example of a present value calculation of several royalty alternatives in a simple situation. Assume, please, that we as licensor have developed a process technology that can save a significant amount of money in the manufacture of a commodity chemical. As the baseline of our analysis, we develop a model representing the economics of the commodity chemical business as it exists for a potential licensee. It is obvious that if we, the licensor, are also in the commodity chemical business, we already know the economics of the industry. If we are not, we will have to do some research to construct this base model. We again recommend the sources of industry data and financial information that are presented in Appendix B.

We have made a ten-year projection of a simple income statement. Sales revenue is driven by an estimate of product quantity and unit price because we may wish to vary these in later estimates. We are not attempting to mirror the licensee's whole business (which may include other products or lines of business), but to capture the typical economics of the business element in which our technology will be licensed.

In order to keep the model as simple as possible, we have not included estimates of capital additions and working capital changes. The reader will recall that these are ingredients of a complete cash flow model and are nearly always present. There are few, if any, business opportunities that do not incorporate the necessity for additional tangible assets or additions to working capital. We are simply eliminating these elements in order to illustrate the technique. The base model is as shown in Figure 7.4.

At a discount rate of 12%, the present value of this business element is $423,016. For the purpose of this example, we have not included any consideration of inflationary price or expense increases.

We then inject our cost-saving technology into this base model. The effect is to change Cost of Goods Sold from $875,000 to $800,000. We then calculate the present value of this new scenario in Figure 7.5.

We observe that our cost-saving technology improves the present value of this operation by $253,810 to $676,826. So, if we were to *give* the technology to the owners of this enterprise, we would have enriched them by something more than a quarter of a million dollars. Obviously, this is not the objective of an intellectual property owner. We require compensation for making available some rights to our property. Further calculations will show that the maximum we could expect to receive from the licensee would be a compensation with a present value of $253,810. We illustrate this by introducing a royalty of $0.15/lb into the model, and observe that the present value of the business element to the licensee returns to $423,016, where it was without the technology. See Figure 7.6.

The present value of this scenario, to the licensor, is seen to be $423,016, which is equivalent to approximately $253,810 after tax. To make this comparison, it is necessary to consider the tax benefit of the royalty payment made by the licensee. Tax considerations are not a part of any of the calculations and examples which follow.

The licensee, however, would have little motivation to enter into an agreement such as that unless he anticipates additional benefits that we have missed. A more likely scenario would be

		1	2	3	4	5	6	7	8	9	10
QUANTITY (lb 000s)		500	500	500	500	500	500	500	500	500	500
PRICE PER UNIT ($)		2.50	2.50	2.50	2.50	2.50	2.50	2.50	2.50	2.50	2.50
REVENUE ($000s)		1,250	1,250	1,250	1,250	1,250	1,250	1,250	1,250	1,250	1,250
Cost of Goods Sold		875	875	875	875	875	875	875	875	875	875
Gross Profit		375	375	375	375	375	375	375	375	375	375
SG & A Expense		200	200	200	200	200	200	200	200	200	200
Other Expense		50	50	50	50	50	50	50	50	50	50
Pretax Income		125	125	125	125	125	125	125	125	125	125
Taxes		50	50	50	50	50	50	50	50	50	50
Net Income		75	75	75	75	75	75	75	75	75	75
Present Value	12%	70.36	61.91	54.48	47.95	42.19	37.13	32.67	28.75	25.30	22.27
Total Present Value ($)		423,016									

Figure 7.4 Base Case for Licensee

		1	2	3	4	5	6	7	8	9	10
QUANTITY (lb 000s)		500	500	500	500	500	500	500	500	500	500
PRICE PER UNIT ($)		2.50	2.50	2.50	2.50	2.50	2.50	2.50	2.50	2.50	2.50
REVENUE ($000s)		1,250	1,250	1,250	1,250	1,250	1,250	1,250	1,250	1,250	1,250
Cost of Goods Sold		800	800	800	800	800	800	800	800	800	800
Gross Profit		450	450	450	450	450	450	450	450	450	450
SG & A Expense		200	200	200	200	200	200	200	200	200	200
Other Expense		50	50	50	50	50	50	50	50	50	50
Pretax Income		200	200	200	200	200	200	200	200	200	200
Taxes		80	80	80	80	80	80	80	80	80	80
Net Income		120	120	120	120	120	120	120	120	120	120
Present Value	12%	112.57	99.06	87.17	76.71	67.51	59.41	52.28	46.00	40.48	35.63
Total Present Value ($)		676,826									

Figure 7.5 Effect of Technology to Licensee

		1	2	3	4	5	6	7	8	9	10
QUANTITY (lb 000s)		500	500	500	500	500	500	500	500	500	500
PRICE PER UNIT ($)		2.50	2.50	2.50	2.50	2.50	2.50	2.50	2.50	2.50	2.50
REVENUE ($000s)		1,250	1,250	1,250	1,250	1,250	1,250	1,250	1,250	1,250	1,250
Cost of Goods Sold		800	800	800	800	800	800	800	800	800	800
Gross Profit		450	450	450	450	450	450	450	450	450	450
Royalty		75	75	75	75	75	75	75	75	75	75
SG & A Expense		200	200	200	200	200	200	200	200	200	200
Other Expense		50	50	50	50	50	50	50	50	50	50
Pretax Income		125	125	125	125	125	125	125	125	125	125
Taxes		50	50	50	50	50	50	50	50	50	50
Net Income		75	75	75	75	75	75	75	75	75	75
Present Value	12%	70.36	61.91	54.48	47.95	42.19	37.13	32.67	28.75	25.30	22.27
Total Present Value ($)		423,016									
Present Value of Royalties		70.36	61.91	54.48	47.95	42.19	37.13	32.67	28.75	25.30	22.27
Total Present Value ($)		423,016									

Figure 7.6 Introduce $0.15/lb Royalty (Equal to Economic Benefit)

to consider a division of the apparent benefits. Figure 7.7 shows the effect of an equal split of the benefits between licensee and licensor.

This reduces the present value of the business to the licensee to $549,921, and provides a royalty stream to the licensor with a present value of $211,508. These calculations all use a running royalty based on product quantity.

If, for some reason (perhaps we require the money or we have doubts about the licensee's commitment), we want a lump sum royalty upon signing the license, we can use the model (on a trial-and-error basis) to determine the appropriate amount. That amount would be $225,000 in order to maintain the same present value. See Figure 7.8.

If, in negotiations, we have to give up the notion of a 100% lump sum royalty on signing and the licensee is willing to pay about half that, we can again utilize the model to test different assumptions. No doubt, quite a number of results will meet the requirements, but we can show that a $0.04/lb running royalty and a $125,000 up- front payment will maintain the target present value represented by the 50–50 split of economic benefit. See Figure 7.9.

In these examples, the royalty base has been the *quantity* of output. We might choose this royalty base for several reasons:

We forecast price erosion in the commodity chemical market due to new capacity coming on line or because the product is in the "September" of its life cycle.

The licensee is selling internationally, and we do not want to incur currency risk.

We expect the licensee to achieve other productivity improvements.

Quantity produced is cheaper and easier to audit.

		1	2	3	4	5	6	7	8	9	10
QUANTITY (lb 000s)		500	500	500	500	500	500	500	500	500	500
PRICE PER UNIT ($)		2.50	2.50	2.50	2.50	2.50	2.50	2.50	2.50	2.50	2.50
REVENUE ($000s)		1,250	1,250	1,250	1,250	1,250	1,250	1,250	1,250	1,250	1,250
Cost of Goods Sold		800	800	800	800	800	800	800	800	800	800
Gross Profit		450	450	450	450	450	450	450	450	450	450
Royalty		38	38	38	38	38	38	38	38	38	38
SG & A Expense		200	200	200	200	200	200	200	200	200	200
Other Expense		50	50	50	50	50	50	50	50	50	50
Pretax Income		163	163	163	163	163	163	163	163	163	163
Taxes		65	65	65	65	65	65	65	65	65	65
Net Income		98	98	98	98	98	98	98	98	98	98
Present Value	12%	91.46	80.49	70.83	62.33	54.85	48.27	42.48	37.38	32.89	28.95
Total Present Value ($)		549,921									
Present Value of Royalties		35.18	30.96	27.24	23.97	21.10	18.56	16.34	14.38	12.65	11.13
Total Present Value ($)		211,508									

Figure 7.7 50–50 Economic Benefit Split to $0.075/lb Royalty

		1	2	3	4	5	6	7	8	9	10
QUANTITY (lb 000s)		500	500	500	500	500	500	500	500	500	500
PRICE PER UNIT ($)		2.50	2.50	2.50	2.50	2.50	2.50	2.50	2.50	2.50	2.50
REVENUE ($000s)		1,250	1,250	1,250	1,250	1,250	1,250	1,250	1,250	1,250	1,250
Cost of Goods Sold		800	800	800	800	800	800	800	800	800	800
Gross Profit		450	450	450	450	450	450	450	450	450	450
Royalty		225	0	0	0	0	0	0	0	0	0
SG & A Expense		200	200	200	200	200	200	200	200	200	200
Other Expense		50	50	50	50	50	50	50	50	50	50
Pretax Income		(25)	200	200	200	200	200	200	200	200	200
Taxes		(10)	80	80	80	80	80	80	80	80	80
Net Income		(15)	120	120	120	120	120	120	120	120	120
Present Value	12%	-14.07	99.06	87.17	76.71	67.51	59.41	52.28	46.00	40.48	35.63
Total Present Value ($)		550,185									
Present Value of Royalties		211.07	0.00	0.00	0.00	0.00	0.00	0.00	0.00	0.00	0.00
Total Present Value ($)		211,069									

Figure 7.8 50–50 Economic Benefit Split, Lump Sum Royalty

		1	2	3	4	5	6	7	8	9	10
QUANTITY (lb 000s)		500	500	500	500	500	500	500	500	500	500
PRICE PER UNIT ($)		2.50	2.50	2.50	2.50	2.50	2.50	2.50	2.50	2.50	2.50
REVENUE ($000s)		1,250	1,250	1,250	1,250	1,250	1,250	1,250	1,250	1,250	1,250
Cost of Goods Sold		800	800	800	800	800	800	800	800	800	800
Gross Profit		450	450	450	450	450	450	450	450	450	450
Royalty		125	20	20	20	20	20	20	20	20	20
SG & A Expense		200	200	200	200	200	200	200	200	200	200
Other Expense		50	50	50	50	50	50	50	50	50	50
Pretax Income		75	180	180	180	180	180	180	180	180	180
Taxes		30	72	72	72	72	72	72	72	72	72
Net Income		45	108	108	108	108	108	108	108	108	108
Present Value	12%	42.21	89.16	78.46	69.04	60.76	53.47	47.05	41.40	36.44	32.06
Total Present Value ($)		550,044									
Present Value of Royalties		117.26	16.51	14.53	12.79	11.25	9.90	8.71	7.67	6.75	5.94
Total Present Value ($)		211,303									

Figure 7.9 50–50 Economic Benefit Split, Lump Sum and Running Royalty

We may, however, for our own reasons or as a result of negotiation want to shift to a sales revenue royalty base. Reasons for this might include:

Increasing demand for the product will enable the licensee to increase price.

Other, nonlicensed product enhancements will result in price increase.

Sales revenue is cheaper and easier to audit.

The model allows us to make a shift to net sales as a royalty base. With some experimentation, we discover that a running royalty of 3% of sales will net us the same present value (as licensor) as the 50–50 split of economic benefit. See Figure 7.10.

Another strategy that can be tested involves lowering the royalty amount so that diffusion of the technology will be greater and more rapid. It is nice to sell ten items for $2 each, but it is better yet to sell 30 items for $1 each. A lower royalty rate might encourage the licensee to lower the price of the product and increase the market penetration, for his own benefit as well as ours. We can use the model to test out this strategy. If we recast it to a quantity royalty base and estimate increasing sales, we can test whether this structure has merit for us. In Figure 7.11, the present value of the royalty stream (on a pretax basis to keep it simple) has dropped to $131,905. On this basis, it appears that this is not an attractive alternative for us. Perhaps a further drop in price would increase the licensee's market share even more. To make that judgment, we would have to have more facts about the size of the market, the competition, and the licensee's capacity to supply a larger share.

Since the licensed technology results in cost savings for the licensee, a logical form of compensation to us would be a percentage of the cost savings. Let us further assume that the

		1	2	3	4	5	6	7	8	9	10
QUANTITY (lb 000s)		500	500	500	500	500	500	500	500	500	500
PRICE PER UNIT ($)		2.50	2.50	2.50	2.50	2.50	2.50	2.50	2.50	2.50	2.50
REVENUE ($000s)		1,250	1,250	1,250	1,250	1,250	1,250	1,250	1,250	1,250	1,250
Cost of Goods Sold		800	800	800	800	800	800	800	800	800	800
Gross Profit		450	450	450	450	450	450	450	450	450	450
Royalty		38	38	38	38	38	38	38	38	38	38
SG & A Expense		200	200	200	200	200	200	200	200	200	200
Other Expense		50	50	50	50	50	50	50	50	50	50
Pretax Income		163	163	163	163	163	163	163	163	163	163
Taxes		65	65	65	65	65	65	65	65	65	65
Net Income		98	98	98	98	98	98	98	98	98	98
Present Value	12%	91.46	80.49	70.83	62.33	54.85	48.27	42.48	37.38	32.89	28.95
Total Present Value ($)		549,921									
Present Value of Royalties		35.18	30.96	27.24	23.97	21.10	18.56	16.34	14.38	12.65	11.13
Total Present Value ($)		211,508									

Figure 7.10 50–50 Economic Benefit Split to % of Sales Royalty

		1	2	3	4	5	6	7	8	9	10
QUANTITY (lb 000s)		600	720	792	871	958	1,054	1,160	1,276	1,403	1,543
PRICE PER UNIT ($)		2.40	2.40	2.40	2.40	2.40	2.40	2.40	2.40	2.40	2.40
REVENUE ($000s)		1,440	1,728	1,901	2,091	2,300	2,530	2,783	3,061	3,367	3,704
Cost of Goods Sold		960	1,152	1,267	1,394	1,533	1,687	1,855	2,041	2,245	2,469
Gross Profit		480	576	634	697	767	843	928	1,020	1,122	1,235
Royalty		15	18	20	22	24	26	29	32	35	39
SG & A Expense		240	288	317	348	383	422	464	510	561	617
Other Expense		60	72	79	87	96	105	116	128	140	154
Pretax Income		165	198	218	240	264	290	319	351	386	424
Taxes		66	79	87	96	105	116	128	140	154	170
Net Income		99	119	131	144	158	174	191	210	232	255
Present Value	12%	92.87	98.07	94.93	91.89	88.95	86.11	83.35	80.68	78.10	75.60
Total Present Value ($)		870,575									
Present Value of Royalties		14.07	14.86	14.38	13.92	13.48	13.05	12.63	12.22	11.83	11.46
Total Present Value ($)		131,905									

Figure 7.11 Drop Royalty to $0.025/lb, Licensee Drops Price and Increases Market Share

licensee will be able to increase the amount of those savings by successful enhancement of the technology. If the royalty is set at an amount equal to one-half of the savings, Figure 7.12 results.

With a present value of $309,662, this option looks attractive. We must consider several points, however, before proposing this option. Cost savings can be very difficult to quantify and monitor. There is a myriad of inputs to a chemical process, and isolating the effect of one of them is difficult. The licensee is going to be continually "tinkering" with the process to improve it, and may have to change it to accommodate feedstocks of different quality or to meet new environmental restrictions, and so forth. One option is to establish benchmarks of cost with and without the licensed technology at the outset and convert the difference to a royalty on a quantity base. The risk to us here is whether or not the licensee may in the future further improve the technology, and we would not share in this "upside."

Nearly endless possibilities exist. We can test out the royalty based on cost sharing with the possibility of the licensee dropping the price to increase the market share, and observe that this improves our present value even more. See Figure 7.13.

These are but a few of the royalty structure possibilities that can be tested with this simple discounted cash flow model. There are almost endless permutations of sales forecasts, royalty base, and royalty structure that can be quantified. There are, in addition, other positive cash flow license provisions that should be considered.

Grantback to the licensor of improvements to the technology is another provision with potential for altering the amount of cash flow. Here, the effect can take a variety of forms. The grantback of improvements can extend the economic life of the intellectual property, and therefore the strength and duration of the royalty stream. A more likely basis for an estimate of enhanced cash flow would be the likelihood of the licensor being able to grant additional licenses or, if the grantbacks broaden the

		1	2	3	4	5	6	7	8	9	10
QUANTITY (Lbs. 000's)		500	500	500	500	500	500	500	500	500	500
PRICE PER UNIT ($)		2.50	2.50	2.50	2.50	2.50	2.50	2.50	2.50	2.50	2.50
REVENUE ($ 000's)		1,250	1,250	1,250	1,250	1,250	1,250	1,250	1,250	1,250	1,250
Cost of Goods Sold		800	775	775	750	750	750	750	750	750	750
Gross Profit		450	475	475	500	500	500	500	500	500	500
Royalty		38	50	50	63	63	63	63	63	63	63
SG & A Expense		200	200	200	200	200	200	200	200	200	200
Other Expense		75	75	75	75	50	50	50	50	50	50
Pre–tax Income		138	150	150	163	188	188	188	188	188	188
Taxes		55	60	60	65	75	75	75	75	75	75
Net Income		83	90	90	98	113	113	113	113	113	113
Present Value	12%	77.39	74.30	65.38	62.33	63.29	55.69	49.01	43.13	37.95	33.40
Total Present Value ($)		561,874									
Present Value of Royalties		35.18	41.28	36.32	39.95	35.16	30.94	27.23	23.96	21.09	18.56
Total Present Value ($)		309,662									

Figure 7.12 Royalty Set at One-Half of Cost Savings

		1	2	3	4	5	6	7	8	9	10
QUANTITY (lb 000s)		600	720	864	950	1,045	1,150	1,265	1,391	1,531	1,684
PRICE PER UNIT ($)		2.40	2.40	2.40	2.40	2.40	2.40	2.40	2.40	2.40	2.40
REVENUE ($000s)		1,440	1,728	2,074	2,281	2,509	2,760	3,036	3,340	3,674	4,041
Cost of Goods Sold		960	1,152	1,382	1,521	1,673	1,840	2,024	2,226	2,449	2,694
Gross Profit		480	576	691	760	836	920	1,012	1,113	1,225	1,347
Royalty		45	54	65	71	78	86	95	104	115	126
SG & A Expense		240	288	346	380	418	460	506	557	612	673
Other Expense		60	72	86	95	105	115	126	139	153	168
Pretax Income		135	162	194	214	235	259	285	313	344	379
Taxes		54	65	78	86	94	103	114	125	138	152
Net Income		81	97	117	128	141	155	171	188	207	227
Present Value	12%	75.98	80.24	84.73	82.02	79.40	76.86	74.40	72.02	69.71	67.48
Total Present Value ($)		762,840									
Present Value of Royalties		42.21	44.58	47.07	45.57	44.11	42.70	41.33	40.01	38.73	37.49
Total Present Value ($)		423,800									

Figure 7.13 Royalty Set at One-Half of Cost Savings, Licensee Drops Price and Increases Market Share

technology, licenses in additional fields of use. We can utilize a simpler calculation to reflect these potential cash flows. See Figure 7.14.

A *sublicense* provision can have significant positive cash flow implications. Typically, it would cause the licensee to become the licensor's agent, and they would divide the license fees charged to the ultimate licensees. Sublicenses usually provide royalty income to both the original licensor and licensee. An estimate of cash flows from sublicensing begins with a forecast of potential sublicensee sales as a royalty base. To us, as original licensor, the income is a portion of the royalty income that results, less the costs of administration. These costs could be expected to be less than those to administer the original license because one would expect that our licensee would participate, at his own cost, in the process. An example is shown in Figure 7.15.

Negative Cash Flow Provisions

The remaining provisions commonly found in an intellectual property license agreement have negative cash flow implications. These are very difficult to quantify, as they relate to obligations of the licensor which may only be activated in unusual circumstances. There are two situations, however, which are fairly straightforward and relate to the cost of administration and providing technical assistance.

Administration, auditing, and *quality control* are, to some extent, part of every license transaction. Even if the licensor makes no attempt to audit the licensee's accounting for the royalty base and royalty payments, these payments represent a receivable to the licensor, and some cost is incurred to enter it in the accounts. At the other extreme, a licensor can experience significant expense with a recalcitrant licensee, especially one in another country where travel expense, culture, accounting practices, and record keeping can be barriers. Even under normal

		1	2	3	4	5	6	7	8	9	10
Positive Cash Flow		0	0	25	25	50	50	50	75	75	75
Negative Cash Flow		0	0	0	0	0	0	0	0	0	0
		---------	---------	---------	---------	---------	---------	---------	---------	---------	---------
Net Cash Flow		0	0	25	25	50	50	50	75	75	75
Present Value	20%	0.00	0.00	14.31	11.45	18.32	14.65	11.72	14.07	11.25	9.00
Total Present Value ($)		104,781									

Figure 7.14 Grantback Provision

		1	2	3	4	5	6	7	8	9	10
Sublicensee Net Sales		0	125	175	250	350	500	750	750	750	750
Royalty @	3%	0	4	5	8	11	15	23	23	23	23
Negative Cash Flow		10	2	2	2	2	2	2	2	2	2
Net Cash Flow		(10)	2	3	6	9	13	21	21	21	21
Present Value	20%	-8.94	1.25	1.86	2.52	3.11	3.81	4.81	3.85	3.08	2.46
Total Present Value ($)		17,800									

Figure 7.15 Sublicense

circumstances, there are professional fees, supplies, and communications expenses, as well as the cost of diverting accounting, manufacturing, and engineering personnel from their regular duties. Then, too, one certainly cannot ignore the cost of creating the license in the first place. This is a cost of doing business, and one should not wait until the license is in place to "start the meter." In fact, if one is making a very precise forecast, some of the early development expenses take place considerably before any positive cash flow from royalties can be expected. There can easily be six months of negotiation before a license is consummated. We have not attempted to introduce this precision into our examples, but it is a real consideration.

In a copyright or trademark licensing agreement, the cost of proper administration can be significant and involve extensive approvals of products and packaging, sample examination, quality control activities, and inspection of manufacturing facilities. The licensor in this case has a considerable stake in assuring the maintenance of the goodwill embodied in the intellectual property. We are aware of some licensing practitioners who feel that $25,000 per license per year is a realistic rule-of-thumb for administration expenses. These potential costs (which for the purpose of our manufacturing technology example are rather modest) can be reflected in the model as shown in Figure 7.16.

Many licenses call for *technical assistance* to be provided by the licensor. In some cases, the license may be for know-how or "show-how" alone, in which case the efforts required by the licensor may be substantial. In our example, we will assume that the granting of a patent license conveys the intellectual property satisfactorily, and that not much in the way of technical support will be needed. We are, however, willing to invest some time with the licensee, since we foresee some future benefits from grantbacks. See Figure 7.17.

The most troublesome license provisions to quantify are those which require of the licensor some form of indemnification.

		1	2	3	4	5	6	7	8	9	10
Positive Cash Flow		0	0	0	0	0	0	0	0	0	0
Negative Cash Flow		25	5	5	5	5	5	5	5	5	5
		---------	---------	---------	---------	---------	---------	---------	---------	---------	---------
Net Cash Flow		(25)	(5)	(5)	(5)	(5)	(5)	(5)	(5)	(5)	(5)
Present Value	12%	-23.45	-4.13	-3.63	-3.20	-2.81	-2.48	-2.18	-1.92	-1.69	-1.48
Total Present Value ($)		(46,963)									

Figure 7.16 Administration, Auditing, Quality Control

		1	2	3	4	5	6	7	8	9	10
Positive Cash Flow		0	0	0	0	0	0	0	0	0	0
Negative Cash Flow		35	25	10	5	5	5	5	5	5	5
		--------	--------	--------	--------	--------	--------	--------	--------	--------	--------
Net Cash Flow		(35)	(25)	(10)	(5)	(5)	(5)	(5)	(5)	(5)	(5)
Present Value	12%	-32.83	-20.64	-7.26	-3.20	-2.81	-2.48	-2.18	-1.92	-1.69	-1.48
Total Present Value ($)		(76,486)									

Figure 7.17 Technical Assistance

Understandably, licensees want to be held harmless in the event that the ownership or validity of the licensed intellectual property is challenged, or in the event of product liability. Licensors are rarely willing to provide such protection, but some intermediate levels of commitment are often negotiated. To quantify this element, one needs to form an opinion about: 1) the likelihood of the damaging event, and 2) the potential cost. Each of these estimates must be based on subjective judgment, responding to such questions as:

Is the proposed field of use one in which there is heavy competition and a history of infringement litigation?

Was the granting of the licensed intellectual property made difficult by nearly conflicting patents, trademarks, etc.?

Is the license going to place the licensee in a dominant, high-profit business segment that is likely to attract competition (and litigation)?

Are there large competitors to the licensee who can fund litigation?

Are there large competitors to the licensee whose competing business is so large that a damage award could be massive?

Is the licensee's product in an area that is likely to engender product liability claims, based on past experience? Are they going to use the plastic to make football helmets, acoustic tiles, or pipe insulation?

We suggest that one attempt to estimate these eventualities in the form of ranges or optimistic/pessimistic scenarios. Obviously, the most optimistic view is that none of these bad things will happen. The reader will have to judge for his or herself whether that is a prudent assumption. In the quantification, however, one can reflect the great uncertainty surrounding the event by either introducing an estimate of *probability* into the calculation, or by assuming a *high rate of discount*, as we have done in Figure 7.18.

In this calculation, we have made two estimates. One, which we have called the "Base Case," represents a legal "skirmish," settled without damages, and is quantified at $100,000 and estimated to take place in year 3 of the license. Most likely, this sort of problem will arise fairly early in the license, unless there will be considerable development time required before the licensee's products get to market and attract attention.

In a second calculation, we estimate more of a full-blown litigation, with a cost of $1 million, again in year 3. To reflect the relative unlikelihood of these events, we have used a discount rate of 25% for both, which substantially reduces their present value. One could use a different rate for each, depending on the judgment of their relative likelihood.

An important strategy that can be applied in these provisions

		1	2	3	4	5
Base Case						
Negative Cash Flow		0	0	100	0	0
		--------	--------	--------	--------	--------
Net Cash Flow		0	0	(100)	0	0
Present Value	25%	0.00	0.00	-48.71	0.00	0.00
Total Present Value ($)		(48,714)				
Worst Case						
Negative Cash Flow		0	0	1,000	0	0
		--------	--------	--------	--------	--------
Net Cash Flow		0	0	(1,000)	0	0
Present Value	25%	0.00	0.00	-487.14	0.00	0.00
Total Present Value ($)		(487,139)				

Figure 7.18 Indemnification

is a "stop-loss" element. This simply sets limits on the monetary participation of the licensor or gives the licensor control over the proceedings so that it has the option of whether to pursue litigation, to settle, and so forth. Insurance can also play a role, although this type of insurance is expensive and can be unavailable as a practical matter. A licensor could, as an example, require the licensee to carry product liability insurance.

SECONDARY ECONOMIC DRIVERS

Exclusivity is a secondary economic driver relative to the amount of positive cash flow. All things equal, a licensee ought to be willing to pay more for an exclusive license than a nonexclusive one. This would be especially true if the licensee:

> Is in a very competitive situation and the licensed intellectual property will provide an instant advantage in the market.
>
> Has, or is willing to build, the capacity to serve the large market that exclusivity will make available.
>
> Has its own intellectual property that complements the licensed intellectual property, and synergistic benefits will result.

Generally, if these statements are not true, the licensee may well be indifferent to exclusivity and not willing to pay a premium for it. For more on this subject, we refer the reader to the article by Mark Kleinginna and Lawrence Shanda, "Making the Exclusivity Decision," *Les Nouvelles*. We can, however, use the model developed above to test the results of granting exclusivity. In Figure 7.19, we determine the level of increased sales necessary to preserve the present value of the 50–50 split of economic

		1	2	3	4	5	6	7	8	9	10
QUANTITY (lb 000s)		1,000	1,000	1,000	1,000	1,000	1,000	1,000	1,000	1,000	1,000
PRICE PER UNIT ($)		2.50	2.50	2.50	2.50	2.50	2.50	2.50	2.50	2.50	2.50
REVENUE ($000s)		2,500	2,500	2,500	2,500	2,500	2,500	2,500	2,500	2,500	2,500
Cost of Goods Sold		1,600	1,600	1,600	1,600	1,600	1,600	1,600	1,600	1,600	1,600
Gross Profit		900	900	900	900	900	900	900	900	900	900
Royalty		38	38	38	38	38	38	38	38	38	38
SG & A Expense		400	400	400	400	400	400	400	400	400	400
Other Expense		100	100	100	100	100	100	100	100	100	100
Pretax Income		363	363	363	363	363	363	363	363	363	363
Taxes		145	145	145	145	145	145	145	145	145	145
Net Income		218	218	218	218	218	218	218	218	218	218
Present Value	12%	204.03	179.55	158.00	139.04	122.36	107.67	94.75	83.38	73.38	64.57
Total Present Value ($)		1,226,747									
Present Value of Royalties		35.18	30.96	27.24	23.97	21.10	18.56	16.34	14.38	12.65	11.13
Total Present Value ($)		211,508									

Figure 7.19 Royalty $0.0375/lb (Nonexclusive); What Additional Sales Needed?

benefit illustrated in Figure 7.7. If, for whatever reason, the licensee will not agree to a royalty of $0.075/lb for an exclusive license, and if we can agree on a royalty of $0.0375/lb for nonexclusive rights, 1,000,000 lb of product will need to be sold in order for us to preserve the present value of about $211,000. If this licensee can only produce 500,000 lb annually, we will have to locate another licensee to make up the difference or search for another licensee who will pay the premium for exclusivity.

A "Most Favored Nations" (MFN) provision can also have an effect on positive cash flow. If we anticipate granting a series of licenses (say, to manufacturers in various parts of the world), it is not unreasonable to assume that royalties may be negotiated downward over time. If compensation is one of the terms covered by an MFN provision, then there will be an erosion of cash flow unless quantities increase to compensate. An example is shown in Figure 7.20.

In this case, volume must increase from 500,000 lb annually to 1,250,000 in order to compensate for a royalty erosion from $0.075/lb to $0.03/lb during the ten-year period.

Grant of License

Definitions

Field of Use

Territorial Rights

Currency Exchange

Taxation

Dispute Resolution

Guarantees/Warranties

Assignability

Bankruptcy

		1	2	3	4	5	6	7	8	9	10
QUANTITY (lb 000s)		500	500	500	750	750	940	940	1,250	1,250	1,250
PRICE PER UNIT ($)		2.50	2.50	2.50	2.50	2.50	2.50	2.50	2.50	2.50	2.50
REVENUE ($000s)		1,250	1,250	1,250	1,875	1,875	2,350	2,350	3,125	3,125	3,125
Cost of Goods Sold		800	800	800	1,200	1,200	1,504	1,504	2,000	2,000	2,000
Gross Profit		450	450	450	675	675	846	846	1,125	1,125	1,125
Royalty		38	38	38	38	38	38	38	38	38	38
SG & A Expense		200	200	200	300	300	376	376	500	500	500
Other Expense		50	50	50	75	75	94	94	125	125	125
Pretax Income		163	163	163	263	263	338	338	463	463	463
Taxes		65	65	65	105	105	135	135	185	185	185
Net Income		98	98	98	158	158	203	203	278	278	278
Present Value	12%	91.46	80.49	70.83	100.69	88.60	100.52	88.45	106.39	93.62	82.39
Total Present Value ($)		903,430									
Present Value of Royalties		35.18	30.96	27.24	23.97	21.10	18.61	16.38	14.38	12.65	11.13
Total Present Value ($)		211,601									

Figure 7.20 Royalty Erosion from "Most Favored Nation"; What Additional Sales Needed?

These are but some of the license provisions that are in common use. They are Secondary Economic Drivers in that they can strengthen and buttress those provisions directly affecting the economics of the deal. Carefully crafted, they can have the effect of reducing the risk of the licensor. They must be carefully considered in the quantification for their effect on the discount rates utilized, as an example. We, by categorizing them as "secondary," are not at all implying that they are unimportant. A critical omission here can cause the whole license to "crash and burn." They are secondary because their economic effect is measured in the quantification related to other clauses.

EVALUATING THE NET PRESENT VALUE

To this point, we have concentrated on quantifying individual license provisions. In order to know where we are, it is necessary to integrate these valuations into a single conclusion. We suggest doing that by restating the individual discounted cash flow calculations into one in the form of a license. One therefore goes back and extracts from the DCFs, the calculation of present value, year by year. We do so, utilizing the data from previous figures in Figure 7.21.

We can now observe the collective effect of the individual judgments made. The Net Present Value (NPV) is $260,081, using the base case of the Indemnification Provision. If the worst case were used, the total NPV would be negative. We are now in a position to evaluate whether this license transaction, if it were structured as we have done, is an acceptable one.

We have adopted, as a Royalty scheme, that shown in Figure 7.12, with royalty set at one-half of cost savings, with the assumption that further cost saving will be achieved by the efforts of the licensee, and by us, through technical assistance. Of the total

	1	2	3	4	5	6	7	8	9	10
Positive Cash Flows	Present Value ($000's)									
ERR	35	41	36	40	35	31	27	24	21	19
Sublicense	(9)	1	2	3	3	4	5	4	3	2
Grantback Provision	0	0	14	11	18	15	12	14	11	9
	-----	-----	-----	-----	-----	-----	-----	-----	-----	-----
	26	42	52	54	56	50	44	42	35	30
Negative Cash Flows										
Administration, etc.	(23)	(4)	(4)	(3)	(3)	(2)	(2)	(2)	(2)	(1)
Technical Assistance	(33)	(21)	(7)	(3)	(3)	(2)	(2)	(2)	(2)	(1)
Indemnification	0	0	(49)	0	0	0	0	0	0	0
	-----	-----	-----	-----	-----	-----	-----	-----	-----	-----
	(56)	(25)	(60)	(6)	(6)	(4)	(4)	(4)	(4)	(2)
	-----	-----	-----	-----	-----	-----	-----	-----	-----	-----
Net Present Value	(30)	17	(8)	48	50	46	40	38	31	28
Total Present Value ($)	260,081									

Figure 7.21 License Summary

positive present value ($432,000) forecasted on Figure 7.21, the present value of royalties represents about 75%.

Of the total positive present value of $432,000, approximately 25%, or $104,000, is attributed to the present value of grantbacks. Without this present value, the total present value would be significantly less—perhaps to the point where we would not wish to consummate the transaction as structured here. We can, however, take some comfort in the fact that we utilized a discount factor of 20% in the calculation of the grantback's present value, making the estimate of this contribution more conservative. We might, however, wish to take a second look at our assumptions since this element of present value is so important in the total.

We should also take a second look at the indemnification provision and present value. Perhaps some "stop-loss" element might this more palatable. Remember, we used a discount rate of 25% on this element. When the element is a potential *expense,* the use of a high discount rate ends up being aggressive in terms of the total. It has the effect of minimizing a potential cost.

If all of the individual provision elements are linked in the model (probably by using a computer), then changes to individual provisions can result in instant change in the total for decision-making use.

SUMMARY

Is a model such as this going to reduce the licensing process to a laptop computer exercise? Will we someday negotiate a license by simply saying, "let my computer talk to your computer? We cannot envision that ever happening. An intellectual property license represents a "marriage" of sorts between two (or more) entities, each represented by a number of individuals who bring to the negotiating table their own peculiarities, their respective corporate (and national) cultures, and a host of economic strategies and objectives. We do not see that being reduced to a computer program, although perhaps we should not be *too* positive (after all, they are designing robots to do surgery!).

What we have attempted to present is a tool or, more importantly, a systematic way of looking at the value or costs associated with particular license provisions. It can serve to both organize our thought process relative to the economic implications of what we are doing in the licensing process, and help apply return on investment principles to that process. Many of the features of this system can be, and deserve to be, further refined. Certainly, the skills involved in forecasting are much more highly developed than we have presented. Also, there are available much more sophisticated methods for reflecting the probabilities of future events, such as "Monte Carlo" techniques. It is, however, a start.

8

Joint Venture Equity Allocations

Time savings, cost savings, and risk reduction strategies are bringing together corporate partners from all over the world as they expand into new product lines and new global markets. Joint venture partners share secrets and economic benefits. More accurately, they pool valuable intellectual property into businesses in which the partners own equity and share profits.

Some companies bring manufacturing capabilities to a venture, while other partners bring research capabilities or marketing know-how. A recent joint venture between Merck & Co. and Johnson & Johnson allows the optimization of unique intellectual property. Merck & Co. is using its unparalleled research center to develop a new product line of over-the-counter drugs. Merck has expertise in development, commercialization, and in the special skills needed to efficiently obtain Food & Drug Administration approvals. Merck, however, does not possess a well-recognized trademark among general consumers. It also lacks the distribution network required to get the new products onto store shelves. Johnson & Johnson possesses the perfect complementary intellectual property in the form of world-class trademarks, along with a well-developed distribution network that has access to store shelves across the country.

Joint ventures are accelerating because plain vanilla licensing deals cannot provide for all of the complexities of starting new ventures. Licensing basic embryonic technology does not help a mature manufacturing company unless they also receive assistance in building prototypes, establishing mass-manufacturing techniques, and penetrating new markets. Licensing deals also end, very often leaving the licenser with a new and well-educated competitor. Joint ventures, on the other hand, can provide superior benefits:

1) Permanent access to the intellectual property of another company, access that might not otherwise be available.
2) Continued contribution of expertise for the mutual benefit of the partners.
3) Continued loyalty to the joint venture by the contributing parents.
4) Immediate access to intellectual property that fills a gap in company capabilities.
5) Elimination of the costs required to create similar or duplicative intellectual property.
6) Reduction in the potential for failure due to the contribution of partially or completely developed intellectual property.

These benefits are valuable. Research funds can be saved by finding a joint venture partner. When new drug development costs $250 million, a joint venture partner possessing a newly developed drug and FDA approvals is a valuable ally. Quicker market entry is also a huge advantage. Very often, the first company into the market with a new product can establish a formidable market share position. Followers, even those possessing improved products, can have a tough time turning the heads of consumers away from the perceived product innovator. Sharing investment risks is also highly desirable in a fast-paced market where new product introductions can cost $100 million for promotional campaigns. Not many companies can afford to lose more than one or two new product introductions and remain in existence. A partner with which to share the risks is becoming ever more popular.

Some of the types of assets that are being pooled include:

Research expertise
Embryonic technology
Proven technology
Manufacturing capabilities
Commercialization capabilities
Trademarks
Distributions networks
Customer lists.

A successful business enterprise is comprised of the following basic components: monetary assets, tangible assets, intangible assets, and intellectual property. In joint ventures, monetary assets are rarely a driving force for completing a deal among well-established companies. Merck and Johnson & Johnson are not really in need of each other's cash. The same is true for tangible assets, such as manufacturing facilities, trucks, and warehouses. Assets that are driving joint ventures come from the intangible asset category and the intellectual property of joint venture partners. Some examples of complementary intellectual property exploitation include:

- Mattel's ability to turn the movie characters of Warner Brothers into profitable toy lines. Warner creates the characters in the movies, and Mattel turns them into worldwide toy sales. Mattel has commercialization capabilities and a well-established distribution network.
- Genentech's expertise for successfully commercializing new biotech products. Inventors develop new gene-splicing therapeutics, and Genentech gets these new medi-

cines past all the requisite regulatory and commercial hurdles and into the hospital for patient use.

- Dow Chemical's development of sophisticated composite materials that United Technologies can use in its Sikorski Aircraft Division. Dow is contributing advanced materials technology to the joint venture, and United Technology is contributing its research and manufacturing capabilities. United Technologies is also bringing an order book of spare parts contracts from the customers of previously sold aircraft.

The successful venturing experiences at the Massachusetts Institute of Technology also highlight the central focus on intellectual property. M.I.T. is a large research university with 1,000 professors, 3,000 research scientists, 4,500 graduate students, and 4,000 undergraduate students. The annual research budget exceeds $700 million. The most dramatic evidence of M.I.T.'s research success is measured by the 636 companies that have emerged from the university. They include Digital Equipment, Raytheon, Analog Devices, and Lotus Development Corporation. Together, these companies employ approximately 200,000 people and have annual sales of about $40 billion. All of these successes are based on the integrated exploitation of different intellectual properties.

A study of 12 recent start-ups that emerged from M.I.T. identified the major characteristics that were possessed by successful spin-offs. The study found that large sums of venture capital alone did not guarantee success. More important was that the venture capitalists involved with the start-up had a network of connections to people and other companies that might eventually make good strategic partners, partners that might be able to advance the process toward commercialization by introducing marketing know-how, distribution networks, and manufacturing expertise.

OWNERSHIP SPLIT

A crucial issue at the core of all joint ventures centers on the ownership split. Joint ventures provide great opportunities. Unrelated intellectual property can be combined in a nurturing business environment and provide the partners with enormous economic benefits. But who gets what? The remainder of this chapter presents a fictitious company, based on numerous consulting assignments, that uses a financial model for isolating the relative contribution from different intellectual properties for a new venture. It provides guidance about joint venture equity splits by considering factors such as expected profits, capital expenditure investments, and cash flow timing. It also captures the economic benefits of joint ventures associated with time savings, cost savings, and risk reduction.

EXPANSION AT OVERBOARD INDUSTRIES, INC.

> Our goal is to increase shareholder value. . . Our strategy will be to enter new markets. . . Our plan is to focus on innovative new products that will allow us to exploit our proprietary know-how and thereby create new value for you, our shareholders.—*Roger J. Weatherson Jr., Chairman of the Board and Chief Executive Officer, Overboard Industries, Inc.*

Amid thunderous applause, the newly appointed CEO of Overboard Industries, Inc. rapidly left the auditorium where he had just finished delivering his first address to shareholders. Instead of being delighted with his performance, Weatherson was troubled. He had just promised to add new shareholder value to the company. Unlike many chief executives, Weatherson was sincerely worried about his ability to deliver on his promise. Wall

Street had decried his appointment because it believed that a long-time insider at Overboard would not have the expansive vision necessary to lead the company through its next stage of growth. Weatherson was determined to prove himself, but had not yet selected the proper product or markets for achieving his announced goal. Driving back to headquarters, Roger Weatherson, considered the extraordinary history of Overboard.

Overboard Industries, Inc. was founded by Roger J. Weatherson, Sr. on a revolutionary product that allowed offshore oil drillers to know the exact location of their drilling bits at all times. The first generation of the product occupied every square foot of a 200-foot barge, and required another 75-foot service boat for power and control. The product was a computer-controlled probe that integrated sonar, electronics, and gyroscope technology, all of which added to the dimensions of the product. Giant winches on board the barge positioned the drill bit probe into the ocean. The submerged device scanned for the sounds of the drill bit, and transmitted periodic data readings through large coaxial cables back to a minicomputer on the service boat. The drill bit locater system was a great success. Offshore drillers had always wanted to know where they were drilling and were never exactly sure. With the Overboard product, they could accurately control the drilling process and thereby save time and money. More importantly, the drillers could be sure they were exploring their own fields, and not drilling into oil fields owned by competitors.

Over the years, the product evolved into a portable device. The probe was miniaturized, the controls were packaged into the latest notebook computers, and the locater system was priced so that even small drillers could afford the extraordinary benefits of the product. From its founding in 1972, sales had grown from nothing to nearly $500 million. Profit margins were an extraordinary 15% of sales after taxes. Overboard had developed excellent manufacturing controls as it grew. Managers at the company often boasted that no other company could build sophisticated electronics products cheaper. Not even the Japanese.

New shareholder value, however, was not likely to come from further refinements to the locater product. Weatherson knew that Overboard had the lion's share of a market which could not be expected to grow at a pace that would allow the company to continue its previous rate of rapid growth. His goal of adding to shareholder value would require that he devise a plan to exploit the strengths of Overboard in markets that were new to the company.

CONSUMER ELECTRONICS

> I've decided that our best opportunity lies in the consumer electronics products industry. I want to make the Pin-Point.

Roger J. Weatherson, Jr. abruptly interrupted the strategic planning meeting he and his top executives were having in his office. Consumer electronics was the new market he had decided Overboard would pursue. During one of their previous strategy meetings, the group had considered manufacturing and selling a product for hikers that would identify their exact location relative to a preset position. It was called "Pin-Point," and had been invented by an electrical engineering professor at Rutgers. The professor had made a convincing presentation about the potential for the product, but needed manufacturing capabilities. A prototype was flawlessly demonstrated. Commercialization required miniaturization refinements and mass production practices—nothing that Overboard could not easily accomplish. Initially, the group had decided to explore other possible strategies, but during each subsequent strategy meeting, Weatherson's thoughts drifted back to the Pin-Point. Weatherson explained his decision: "I don't want to make any acquisitions into non-manufacturing businesses. Our strength is in manufacturing, and not in any of these other acquisition candidates that you guys keep bringing to these meetings. I'm interested in building something, not buying and managing someone else's business."

The location of someone using the Pin-Point locator product could instantly be determined relative to an anchor point. The anchor point would be set into the product at the beginning of an excursion just by pressing a button. At any time during the trip, hikers could establish their exact position relative to the anchor point. The product would make use of the U.S. Naval Geopositioning Satellite System and internal gyroscopes. The anchor point would be set by reading the signals sent out by the satellite system, and subsequent readings would establish relative positions. It would be electronically controlled and no larger than the average paging device. Hikers would never get lost again, and could also use the device to send a distress signal via the satellite system. Other market potential also looked realistic. Boy Scout troops would be excellent target consumers—so would geological field engineers, and maybe even motorists.

Weatherson was excited about the product. It would allow Overboard to use its current manufacturing capabilities and facilities. The product would tap into the growing naturalist movement among consumers, and it would let him prove to the naysayers that Roger J. Weatherson, Jr. could build a new product that would add to shareholder value.

ACCESS TO THE TECHNOLOGY

Patented technology was key to the Pin-Point. The inventor had developed an extraordinarily small gyroscope device. He had also devised a portable system that could transmit and receive signals to and from a space satellite. Packaged together, these two patented technologies allowed for fantastic product capabilities. The technologies were the foundation of the Pin-Point product, and the prototype proved itself to be effective and reliable.

The only improvements needed for product commercialization were some miniaturization engineering and a limited amount of manufacturing engineering to accomplish mass production. The inventor explained that he could easily accomplish the miniaturization work, but needed more information about large-scale production engineering before miniaturization designs were worth pursuing.

The inventor wanted a joint venture deal: "Mr. Weatherson, my product is developed. It's far more than a mere concept. You've seen it work. A license agreement that pays some nominal royalty does not interest me. It's true that I don't possess manufacturing assets, and it's also true that I would benefit from your production engineering expertise, but I want more than a licensing royalty. . . My contribution to our possible joint venture is extremely valuable."

Listed below are the contributions that the inventor would be making to a joint venture:

1) Reduction of investment risk by providing a proven technology.
2) Accelerated market introduction by saving Overboard the time that would be needed to internally develop the product.
3) Savings of research funds that would be needed to learn about and develop the new technologies.

Acceptance of a joint venture arrangement would save Overboard from having to develop the technology itself. There is no assurance that such efforts would be successful at duplicating the invention. Further, if similar technology were indeed developed at Overboard, there is no assurance that the company would not be infringing on the inventor's patents. Acceptance of a joint venture arrangement would allow for production and miniaturization engineering to immediately begin. Otherwise, the company might need to spend years creating the basic technology for itself. Acceptance of the joint venture arrangement would also save Overboard from spending substantial amounts of research funds to develop the basic technology. The inventor offered to save Overboard time, money, and also offered a reduction of investment risk.

The posture taken by the inventor in this fictional case is becoming much more common. Intellectual property inventors want more than a licensing royalty rate for the contribution of their inventions. They see that entire businesses can be founded on their original contribution. They see that future technologies and products might be spawned from their inventions. Whole industries can be changed. The initial invention can give rise to enhanced inventions, and these in turn can open new business opportunities. A large multinational business can eventually spring from a single new technology. These businesses can earn profits into perpetuity. Inventors are no longer content to take small royalty payments associated with licenses that terminate with the life of the original patent. Inventors are looking for economic benefits from the commercialization of the initial inventions, and participation in the economic benefits that evolve from second, third, and fourth generations of the initial invention.

Alliances with university research centers are becoming a new source of technological development. Some of the trends associated with these alliances mirror the attitudes of inventors that want more equity participation. During an April 1991 conference at the Harvard School of Public Health entitled, "Commercializing Biomedical Technologies," the following trends were reported by participants that included representatives from business and academia:

- Industrial partners are far less eager to commit funds for commercialization of new technologies where the university is offering a nonexclusive license.
- Business partners are looking to the university for technology that can be quickly commercialized. Most companies have their own basic research efforts. They are looking for university technology that can be transformed into profits. Embryonic research programs were reported to be less desirable.
- Joint ventures are becoming more popular. Universities are recognizing that their initial technology contribution can lead to the establishment of an extremely valuable company.
- Universities are starting to look for more equity participation.

Inventors that are offering keystone technological advancements want to participate in the long-term economic benefits derived from their flashes of genius. Companies that want new technology may have to promise much more in the future than a limited stream of royalty payments.

ACCESS TO THE MARKET

Assuming that Roger J. Weatherson, Jr. could gain access to the technology still left Overboard with a major problem. Access to a niche consumer market such as serious hikers, and "wannabees," would not be easily accomplished by Overboard Industries.

While the company is well known in the oil drilling industry, few sporting goods consumers know of the company. An additional problem is that the company sales force is not well connected to the distribution networks needed to place the new Pin-Point product into the proper outlets. Overboard needs two vital intangible assets in order to get to market:

1) A well-established brand name that serious hikers, mountain climbers, hunters, and wilderness enthusiasts regard highly.
2) A well-organized sales force or distribution network that can place the product where it will sell.

A well-regarded brand name can be enormously expensive to build from inception. It requires a huge initial outlay to grab the attention of already overloaded consumers, as well as the normal amount of advertising that all products require. More importantly, association with a brand name that the target market trusts could allow for a higher selling price at retail levels, which would translate to a higher wholesale price. Without a well-known brand name, Overboard would need to risk a big investment on creating their own brand. Also, the company would most likely have to price the product lower than if a well-established brand name were associated with the product.

Joint venturing with a trademark company would also provide Overboard with immediate access to a sales force that had strong ties to the proper wholesale and retail outlets. Marketing consumer products is very different from marketing industrial products. A trademark company joint venture would save Overboard the time and expense required to hire, develop, and grow their own consumer products retail organization.

Access to a well-established brand name would:

1) Save advertising funds that would be needed to create a new name,
2) Save the funds that would be needed to develop a consumer products distribution network,
3) Lower the investment risk associated with launching a new product,
4) Allow for higher product pricing.

MEASURING POTENTIAL VALUE FROM PIN-POINT

Roger J. Weatherson, Sr. had a simple way of creating value. He would often say to his executives, and more times yell: "Grab for market share—control manufacturing costs—the bottom line will take care of itself." The senior Weatherson was a worshiper of earnings per share, and never considered cash flow as the true source of corporate value. He did not have to worry because rapid sales growth and high profits associated with his oil service drilling products showered the company with cash, and Wall Street did the rest.

The new CEO was more attuned to the dynamic relationship between cash flow and value. Before making any commitments, the young Weatherson wanted to know the potential for value creation that the new product would bring to the company. At the next strategic planning meeting, he described the discounted cash flow (DCF) analysis that he wanted, and instructed his marketing, manufacturing, engineering, and operations chiefs to provide the finance vice president with the necessary inputs. Weatherson explained (what we already know from previous chapters) that a DCF valuation model comprehensively captures all of the elements that create value by converting forecasts of net cash flow into a present value using a discount rate that reflects the riskiness of the expected cash flows. The DCF model considers the up-front expenditures that are required and the cash flows to be derived from them in the future. It also considers the timing associated with receipt of cash flows. Weatherson requested that a DCF be performed to show the value creation that would stem from the Pin-Point product. He specified two assumptions for the initial study:

1) Assume that Overboard already has access to the basic technology that was demonstrated by the inventor.
2) Assume that Overboard already possesses a well-recognized consumer trademark under which to launch the product.

Weatherson also indicated that from this first DCF model, he would then show his executives how to determine the value contribution derived from the basic technology and the trademark.

Figure 8.1 represents the Pin-Point Product Line DCF model, assuming that joint venture partners have provided access to the technology and trademarks needed. It shows a ten-year estimate of cash flows, and determines a contribution to value of almost $81 million to Overboard. The first-year forecasts represent nothing more than the costs to set up a small engineering group to take the prototype product and prepare it for commercial manufacturing. The engineering department estimated that the effort would take a year and cost $1 million. General expenses for the new business unit were estimated by the operations chief at $250,000 for the first year. Production was expected to begin in the second year, and the sales staff decided that they could get $100 per unit from distributors, while still allowing the retail price

YEAR		0	1	2	3	4	5	6	7	8	9	10
Units sales (thousands)		0	25	300	1,000	3,000	3,600	4,320	5,184	6,221	7,465	8,958
Price per unit		$0.00	$100.00	$80.00	$75.00	$60.00	$62.40	$64.90	$67.49	$70.19	$73.00	$75.92
Manuf. costs per unit		$0.00	$80.00	$50.00	$35.00	$24.00	$24.96	$25.96	$27.00	$28.08	$29.20	$30.37
Sales		0	2,500	24,000	75,000	180,000	224,640	280,351	349,878	436,647	544,936	680,080
Cost of Sales		0	2,000	15,000	35,000	72,000	89,856	112,140	139,951	174,659	217,974	272,032
Gross Profit		0	500	9,000	40,000	108,000	134,784	168,210	209,927	261,988	326,962	408,048
Gross Profit Margin			*20.0%*	*37.5%*	*53.3%*	*60.0%*	*60.0%*	*60.0%*	*60.0%*	*60.0%*	*60.0%*	*60.0%*
Operating Expenses:												
General & Administrative		250	300	2,880	9,000	21,600	26,957	33,642	41,985	52,398	65,392	81,610
Research & Development		1,000	500	0	0	0	0	0	0	0	0	0
Marketing		0	2,000	2,400	7,500	18,000	22,464	28,035	34,988	43,665	54,494	68,008
Selling		0	500	4,800	15,000	36,000	44,928	56,070	69,976	87,329	108,987	136,016
Operating Profit		(1,250)	(2,800)	(1,080)	8,500	32,400	40,435	50,463	62,978	78,597	98,088	122,414
Operating Profit Margin		*NM*	*NM*	*NM*	*11.3%*	*18.0%*	*18.0%*	*18.0%*	*18.0%*	*18.0%*	*18.0%*	*18.0%*
Income Taxes		0	0	0	3,230	12,312	15,365	19,176	23,932	29,867	37,274	46,517
Net Income		(1,250)	(2,800)	(1,080)	5,270	20,088	25,070	31,287	39,046	48,730	60,815	75,897
Net Profit Margin			*NM*	*NM*	*7.0%*	*11.2%*	*11.2%*	*11.2%*	*11.2%*	*11.2%*	*11.2%*	*11.2%*
Cash Flow Calculation:												
+ Depreciation		0	26	242	753	1,804	2,251	2,810	3,506	4,374	5,458	6,811
- Working Capital Addtns		0	313	2,688	6,375	13,125	5,580	6,964	8,691	10,846	13,536	16,893
- Capital Expenditures		250	250	2,150	5,100	10,500	4,464	5,571	6,953	8,677	10,829	13,514
Net Cash Flow		(1,500)	(3,337)	(5,676)	(5,452)	(1,733)	17,277	21,562	26,909	33,581	41,908	52,300
Discount Factor	20%	1.00000	0.91414	0.76178	0.63482	0.52901	0.44084	0.36737	0.30614	0.25512	0.21260	1.00941
Present Value of Net Cash Flow		(1,500)	(3,050)	(4,323)	(3,461)	(917)	7,617	7,921	8,238	8,567	8,910	52,792
Net Present Value		$80,794										

Figure 8.1 New Pin-Point Product Line: Strategic Business Unit Value with Joint Venture Partner

to stay between $150 and $195. The prestige associated with an assumed trademark would allow such a hefty price. The sales staff also expected that the first year of sales would be only 25,000 units. It would take time for consumer reactions and media promotions to turn the product into a basic piece of hiking equipment.

The manufacturing executives expected to continue the process of refining manufacturing procedures during the first year. They budgeted another $500,000 for this effort, and expected to reduce manufacturing costs as higher sales levels were achieved.

The sales executives expected that competition would surface as soon as the smell of success started to drift around the industry. Therefore, they proposed a reduction in the real selling price of the product as manufacturing techniques lowered production costs. By the fourth year, a 60% gross profit margin was predicted, and everyone planned to hold the gross profit margin steady by indexing selling prices and production costs with the rate of inflation. Unit sales were admittedly a best guess, but demographics research and social trends made the potential for rapid growth quite reasonable. The marketing chiefs decided that sales growth beyond the tenth year should be conservatively expected to grow with inflation.

The assumptions associated with the rest of the line items in the DCF are presented below:

General and administrative expenses, after the initial start-up phase, are expected to run at 12% of sales based on previous company experiences.

Research & development expenses are expected to be negligible after the engineering work for commercialization is completed.

Marketing expenses are budgeted to run at 10% of sales beginning in year 3. Initially, a modest introductory promotional campaign is planned for years 1 and 2. The strength of the assumed trademark provided by one of the joint venture partners is well established and should not require a huge initial advertising campaign.

Selling expenses are expected to represent 20% of sales for salary and commissions. The trademark joint venture partner is expected to provide access to shelf space and other retail outlets through its name and well-established sales force.

Income taxes are estimated at 38% of the operating income for both State and Federal tax obligations.

Depreciation is calculated based on the remaining useful life of the equipment that is purchased for production of the new product. This noncash expense is added to the estimated net income to yield an indication of the gross cash flow to be generated by the new product.

Working capital additions represent the use of future cash flows to increase inventories and account for increased accounts receivable. When offset against rising current liabilities, the net amount of increasing current assets represents a use of cash flows that will not be available to the shareholders. The additions to working capital are investments in the business unit, and they contribute to value by fueling the anticipated growth of the net cash flow.

Capital expenditures simply represent the amounts used in each year to acquire the machinery and equipment needed to meet the anticipated production levels. Just like additions to working capital, this expenditure represents a use of cash flow that will fuel the expected growth. It is subtracted from gross cash flows because the funds are not available for distribution to shareholders.

Net cash flow is estimated for the ten-year period presented in Figure 8.1 as: Net Income *plus* Depreciation *less* Additions to Working Capital *less* Capital Expenditures. The value contribution of the Pin-Point product line equals the discounted value of the estimated net cash flows.

The discount rate is based on using a proper rate of return

requirement that introduces the uncertainty associated with actually receiving the forecasted stream of economic benefits. The required rate of return is that amount which is necessary to compensate investors for accepting various levels of risk.

WEIGHTED AVERAGE COST OF CAPITAL

Corporate investments typically must pass hurdle rates in order to be considered as viable opportunities. Since debt and equity funds are used to finance these investments, the return that is provided must be sufficient to satisfy the interest due on the debt, and also provide a fair rate of return on the equity funds. The hurdle rate must be the weighted average cost of capital, at a minimum.

A corporation that is financed with both debt and equity might have a capitalization structure that is comprised of 25% debt and 75% equity. A good bond rating might allow the corporation to finance debt at 11%. An appropriate equity rate, as determined from one of the models presented in Appendix A, "Investment Rate of Return Requirements," might be 20%.

The weighted average cost of capital is an averaging of the different rates of return that are required by the different capital providers. The average is calculated with respect to the different proportions of debt and equity capital invested in the enterprise, and also reflects the tax deductibility of the interest payments associated with debt. Once an appropriate rate of return is determined, discount factors can be calculated that will convert each year of future cash flow into a present value.

The final year of the projected cash flow most likely does not mean that all cash flows will cease, but represents a point at which specific forecasts beyond the final year are not possible. Still, the business enterprise can be expected to generate cash flows into perpetuity. The discount factor in the final year of the forecast represents a capitalization that discounts the perpetual cash flows into present value without having to show specific cash flow amounts into infinity. In Figure 8.1, the cash flows of the final year are expected to grow at a constant rate of 4% per year into perpetuity. The discount factor selected is the aggregate of the perpetual cash flow, growing at 4%, discounted to the present value at the selected discount rate.

A comprehensive discussion of modern investment theory goes beyond the purpose and scope of this book. Complete books and careers are dedicated to the study of the relationship between risk and return. Indeed, significant differences of academic opinion exist as to the proper measure of risk, as well as the proper measure of return. The reference list in Appendix A provides a rich collection of books and articles that should be studied to further appreciate the relationship among risk, return, and present value.

INTERNAL TECHNOLOGY DEVELOPMENT

Having the basic technology for the satellite transmission and reception immediately available provides Overboard with two important advantages:

1) Basic research and development expenditures can be avoided, and
2) Market entry can be accomplished much sooner because the time to develop the basic technology is saved.

All that needs to be completed is commercialization engineering. Overboard has extensive experience in this area, which would be further complemented by the consulting efforts of the inventor. The required product development investment is therefore low, and the time needed to get the product to market is low.

These two factors, coupled with the assumption about access to a well-known trademark, make the value of the business unit almost $81 million.

> He wants too much. . . it's unheard of for an inventor to get a 25% joint venture interest in the business unit.—*Frank Counter, Overboard Vice President of Finance.*

Back in Weatherson's office, the strategic planning committee was reviewing a number of financial analyses. Each was a DCF analysis using different scenarios. The financial vice president was a bit disturbed that the committee was actually going to consider handing such a large piece of the Pin-Point business unit to the inventor: "Holy Cow, he's not even going to be putting money into the deal!"

Weatherson sorted through the presentation folder that contained the DCF analysis and waved Figure 8.2 at Frank Counter: "That's why I asked you to prepare this second analysis assuming we had to develop the basic technology ourselves. This schedule shows that our engineering guys expect a two year delay and additional up-front research and development costs of $5 million. Some of the costs are for outside consultants to help us develop our own satellite communications capabilities. The rest of the added costs are for our internal engineers to interface the satellite communications with our own technology into a prototype product. Not having the prototype delays market entry for two years. The drop in value is enormous."

Figure 8.2 shows the same input components as previously presented, except for a two-year delay for market entry and added research and development costs of $2.5 million for each of the first two years. The DCF shows that positive cash flows are not generated by the business unit until year 7. The present value drops by almost $44.3 million to a value of $36.5 million.

YEAR	0	1	2	3	4	5	6	7	8	9	10
Units sales (thousands)	0	0	0	25	300	1,000	3,000	3,600	4,320	5,184	6,221
Price per unit	$0.00	$0.00	$0.00	$100.00	$80.00	$75.00	$60.00	$62.40	$64.90	$67.49	$70.19
Manuf. costs per unit	$0.00	$0.00	$0.00	$80.00	$50.00	$35.00	$24.00	$24.96	$25.96	$27.00	$28.08
Sales	0	0	0	2,500	24,000	75,000	180,000	224,640	280,351	349,878	436,647
Cost of Sales	0	0	0	2,000	15,000	35,000	72,000	89,856	112,140	139,951	174,659
Gross Profit	0	0	0	500	9,000	40,000	108,000	134,784	168,210	209,927	261,988
Gross Profit Margin				*20.0%*	*37.5%*	*53.3%*	*60.0%*	*60.0%*	*60.0%*	*60.0%*	*60.0%*
Operating Expenses:											
General & Administrative	250	250	250	300	2,880	9,000	21,600	26,957	33,642	41,985	52,398
Research & Development	2,500	2,500	1,000	500	0	0	0	0	0	0	0
Marketing	0	0	0	2,000	2,400	7,500	18,000	22,464	28,035	34,988	43,665
Selling	0	0	0	500	4,800	15,000	36,000	44,928	56,070	69,976	87,329
Operating Profit	(2,750)	(2,750)	(1,250)	(2,800)	(1,080)	8,500	32,400	40,435	50,463	62,978	78,597
Operating Profit Margin	*NM*	*NM*	*NM*	*NM*	*NM*	*11.3%*	*18.0%*	*18.0%*	*18.0%*	*18.0%*	*18.0%*
Income Taxes	0	0	0	(1,064)	(410)	3,230	12,312	15,365	19,176	23,932	29,867
Net Income	(2,750)	(2,750)	(1,250)	(1,736)	(670)	5,270	20,088	25,070	31,287	39,046	48,730
Net Profit Margin		*NM*	*NM*	*NM*	*NM*	*7.0%*	*11.2%*	*11.2%*	*11.2%*	*11.2%*	*11.2%*
Cash Flow Calculation:											
+ Depreciation	0	26	52	78	294	805	1,856	2,303	2,862	3,558	4,426
– Working Capital Addtns	0	0	0	313	2,688	6,375	13,125	5,580	6,964	8,691	10,846
– Capital Expenditures	250	250	250	250	2,150	5,100	10,500	4,464	5,571	6,953	8,677
Net Cash Flow	(3,000)	(2,974)	(1,448)	(2,221)	(5,213)	(5,400)	(1,681)	17,329	21,614	26,961	33,633
Discount Factor 20%	1.00000	0.91414	0.76178	0.63482	0.52901	0.44084	0.36737	0.30614	0.25512	0.21260	1.00941
Present Value of Net Cash Flow	(3,000)	(2,719)	(1,103)	(1,410)	(2,758)	(2,381)	(618)	5,305	5,514	5,732	33,950
Net Present Value	$36,513										

Figure 8.2 New Pin-Point Product Line: Strategic Business Unit Value Without Joint Venture Partner for Technology

The value drops over 50% because of the added up-front costs and the delay of market entry. Weatherson explains to his committee: "If we can't talk this inventor into a low industry royalty rate like those associated with a license agreement, his request for 25% of the equity isn't all that unreasonable. In fact, we'd better hope that he doesn't perform a similar analysis. He'll find out just how important his contribution is to the value of this project. If he can actually get us into the market sooner than the time frame shown in Figure 8.2 and save us the added $5 million of R&D costs, then I don't care if he puts money into the deal. . . His contribution is the basic technology, the $5 million research savings and the earlier market entry."

INTERNAL TRADEMARK DEVELOPMENT

> Roger, we still have to deal with the trademark partner. They want 25% of the deal too and they won't split the costs of advertising and promotion.—*Tom Handler, Overboard Vice President, Marketing and Sales.*

Just as the marketing vice president finished his complaint Weatherson handed him a copy of Figure 8.3 and pointed out: "Tom, your own estimates show that we'll need to launch a substantial advertising and promotional campaign if we decide to establish our own trademark. You're also indicating that we won't be able to get the same premium price for the product without the big name. It means that we need to spend $15 million more in up-front money and that we'll never get the 60% gross profit margin. The selling price will drop without a big name, but our production costs aren't going to change. Without a joint venture partner for the trademark, the value drops big-time."

Figure 8.3 is the same as Figure 8.1, except that early marketing expenses are shown for the establishment of a new trade-

YEAR		0	1	2	3	4	5	6	7	8	9	10
Units sales (thousands)		0	25	300	1,000	3,000	3,600	4,320	5,184	6,221	7,465	8,958
Price per unit		$0.00	$90.00	$70.00	$65.00	$55.00	$57.20	$59.49	$61.87	$64.34	$66.92	$69.59
Manuf. costs per unit		$0.00	$80.00	$50.00	$35.00	$24.00	$24.96	$25.96	$27.00	$28.08	$29.20	$30.37
Sales		0	2,250	21,000	65,000	165,000	205,920	256,988	320,721	400,260	499,525	623,407
Cost of Sales		0	2,000	15,000	35,000	72,000	89,856	112,140	139,951	174,659	217,974	272,032
Gross Profit		0	250	6,000	30,000	93,000	116,064	144,848	180,770	225,601	281,550	351,375
Gross Profit Margin			*11.1%*	*28.6%*	*46.2%*	*56.4%*	*56.4%*	*56.4%*	*56.4%*	*56.4%*	*56.4%*	*56.4%*
Operating Expenses:												
General & Administrative		250	270	2,520	7,800	19,800	24,710	30,839	38,487	48,031	59,943	74,809
Research & Development		1,000	500	0	0	0	0	0	0	0	0	0
Marketing		0	10,000	5,000	6,500	16,500	20,592	25,699	32,072	40,026	49,952	62,341
Selling		0	450	4,200	13,000	33,000	41,184	51,398	64,144	80,052	99,905	124,681
Operating Profit		(1,250)	(10,970)	(5,720)	2,700	23,700	29,578	36,913	46,067	57,492	71,750	89,544
Operating Profit Margin		*NM*	*NM*	*NM*	*4.2%*	*14.4%*	*14.4%*	*14.4%*	*14.4%*	*14.4%*	*14.4%*	*14.4%*
Income Taxes		0	0	0	1,026	9,006	11,239	14,027	17,506	21,847	27,265	34,027
Net Income		(1,250)	(10,970)	(5,720)	1,674	14,694	18,338	22,886	28,562	35,645	44,485	55,517
Net Profit Margin			*NM*	*NM*	*2.6%*	*8.9%*	*8.9%*	*8.9%*	*8.9%*	*8.9%*	*8.9%*	*8.9%*
Cash Flow Calculation:												
+ Depreciation		0	26	242	753	1,804	2,251	2,810	3,506	4,375	5,458	6,811
– Working Capital Addtns		0	281	2,344	5,500	12,500	5,115	6,384	7,967	9,942	12,408	15,485
– Capital Expenditures		250	250	2,150	5,100	10,500	4,464	5,571	6,953	8,677	10,829	13,514
Net Cash Flow		(1,500)	(11,475)	(9,972)	(8,173)	(6,502)	11,011	13,741	17,148	21,400	26,706	33,329
Discount Factor	20%	1.00000	0.91414	0.76178	0.63482	0.52901	0.44084	0.36737	0.30614	0.25512	0.21260	1.00941
Present Value of Net Cash Flow		(1,500)	(10,490)	(7,596)	(5,188)	(3,440)	4,854	5,048	5,250	5,460	5,678	33,642
Net Present Value		$31,717										

Figure 8.3 New Pin-Point Product Line: Strategic Business Unit Value with Joint Venture Partner for Trademark

mark. Market entry is not different because this third scenario assumes access to the technology. The differences are: 1) the need to spend initially for the creation of a new trademark, and 2) the selling price of the product is lower due to the lack of implied endorsement from association with a well-known trademark. The value drops to $31.7 million if Overboard decides to internally develop their own trademark. This represents a $49 million drop in value—almost 60%.

"We need a trademark partner," announced Weatherson, "if they hold out for 25% of the new business unit, we'll just have to give it up. . . What alternatives do we have?"

GOING IT ALONE

> None. —*Roger J. Weatherson, Sr., Overboard retired Chairman of the Board and company consultant.*

The elder Weatherson passed out copies of Figure 8.4 and explained: "I asked Frank Counter to take a look at your plans assuming that Overboard doesn't use any joint venture partners. I asked Frank to calculate the present value of the new business unit assuming that Overboard will need to develop its own basic technology and create its own trademark. This scenario incorporates the added expenses for both endeavors, the time delay for technology development, and the reduced selling price associated with lacking a well-known trademark. The present value drops to less than $11 million. The project still adds shareholder value by going it alone, but far less than we've been talking about, and I'm not sure that $11 million is the right value. We're talking about accepting substantially more risk. We're now talking about three major endeavors, none of which is guaranteed."

The elder Weatherson surprised everyone with his command of the DCF analyses. The retired chairman also explained

YEAR		0	1	2	3	4	5	6	7	8	9	10
Units sales (thousands)		0	0	0	25	300	1,000	3,000	3,600	4,320	5,184	6,221
Price per unit		$0.00	$0.00	$0.00	$90.00	$70.00	$65.00	$55.00	$57.20	$59.49	$61.87	$64.34
Manuf. costs per unit		$0.00	$0.00	$0.00	$80.00	$50.00	$35.00	$24.00	$24.96	$25.96	$27.00	$28.08
Sales		0	0	0	2,250	21,000	65,000	165,000	205,920	256,988	320,721	400,260
Cost of Sales		0	0	0	2,000	15,000	35,000	72,000	89,856	112,140	139,951	174,659
Gross Profit		0	0	0	250	6,000	30,000	93,000	116,064	144,848	180,770	225,601
Gross Profit Margin					*11.1%*	*28.6%*	*46.2%*	*56.4%*	*56.4%*	*56.4%*	*56.4%*	*56.4%*
Operating Expenses:												
General & Administrative		250	250	250	270	2,520	7,800	19,800	24,710	30,839	38,487	48,031
Research & Development		2,500	2,500	1,000	500	0	0	0	0	0	0	0
Marketing		0	0	0	10,000	5,000	6,500	16,500	20,592	25,699	32,072	40,026
Selling		0	0	0	450	4,200	13,000	33,000	41,184	51,398	64,144	80,052
Operating Profit		(2,750)	(2,750)	(1,250)	(10,970)	(5,720)	2,700	23,700	29,578	36,913	46,067	57,492
Operating Profit Margin		*NM*	*NM*	*NM*	*NM*	*NM*	*4.2%*	*14.4%*	*14.4%*	*14.4%*	*14.4%*	*14.4%*
Income Taxes		0	0	0	(4,169)	(2,174)	1,026	9,006	11,239	14,027	17,506	21,847
Net Income		(2,750)	(2,750)	(1,250)	(6,801)	(3,546)	1,674	14,694	18,338	22,886	28,562	35,645
Net Profit Margin			*NM*	*NM*	*NM*	*NM*	*2.6%*	*8.9%*	*8.9%*	*8.9%*	*8.9%*	*8.9%*
Cash Flow Calculation:												
+ Depreciation		0	26	52	78	294	805	1,856	2,303	2,862	3,558	4,427
- Working Capital Addtns		0	0	0	281	2,344	5,500	12,500	5,115	6,384	7,967	9,942
- Capital Expenditures		250	250	250	250	2,150	5,100	10,500	4,464	5,571	6,953	8,677
Net Cash Flow		(3,000)	(2,974)	(1,448)	(7,255)	(7,746)	(8,121)	(6,450)	11,063	13,793	17,200	21,452
Discount Factor	20%	1.00000	0.91414	0.76178	0.63482	0.52901	0.44084	0.36737	0.30614	0.25512	0.21260	1.00941
Present Value of Net Cash Flow		(3,000)	(2,719)	(1,103)	(4,605)	(4,098)	(3,580)	(2,370)	3,387	3,519	3,657	21,654
Net Present Value		$10,742										

Figure 8.4 New Pin-Point Product Line: Strategic Business Unit Value Without Joint Venture Partner for Trademark or Technology

that the 20% discount rate might not be appropriate when the added risks of going it alone are considered. In addition to entering a new market with a new product, higher risks are introduced by the compound requirements of successfully developing the basic technology at Overboard and also creating their own trademark. The chances of having all three of these major endeavors simultaneously achieved has got to be considered riskier than the 20% discount rate used for the other scenarios. Weatherson, Sr. concluded: "Going it alone has got to be riskier. I don't know that it's as risky as an embryonic venture capital deal, but I sure do know that the discount rate should be higher than 20%. I asked Frank Counter to see what happens to the value if we use a 25% discount, and Figure 8.5 shows the answer. . . It's red ink boys. . . a dead deal if you go it alone."

SUMMARY

Joint venture partners save each other time, money, and reduce business risks. The five different DCF models indicate the relative importance of a well-established trademark, possession of well-defined basic technology, and expertise in manufacturing. In some cases, intellectual property is more important than manufacturing assets and manufacturing expertise. If Overboard can structure a joint venture deal that gives less than 25% to each of the intellectual property partners, then corporate value will be enhanced. If they have to give in and hand over 50% of the joint venture to the two partners, corporate value is still enhanced. If they go it alone, corporate value is most likely to suffer.

Joint venture analysis can be greatly enhanced by using a flexible financial model that shows the effect on value when basic assumptions are adjusted. The DCF analysis allows exploration of many variables that impact the viability of joint ventures and

YEAR		0	1	2	3	4	5	6	7	8	9	10
Units sales (thousands)		0	0	0	25	300	1,000	3,000	3,600	4,320	5,184	6,221
Price per unit		$0.00	$0.00	$0.00	$90.00	$70.00	$65.00	$55.00	$57.20	$59.49	$61.87	$64.34
Manuf. costs per unit		$0.00	$0.00	$0.00	$80.00	$50.00	$35.00	$24.00	$24.96	$25.96	$27.00	$28.08
Sales		0	0	0	2,250	21,000	65,000	165,000	205,920	256,988	320,721	400,260
Cost of Sales		0	0	0	2,000	15,000	35,000	72,000	89,856	112,140	139,951	174,659
Gross Profit		0	0	0	250	6,000	30,000	93,000	116,064	144,848	180,770	225,601
Gross Profit Margin					*11.1%*	*28.6%*	*46.2%*	*56.4%*	*56.4%*	*56.4%*	*56.4%*	*56.4%*
Operating Expenses:												
General & Administrative		250	250	250	270	2,520	7,800	19,800	24,710	30,839	38,487	48,031
Research & Development		2,500	2,500	1,000	500	0	0	0	0	0	0	0
Marketing		0	0	0	10,000	5,000	6,500	16,500	20,592	25,699	32,072	40,026
Selling		0	0	0	450	4,200	13,000	33,000	41,184	51,398	64,144	80,052
Operating Profit		(2,750)	(2,750)	(1,250)	(10,970)	(5,720)	2,700	23,700	29,578	36,913	46,067	57,492
Operating Profit Margin		*NM*	*NM*	*NM*	*NM*	*NM*	*4.2%*	*14.4%*	*14.4%*	*14.4%*	*14.4%*	*14.4%*
Income Taxes		0	0	0	(4,169)	(2,174)	1,026	9,006	11,239	14,027	17,506	21,847
Net Income		(2,750)	(2,750)	(1,250)	(6,801)	(3,546)	1,674	14,694	18,338	22,886	28,562	35,645
Net Profit Margin			*NM*	*NM*	*NM*	*NM*	*2.6%*	*8.9%*	*8.9%*	*8.9%*	*8.9%*	*8.9%*
Cash Flow Calculation:												
+ Depreciation		0	26	52	78	294	805	1,856	2,303	2,862	3,558	4,427
– Working Capital Addtns		0	0	0	281	2,344	5,500	12,500	5,115	6,384	7,967	9,942
– Capital Expenditures		250	250	250	250	2,150	5,100	10,500	4,464	5,571	6,953	8,677
Net Cash Flow		(3,000)	(2,974)	(1,448)	(7,255)	(7,746)	(8,121)	(6,450)	11,063	13,793	17,200	21,452
Discount Factor	25%	1.00000	0.89628	0.71703	0.57362	0.45890	0.36712	0.29369	0.23496	0.18796	0.15037	0.51131
Present Value of Net Cash Flow		(3,000)	(2,666)	(1,038)	(4,161)	(3,555)	(2,981)	(1,894)	2,599	2,593	2,586	10,969
Net Present Value		($549)										

Figure 8.5 New Pin-Point Product Line: Strategic Business Unit Value Without Joint Venture Partner for Trademark or Technology

the reasonableness of proposed equity splits. A few of the questions that can be answered include:

- What happens if the estimated sales price of the product without the trademark partner is determined by market research to be unreasonably high?
- Is the equity participation request of the inventor still reasonable if internal creation of the basic technology can be accomplished for $1 million less than originally estimated?
- Is a "go it alone" strategy viable if a trademark and distribution network can be internally created for $5 million during the first two years of the venture?

By changing the input parameters of the DCF model, all of these questions can be considered. As long as the present value of the expected cash flows is zero or greater, then the weighted average cost of capital has been earned by the venture, and the venture is a worthwhile investment.

Creating a financial model, such as the simple example presented in this chapter, is a miniaturized version of the venture contemplated. The model requires insightful inputs from a diverse group of experts from research, engineering, marketing, sales, manufacturing, and finance. The greatest strength of a discounted cash flow analysis is that it forces a team of insightful experts to comprehensively consider the tough questions of investing in new ventures.

As Peter F. Drucker, Professor at Claremont Graduate School in California, told *Forbes* in an interview ("Roaches Outlive Elephants—An Interview with Peter F. Drucker by Mark Skousen," *Forbes,* August 19, 1991): "Alliances are increasingly the wave of the future. Grass roots development and acquisitions are becoming too expensive." The growing complexities of the many talents required by corporations to compete is much too broad to master alone. Time, costs, and risks make joint ventures the business strategy that will dominate the future. Equity splits are also the wave of the future. They require a comprehensive analysis, and the financial model presented in this chapter can be adapted to assure that fair equity splits foster continued loyalty to the joint venture from the intellectual property partners.

9

Global Exploitation of Intellectual Property

> We are finally living in a world where money, securities, services, options, futures, information and patents, software and hardware, companies and know-how, assets and memberships, paintings and brands are all traded without national sentiments across traditional borders.

So writes Kenichi Ohmae in his book, *The Borderless World* [1].

It is said that in 40,000 B.C., Cro-Magnons migrated to Europe from the Near East. One wonders what they brought with them that may have amazed the local residents that remained alive. About 950 A.D., New Zealand was discovered by Maori sailors. By the early 1500s, Spain was discovering everything in sight, exporting religion and importing silver and gold. All of these and other explorers and migrants carried information and technology with them as they roamed the land and seas.

When the electric telegraph was invented in 1816, a significant amount of information could be transmitted for the first time without someone carrying it. Geography and national boundaries were still barriers, however. Guglielmo Marconi's wireless telegraph finally broke those barriers, and by sending electric signals into the ether, it was possible for information to be transported anywhere. Today, radio, television, and satellite transmissions go everywhere in the fashion of a giant "party line" to which anyone with the proper equipment can connect. We have gotten so accustomed to sending information by "fax" and from computer to computer that one wonders that if we could eavesdrop on international telecommunications traffic, all we would hear is the porpoise-like "beeping" of one fax machine or computer to another, and very little human speech.

Reflecting our commercial existence, we have communicated lifestyles, social standards, and product information over the national, geographic, and ideological boundaries that have existed between us. The world knows about COCA-COLA soft drinks and NIKE athletic shoes and MACDONALD'S hamburgers, even though the majority of the world community has not experienced these products personally. Brand images have flown around the world like "Tinker Bell." Now that national boundaries are more permeable to commerce and geographic barriers are yielding to transportation, the pent-up demand for goods and services created by the advance guard of telecommunications is building. And it will be met, perhaps not as rapidly as we would wish, but it will be.

Manufacturing and distribution must catch up with this demand. There is a great deal of work to do, as anyone who has followed the development of the European Community can attest. Monetary systems and manufacturing standards must be made common; capital must become readily available across national borders, intellectual property protection needs to be consistent, and taxation should be equitable.

IMPACT OF THE INTERNATIONAL ENVIRONMENT

Ever since the first trader set out from his home to sell the products of his labor, we have recognized the added risks of so doing business. At first, it was the possibility of being set upon by robbers or being the victim of a travel accident. We are still setting out from our own turf to do business, and the added risks are still there. The highwaymen are perhaps more subtle, but they are still around, along with a host of other more complicated pitfalls.

We are going to address the many conditions that arise from the international exploitation of intellectual property and analyze how they affect the economics of exploitation. We again will put this analysis in terms of evaluating the present value of future cash flows from exploitation. It is therefore necessary to consider the effect of conditions arising from the international environment. The elements that we must quantify are by now familiar: *duration* (will this condition alter the duration of future cash flows?), the *amount* (how will the international environment change the amount of cash flow?), and the *risk* (has the risk changed by going international?).

The unique effects of exploiting intellectual property internationally can usually be quantified by any one of these factors. In Chapter 7, we used these elements to calculate the present value of cash flows from various licensing scenarios. In Chapter 8, we again used them to evaluate the terms of a joint venture. We will again use them to assist in quantifying the conditions introduced by exploiting intellectual property internationally.

We might, as an example, recognize that there is an element of political risk in doing business in another country. We might, in our projections of cash flow, reflect that in an increased discount rate or in a shorter life of the income stream. Our feeling is that the international elements ought to be reflected in a way that is as close as possible to the potential events. As an example, if the country into which we have licensed technology has a history of unstable government, then the most appropriate way to reflect this is in the discount rate. We do not know what might happen or how this political instability might manifest itself. On the other hand, it is not uncommon for a government, observing the success of a licensee or joint venture within its borders, to effectively "handcuff" that enterprise in order to effectively control the business and obtain the full benefit of the technology for its citizens. If there is any history of this, one ought to reflect this possibility in a shortened economic life of the license or joint venture.

In the discussion that follows, we will provide some example of risk quantification. In some cases, it is impossible to do so without relating to a specific situation. The tools of measurement are the same, however.

ACCOUNTING ISSUES

Any exploitation technique involves, at some point, an analysis or examination of financial records. We previously suggested that an important step in the exploitation process is a financial evaluation of the intended licensee or joint venture partner(s). Some knowledge of accounting standards is necessary to the process. Increasingly, international accounting standards are being homogenized, with the recognition of International Accounting Standards (IAS), but significant differences remain.

Accounting standards vary from very detailed codes such as we are used to in the U.S., to general or very high-level principles that allow considerable latitude on the part of an individual company. Our standards, and those of the U.K., are aimed towards providing complete financial information to stockholders and potential investors, to enable them to make informed investment decisions. These, of course, are precisely the standards that are useful in licensing and joint venturing. In Germany, where businesses have more debt in their capital structure, financial statements are oriented towards lenders' evaluation and towards tax issues since they are used by tax authorities as well. Japanese financial statements tend also to be oriented towards lender and tax matters, and have more latitude in their presentation than do ours. Swedish financial statements are heavily influenced by tax law as opposed to stockholder information.

The point is that there is great variety in the accounting information available about foreign enterprises. There are references cited at the end of this chapter which can guide the reader in the accounting peculiarities of a given country. They can be used to familiarize oneself about them before entering into joint venture negotiations or to estimate the administration costs that are likely to be encountered to monitor a license agreement. In a joint venture, one approach is to attempt to obtain agreement as to which national accounting standards will prevail in the financial reporting.

The primary areas of difference in national accounting standards which affect the type of transaction we are discussing are those applying to depreciation, research and development expense, and the accounting for goodwill. In each case, there is disagreement over how these expenses should be reflected in future periods. At the one extreme, depreciation is reflected as quickly as possible, R&D is expensed when incurred, and goodwill acquired in the purchase of another company is written off immediately. In terms of earnings, one takes the hit now, and future financials do not bear the burdens of the past. The other extreme is to reflect these charges over future periods when the benefits of the expenditure will be realized. There is a great deal of difference of opinion as to how far into the future one should go with this idea. The impact of these opinions is felt on the "bottom line." As we will discuss, if one accounts for a joint venture in the currently recommended way, the manner of the joint venture's accounting may have a marked effect on the books of the parent companies.

Joint Ventures

IAS 31, effective beginning 1/1/92, applies to the financial reporting of interests in joint ventures. This applies to the reporting by the partners to the joint venture. It recommends that joint venturers report their holdings by the *proportionate consolidation* method. In this method, the venturer combines his proportionate share of the joint venture's assets, liabilities, income, and expenses with his own financial statements. Therefore, as an example, if the joint venture shows losses in the early years, those losses will be combined with the earnings of the joint venture partners on their own statements. If the joint venture incurred debt on its own, that debt would be apportioned to the partners' financials. This could have a significant effect on the partners' borrowing power. This is quite different from the *equity* method of joint venture accounting in which only the original equity investment of the partners is shown on their balance sheets.

TAXES

Our purpose is not to provide a reference on the subject of international taxes, but some consideration of taxes is essential in the exploitation of intellectual property on an international scale. Nowhere has the mind of man been more fertile than in devising ways to tax one another. The idea of a required contribution to the common good no doubt surfaced in unrecorded history, and has been steadily enhanced ever since. The Roman emperor Vespasian imposed taxes on many commodities, including urinals, in an effort to restore solvency to the empire. The success of his efforts and the discomfort of his population are unrecorded.

We have, through the centuries, become equally inventive at avoiding taxes. The story of Lady Godiva's ride is well known, but we may forget that she made this trip to reduce taxes. She had long pleaded with her husband, the Earl of Mercia, to reduce the taxes on the people of Coventry. He thought to silence her by offering to do so if she would ride naked through the streets. He did not appreciate the strength of her resolve.

Income Taxes

When the subject of taxes arises, one tends to focus on income taxes. We have come to accept this form of tax as part of our lives, and rightly assume that this holds true internationally as well. We are not going to dwell on the differences between countries with respect to their income taxes because these differences are well documented in other references, and because we do not feel that these differences are especially critical in intellectual property exploitation. We have, as an example, a whole range of state taxation in this country, from no income tax to high income tax. For the most part, however, we are of the opinion that state and local taxes do not control many important business decisions. If, as an example, we wish to serve the northwestern U.S. market by establishing a warehouse and distribution center, the decision on where to locate the facility is more likely to be driven by the availability and cost of real estate and labor, proper access to the transportation system, and potential customers than by the state and local tax structure. Taxation may become a factor if several otherwise equal sites are located. In the same way, the selection of a manufacturing site overseas may be influenced by local income taxes as a secondary consideration.

We do not believe that licensors, licensees, and joint venture partners come together because of the income tax structure of their home countries. They do so because of their respective needs for the subject intellectual property, or because the transaction represents a good marriage of their respective resources. They must be aware, however, of the effect of taxes on income as they affect the net cash flow to licensee, licensor, or joint venture partner. This may relate to the potential structure of the transaction. It may, as an example, be preferable for a given party to receive income in the form of a royalty (from a license) than in the form of dividends (from a joint venture). This desire may stem from a different tax rate on these two forms of income. It may be prudent to domicile a nonoperating holding company in a low tax jurisdiction. These considerations ought to come after the primary business needs are satisfied.

In nearly every country, there is some form of tax withheld on dividends and royalties that are paid to foreign interests. On dividends, it can vary from zero (Ireland, Malaysia, and Taiwan) to 25–35% (Brazil and Mexico). Germany withholds 25% and requires the taxpayer to claim a refund for taxes covered by treaties. Generally, taxes withheld on dividends range around 15%.

Taxes withheld from royalty payments to foreigners also range around 15%, but can vary from zero (Ireland, The Netherlands, Norway, Sweden, Switzerland, Taiwan, and Russia) to 20–35% (China, Italy, Mexico, U.K.), depending on the type of intellectual property on which the royalty is being paid.

Another thought about income taxes relates to the negotiation process. As a licensor, I might recognize that a potential licensee enjoys some income tax breaks in his home country. Could I expect to extract a higher payment for the use of my intellectual property than otherwise? No. I may be able to negotiate it, and my success will probably depend on how much the potential licensee wants the intellectual property or how much competition there is for it. I should not, however, expect it. Conventional wisdom tells us that business people do not pay others for what they bring to the table. A safe assumption is that any "tax breaks" enjoyed by the parties to intellectual property exploitation will remain in their own pockets.

Joint Ventures

Issues relating to taxation are likely to be more critical to joint venture alliances than to other forms of intellectual property exploitation. A joint venture creates a new entity that will be subject to all forms of taxation in its home country. If, as an example, the joint venture is a manufacturing operation that has been granted tax incentives in the host jurisdiction, then the partners will seek to maximize profits in the joint venture. If the joint venture must be located in a high-tax jurisdiction for operations reasons, then the partners will seek to maximize tax-deductible items. The partners must then carefully consider the assets of value (such as intangible assets and intellectual property) that they have provided to the venture and charge the venture as much as is reasonable for them. Royalties, interest, and management fees might be part of this consideration.

We caution, however, as we will note in a subsequent discussion on transfer pricing, that the financial relationship between the joint venture and its partners can introduce "taxable events." We will also discover that efforts to shift profits between entities to minimize taxes is becoming increasingly difficult.

Transfer Pricing

Every collector of income taxes wants the businesses in his jurisdiction to be supremely profitable, and will look with a very jaundiced eye on deductions that reduce taxable income. Tax-deductible payments to related parties (such as royalties or management fees) become very high-profile transactions in this examination.

As a result, nearly all of the major trading countries have transfer pricing rules in effect. In general, these rules require that transactions between related companies be measured against an "arm's length" standard. That is, the price for goods or services between related parties should be comparable to the price that would have been agreed upon by two unrelated parties. If tax authorities become convinced that a transfer pricing arrangement does not meet the arm's length standard, they develop a transfer price that will, in their opinion, and levy income taxes on that basis rather than what was actually paid. These rules are formally defined in the 1979 Report on Transfer Pricing and Multinational Enterprises promulgated by the Organization for Economic Co-operation and Development (OECD), a 25-nation member organization formed in 1960 to provide a forum to discuss common economic issues. All OECD countries have structured their transfer pricing regulations to conform to the 1979 Report.

The United States and Germany are generally regarded to examine transfer pricing issues most rigorously. France, the United Kingdom, and Canada also are very attentive to this issue. Other countries have not focused as sharply on this tax issue, but there is every reason to believe that they will become more attentive.

In the U.S., transfer pricing rules have long been a part of the Internal Revenue Code (IRC), contained in Section 482. The Internal Revenue Service was empowered to restate the taxable income of a taxpayer by reapportioning gross income, deductions, credits, or allowances between affiliated entities in order to prevent tax evasion. In the early 1980s, however, Congress became increasingly concerned that significant tax revenues were being lost due to the transfer pricing strategies of multinational corporations (MNCs). Section 1231 of the Tax Reform Act of 1986 amended Section 482 to strengthen it, and to add the standard that payment for the use of intangible assets transferred between affiliated parties was to be "commensurate with the income attributable to the intangibles." Many practical enforcement details were not clear, and the Treasury Department issued a "White Paper" in 1988 outlining its proposed methodologies for enforcing Section 482 and requesting comments. Comments were detailed and profuse: On January 24, 1992, the IRS issued proposed regulations applying to Section 482. The "commensurate with income" standards are generally effective for tax years beginning after December 31, 1986. These proposed regulations are an IRS attempt to clarify intercompany pricing of tangible and intangible property transfers and cost-sharing arrangements. They also include the introduction of the "comparable profit interval" (CPI) method of estimating appropriate transfer prices within a controlled group. Subsequent comments on the proposed regulations have included substantial criticism of this method, which looks to profitability measures from comparable companies. What is causing the most confusion is the standards for measuring what is "arm's length." The IRS proposed several measurement techniques in the White Paper, some of which were roundly criticized. Subsequent IRS regulations have not clarified the situation. But, while there is some confusion over methodology, there is no question that stringent transfer pricing regulations are here to stay.

In 1989, however, the Omnibus Reconciliation Act of 1989 was signed into law. It contained several provisions aimed at foreign-controlled MNCs with U.S. subsidiaries:

The standard for related party ownership was reduced from 50 to 25%.

A foreign parent will have to maintain (in the U.S.) supporting documentation for the transfer prices.

Penalties for not providing intercompany pricing information have been made more severe.

A foreign parent must designate an agent in the U.S. to receive an IRS summons.

If the above requirements are not met, the IRS can deny the deductibility of related party charges.

The implications of all this for joint venture partners are several. First, there is unquestionably great attention being paid to transfer pricing issues worldwide. One cannot simply gerrymander transfer prices in order to minimize income taxes. Second, transfer prices must be documented and have some supportable "arm's length" origin. Third, the standards for being a "related party" are being reduced. A minority joint venture partner could be subject to transfer pricing scrutiny. In addition, one of the original White Paper provisions that remains is the concept that transfer prices are subject to change over time. One cannot simply "set it and forget it." The IRS has recognized that payments for the use of intangible assets or intellectual property which are at a low level because they represented early-stage technology must be increased if the intangible asset or intellectual property becomes the linch-pin of a marketable and profitable product line. Many taxpayers have ignored the typical price changes that occur as a product moves through its introduction, growth, maturity, and decline phases. Taxpayers have argued that royalty rates customarily do not change during the life of a license agreement between unrelated parties. So far, this assertion has not moved the Treasury Department from its position.

As for other countries, some, like Japan and Canada, tend to follow U.S. tax law in new areas, but we cannot tell how far down the Section 482 road they are likely to go. Others, like Germany and the U.K., pursue transfer pricing issues with a vigor, but seem less concerned about defining specific methodologies for measurement, and permit their tax collectors more latitude in making the arm's length judgment.

Transfer Pricing Reminder

It is essential to recognize that there are very important tax issues attendant to what otherwise might seem to be a straightforward business arrangement. A joint venture is not usually just an investment vehicle. It involves an ongoing relationship between the partners, and often establishes a trade relationship between the joint venture and one or more partners. If so, that trade relationship will likely come under transfer pricing scrutiny. The business people negotiating the joint venture must be aware of the requirements, such as the need for documentation and a U.S. agent. They should also consult with tax advisors as to the acceptable methodologies for establishing transfer prices and address them in the joint venture agreement.

Transfer pricing issues should not be a concern in the typical licensing transaction between *unrelated* parties. These are presumed to be arm's length by their very nature. We suggest, however, that those involved in the exploitation of intellectual property be keenly aware of the potential implications that may be hidden in the transactions they are designing. The royalty rate and license terms to an unrelated party may be used by a tax authority as "proof" of an uncontrolled transfer price that could be used to evaluate other intracompany transfer prices. International taxation is a moving target indeed.

POLITICAL RISK

de la Torre and Neckar [2] describe political risk in terms of an international investor's concern about the potential loss in value of his assets. Remembering that value is equal to the present value of the future economic benefits of ownership, this concept comports nicely with the discounted cash flow model that we have been using. That is, any event that impairs the present value of future cash flows (by reducing them, shortening them, or increasing the uncertainty of their collection) reduces value. They also classify political risk in terms of two types of contingency loss. The first is defined as the involuntary loss of control over assets, without compensation. This might include expropriation, nationalization, destruction by civil war, terrorists, and the like. The second classification of loss results from discriminatory actions by the host government, such as price controls, currency or remittance restrictions, tariffs, and the like. de la Torre and Neckar also cite a number of models and references for assessing political risk, and the reader might wish to consult their paper in full.

The term "political risk" could be construed to cover all types of risk if one assumes that a country's government is in control of all aspects of life. A government can alter the tax structure, the monetary and banking system, impose duties, change tariffs, manufacturing standards, environmental regulations, and nearly every element that might affect doing business there. We will separate some of these elements in our discussion, however. With respect to the involuntary loss of control over assets as defined above, it would appear to us that the best way to reflect this possibility is in a shortening of the expected economic life of the intellectual property transaction. Frankly, one is rarely forewarned of the conditions that might lead to expropriation, as an example, and those who license into a potential situation of this kind usually have a very risky scenario in mind at the start. The second type of loss, by discriminatory actions of a host government, is much more common, and the types of discrimination can take many forms, and while seemingly benign, can severely impair the economic benefit to an outsider doing business in that country. This is perhaps best reflected by adding an "international factor" to the discount rate utilized in the evaluation if there is any history of this sort of action in the host country. We address this again in the "Investment Risk" section.

In the paper cited above, de la Torre and Neckar also note that:

1) Foreign companies involved in extractive or agricultural industries seem to have been more subject to political risk. Many countries, especially LDCs, strongly feel that their natural resources should be exploited only for national welfare.

2) High-tech projects, on the other hand seem to be relatively immune from political risk (again in LDCs) because the reality is that local companies are unprepared to take over and provide their output.

3) Heavily differentiated or branded products are again less likely to be disturbed because of the inherent difficulty of substitution.

We recently became aware of a firm which specializes in the assessment of risk overseas, from a business perspective. Political Risk Services in Syracuse, NY, publishes studies directed towards this specific purpose. We observed summaries of their information in *International Business* magazine, where each month a brief summary of risk information is published for several countries. Included is a forecast for 18 months and for five years. Grades are given for such criteria as "financial transfer" (difficulties in converting or transferring local currency out of the country), "direct investment" (risks to foreign investors in subsidiaries or joint ventures), and "export market" (risks faced by exporters to the country as to delays, difficulty receiving payment, import barriers, etc.). Also shown are GDP average growth rates for different periods of time and inflation rates. We understand that this firm's publications (available on a subscription basis) contain much more information.

NEW MARKETS

The exploitation of intellectual property by means of licensing has a great deal of appeal in the international arena. Generally, a license can be negotiated much more quickly and at far less cost than the creation of a joint venture. Joint ventures involve an intermingling of corporate as well as national cultures. We have already discussed the barriers presented by the marriage of corporate cultures, even in the same country.

Another advantage of the licensing strategy is that there is a much different market for intellectual property on an international scale. There is a much wider diversity between the technological advancement of countries than there is likely to be within a single country.

In a client engagement, several years ago, we analyzed a classic progression of manufacturing technology. The product comprised several simple parts that were assembled without tools. The product was small, manufactured in large numbers, and the unit cost was about $1.50 originally. Obviously, under these conditions, the management of the company devoted considerable resources to streamlining the assembly process, with the objective (given U.S. wage rates) of reducing human labor in the process and also improving quality. The original manufacturing process was in assembly line fashion, with the product being assembled on a moving belt passing in front of a line of workers, each adding a part or testing the partially complete assembly. The company then developed a semi-automatic assembly on a rotating table where parts were delivered and positioned by machine. Several operations still had to be done manually, however. After a fairly expensive period of development and fine tuning this machine, costs were reduced to about $0.85 per unit.

Development continued, and the manufacturing process was fully automated, at considerable cost. It was worth the investment, however, because by this time, the company had established itself in the market, and so the reduction of manufacturing cost, ultimately to about $0.35 per unit, went straight to the bottom line in profits.

As far as our client was concerned, the know-how connected with the manual and the semi-automatic manufacturing was of no value. We might reexamine that opinion relative to an international market, however. Suppose there was an entrepreneur in another country who was interested in entering this business and had approached our client. Knowing the cost spent in development and the substantial cost savings represented by the fully automatic technology, the price for the current system would be high indeed. If the potential licensee was from a less developed country (LDC), the fully automated technology might not be attractive because of its cost and complex maintenance, but the previous technologies might be very attractive as a way to start into the business since the cost of labor would not be critical initially, and it would permit testing the market without a back-breaking financial risk.

There are many "semi-automatic technologies" gathering dust in the engineering departments and boneyards of industry everywhere. The international marketplace opens renewed opportunities that have not existed before. As some readers may be aware, this situation has not been without abuse. Some LDCs have found it necessary to establish extensive inspection procedures for goods and equipment being imported. This was necessary in order to prevent the import of old, outmoded, run-out machines. We are not referring to this type of transaction. We are calling attention to the expanded market that exists for what may be to us "second-tier" technology, but for others may be a perfect match for their production needs and relative cost structure. This market is not likely to exist for long.

A more recent example of this is the transaction announced by Texaco, Inc., in which it licensed its coal gasification technology to the Shanghai Coking and Chemical Plant (SCCP). SCCP will build a new plant to utilize the technology to produce domestic gas and chemicals from coal. This technology is not obsolete or "second-tier," but our energy costs have declined since the 1970s when there was great impetus to refine such technology, and so it is not in wide use at this time here. It fits a niche in China perfectly since she has an abundance of coal versus natural gas, and the burning of coal for domestic use is a heavy contributor to air pollution problems. Conditions in China are ideal for the use of this technology, which is currently dormant here.

China is to spend $6.2 billion this year alone on electric generating capacity, and plans to build 80 or so hydroelectric facilities over the next ten years at a cost of $2–$3 billion annually. We suspect that there is a great deal of hydro know-how dormant in the U.S., although we might find that Canada and the Scandinavian countries would be strong competitors in the exploitation of such technology in the Chinese market. China plans to spend $4 billion on rural food processing facilities between now and 1996. This would seem an ideal opportunity for "semi-automatic technology." By contrast, China's modernization of its telecommunications system is an opportunity only for the owners of the very newest technology. There is no benefit in doing anything else but going right to "state-of-the-art."

REPATRIATION

For the most part, funds can be moved internationally without problems. There can be delays and costs, but the deed can be done. Sometimes there are hidden barriers, such as one encounters doing business in Russia, in not being able to easily convert the ruble to other currencies. Licensing into Russia or being a partner in a Russian-located joint venture then carries with it the necessity of developing a means around this difficulty. Some techniques include receiving the economic benefit by barter, reinvesting the funds in Russia (hoping for better days in the future), buying commodities in Russia and exporting them, or helping your partner or licensee earn *your currency* so they will have the wherewithal to pay. The important thing to remember is that, while these techniques work, they introduce costs, delays, and risks that otherwise would not be part of the evaluation equation.

The reader is referred back to Chapter 7 and the discussion of quantifying the present value of the economic benefits of a licensing transaction. The added costs, delays, and risks would have to be reflected in the calculation of the present value of positive cash flows. The reader may recall the examples given in Chapter 7 calculating the present value of various positive cash flows resulting from licensing. One of these made examples that calculation as shown in Figure 9.1.

In the previous discussion, we decided that this option provided the most attractive alternative from the licensor's point of view. The present value of the positive cash flow from royalties is shown to be $309,662. This present value calculation was made using a half-year convention. That is, we assumed that each year's royalties would be received in midyear. Let us now transplant that license to Russia (or any other country where there would be a problem converting the home country currency). Let us further assume that the decision has been made that the best way for us to deal with the problem is to purchase a commodity in the licensee's country, using the royalty proceeds in local currency. That commodity will be shipped to our home country and sold. We therefore must reflect the costs to purchase, transport, and sell the commodity. We must also reflect the loss in present value that results from the time delay to accomplish all of this. The result is a sharply lower present value of $197,186. See Figure 9.2.

In this example, we have estimated the direct costs of the transactions in the form of commissions, duties, insurance, freight, taxes, and sales expense. We have reflected the delay by calculating the present value assuming a six-month delay in receipt of the funds. We must also recognize that by turning this into a series of buy–sell transactions, we have increased the risk associated with receiving the economic benefit. We are now subject to commodity market risks, shipping problems, additional currency risk, and the like. We therefore have increased the

	1	2	3	4	5	6	7	8	9	10
QUANTITY (lb 000s)	500	500	500	500	500	500	500	500	500	500
PRICE PER UNIT ($)	2.50	2.50	2.50	2.50	2.50	2.50	2.50	2.50	2.50	2.50
REVENUE ($000s)	1,250	1,250	1,250	1,250	1,250	1,250	1,250	1,250	1,250	1,250
Cost of Goods Sold	800	775	775	750	750	750	750	750	750	750
Gross Profit	450	475	475	500	500	500	500	500	500	500
Royalty	38	50	50	63	63	63	63	63	63	63
Discount Rate 12.00%										
Present Value of Royalties	35.18	41.28	36.32	39.95	35.16	30.94	27.23	23.96	21.09	18.56
Total Present Value ($)	309,662									

Figure 9.1 Royalty Set at One-Half of Cost Savings (with Licensee Enhancement)

	1	2	3	4	5	6	7	8	9	10
Royalty	38	50	50	63	63	63	63	63	63	63
Less:										
Commodity Purchase Exp.	3	4	4	5	5	5	5	5	5	5
Transportation Exp.	1	1	1	1	1	1	1	1	1	1
Commodity Selling Exp.	4	5	5	6	6	6	6	6	6	6
	-----	-----	-----	-----	-----	-----	-----	-----	-----	-----
Net Royalty	30	40	40	50	50	50	50	50	50	50
Discount Rate 15.00%										
Present Value of Royalties	25.50	28.90	24.57	26.10	22.19	18.86	16.03	13.62	11.58	9.84
Total Present Value ($)	197,186									

Figure 9.2 Royalty Converted to Commodity for Sale in Home Country

discount rate to 15% from the 12% in the base case. If we planned to sell the commodity in yet a third country and repatriate the funds from there, there might well be an additional layer of direct costs and an added risk factor.

CULTURAL ISSUES

In spite of the best efforts of everyone involved in a joint venture or licensing transaction, there are cultural and language barriers in the international arena that can impede full understanding and contribute to greater risk of success. During a sojourn in France, Benjamin Franklin was invited to a literary society meeting. The conversation in French was going a bit fast for him and was punctuated by applause. He was uncertain about joining in, and decided to join the applause when a lady of his acquaintance applauded. All seemed to be well until the gathering was over, at which time his grandson told him, "But, Grandpapa, you always applauded, and louder than anyone else, when they praised you."

It is obviously impossible to precisely quantify the additional risk that this introduces into a transaction, but we cannot ignore the possibilities. We suggest that this can take two forms. First, introduce more lead time in the DCF calculation to allow for more protracted negotiations. Second, increase the discount rate applied to positive cash flows. Increase it more as the licensee's (or joint venture partners') culture differs from your own. Or, increase the administrative costs in the projection (at least by the cost of an interpreter).

INVESTMENT RISK

By this term, we refer to the perception of the investor of the relative risk associated with committing funds to an investment opportunity. In essence, someone who is in the position of exploiting intellectual property is an investor—either on his own if he owns the intellectual property, or in the role of a trustee if he is acting on behalf of shareholders or other owners. The responsibility is the same.

More specifically, we refer to the discount rate to be applied to positive cash flow associated with licensing or joint venturing. For the most part, it is the *positive* cash flows that are affected by international conditions. The negative cash flows—the expenses of the transaction—are going to be there no matter what, and their discount rate will be dictated by the risk of our business in our home country.

All of the other risks we have discussed, accounting standards, tax regulations, political situations, the ability to repatriate funds, and the like, eventually find their way into how we, as the potential investor, view the risks and rewards of a potential transaction. In the end, it is a subjective process. We are not totally without a framework, however. Standard & Poor's Corporation, for one, publishes ratings of various investments, including corporate bonds. These ratings are for the guidance of investors. The highest rating, "AAA," is reserved for debt issues of companies whose "capacity to pay interest and repay principal is extremely strong." At the other end of the scale, bonds rated "CCC" ". . . have a currently identifiable vulnerability to default . . ." and are ". . . dependent upon favorable business, financial, and economic conditions to meet timely payment of interest and repayment of principal." These descriptions are from their *Bond Guide* (see Appendix B), and provide a picture of the two ends of the risk spectrum. At the present time, industrial bonds rated "AAA" by Standard & Poor's are priced in the marketplace to yield about 8.5% to maturity. Those rated "BBB" yield about 9.25%, and those rated "CCC" about 13.25%. Thus, the difference between a "blue chip" debt investment and one in some sort of trouble is a bit less than five percentage points.

This is not an absolute yardstick, but if one refers back to Chapters 7 and 8, we use a discount rate in the calculation of the present value in order to quantify relative uncertainty. In Chapter 7, we decided on an appropriate royalty scheme, and we made some decisions about the present value of future expenses and obligations. We then calculated the net present value of all of the elements of a potential license agreement. If we were to transplant that transaction to an international setting and decide that the risk of realizing the positive cash flows was greater than in our domestic model, it is possible that the transaction "would not fly." That is, the present value might be negative, or not high enough to attract us. There is no "cookbook" to offer that will make these decisions. Elsewhere, we discussed the use of investment rates of return in the 30–40% range used by venture capitalists. This was to reflect the inherent risk of a new and untested technology. Even this range of rate of return might be applicable to reflect international risk under some circumstances. One must be sensitive to all of the available measures of investment risk, and must come to a conclusion about their effect on the transaction being designed.

LEGAL PROTECTION

There is a wealth of information published about the legal protection (or lack thereof) of intellectual property in various countries of the world. This situation is closely monitored by professional organizations such as the United States Trademark Association and the Licensing Executives Society. We do not intend to duplicate that coverage. The reader should, however, add the aspect of legal protection to the list of elements to consider in evaluating the economics of a transaction. Typically, we shun those countries that do not adequately protect intellectual property. There may, however, be valid business reasons to license into or form a joint venture with an entity in such a country. Perhaps the technology is moving so fast that the "pirates" will not be able to catch up. Perhaps the key to the success of the product is an ingredient that we can control, and we are free to license the rest. Whatever the reason, we must factor this condition into our evaluation. Most frequently, this should be reflected in a shorter economic life than otherwise, either because of the short life of the technology, or because unrestricted "knock-off artists" will gather the resources to erode the sales of our licensee or joint venture. If we take this calculated risk, the calculation should be to foreshorten the duration of positive cash flow.

SUMMARY

It is most difficult to quantify the risks of international investment. We can only provide guidelines and a sort of checklist of things to consider. If we go back and put ourselves in the place of the inventor of the "super putter" described in Chapter 3, we can add the international complexity. Let us assume that Cougar Club Company is based in Singapore, and that Golden Shark Enterprises is located in Germany. Both companies, as well as Zing Golf Corporation, the U.S. contender for license rights, have assured us that they have the necessary manufacturing capacity and distribution channels to ensure worldwide coverage. They seem to be equally competent technically, and are on a par (sorry!) financially. Our decision must now be based on their geographical and political location, and we must evaluate these investment opportunities on that basis, carefully considering the elements we have discussed in this chapter, as well as evaluating the specific license provisions as we did in Chapter 7.

REFERENCES

[1] Ohmae, Kenichi, *The Borderless World*. (McKinsey & Company, 1990).

[2] de la Torre, Jose and Neckar, David H., "Forecasting Political Risks for International Operations," in *The Handbook of Forecasting,* Spyros Makridakis and Steven C. Wheelwright, Eds. (New York: John Wiley & Sons, 1987).

OTHER INFORMATION SOURCES

Choi, Frederick D. S., *Handbook of International Accounting*. (New York: John Wiley & Sons, Inc., 1991).

Coopers & Lybrand (International), *International Accounting Summaries*. (New York: John Wiley & Sons, Inc., 1991).

Sweeney, Allen and Robert Rachlin, *Handbook of International Financial Management*. (New York: McGraw-Hill, Inc., 1984).

Ingo, Walter, ed., *Handbook of International Business*. (New York: John Wiley & Sons, Inc., 1988).

Taxation of Cross-Border Mergers and Acquisitions (The Netherlands: Klynveld Peat Marwick Goerdeler, 1991).

Taxation of International Transfers of Technology. (The Netherlands: Klynveld Peat Marwick Goerdeler, 1990).

MacLaren, Terence F., *1990 Licensing Law Handbook*. (New York: Clark Boardman Company, Ltd., 1990).

MacLaren, Terence F., *1992 Licensing Law Handbook*. (New York: Clark Boardman Callaghan, 1992).

International Business. (Harrison, NY: American International Publishing Corp.).

10

Exploitation Begins With Mapping

The greatest business challenge in the future will be to assure that intellectual property is optimally exploited. This goal is more complicated for many companies because they are not aware of all the intellectual property they possess. Vague references to intellectual property are becoming a common theme among top executives and consultants —they have the basic concept, but do not seem to understand the details. . .

> "U.S. corporations must begin to leverage their competencies across businesses."

> "We plan to form alliances with partners that possess complementary knowledge capital."

Empires sometimes rise from such grand and visionary phraseology, but most often, nothing happens because vague concepts do not get new products out the door ahead of competitors. High royalties are paid for property such as materials technology, pharmaceutical therapies, access to customer lists, and the use of famous brands. Knowledge capital and competencies will not earn a dime unless they are better defined to more clearly show how they will contribute to increased sales, generate higher profits, and ultimately create corporate value. Before something can be exploited, it must be identified. This chapter will attempt to provide some guidance for finding the intellectual property that can be licensed, traded, sold, joint ventured, or otherwise serve as the admission price into a potentially lucrative strategic alliance.

Intellectual property represents the keystone to success for most companies. Trademarks capture market share, and patented technologies often command premium prices for the products they represent. In some cases, 80% of a company's value is derived from the intellectual property that it owns. Yet, enormous and expensive management information systems are better equipped to count and control raw materials or manufacturing equipment. Rarely is there a means for capturing the existence of intellectual property. Admittedly, the intangible nature of keystone intellectual property complicates the task. Yet, a rather serious effort is warranted when the lion's share of corporate value lies among patents, trademarks, distribution networks, and other intangibles. Over 80% of the RJR Nabisco purchase price was attributed to intangible assets and intellectual property. Most successful companies would find themselves in the same position as RJR if they assessed their corporate value and identified its different sources.

MAPPING INTELLECTUAL PROPERTY

An inventory of intellectual property is a realistic goal, but is complicated by the multifaceted nature of these intangible assets. Intellectual property cuts across many aspects of a business, and often interplays with other intangible assets. When intellectual property does not cut across business boundaries, new questions arise, like: Why not?

The trademark of a company with various divisions and products, all using the same trademark banner, cannot be conveniently placed in an inventory account that is associated with one of the manufacturing plants or one of the divisions. But customer lists are often associated with a single business division. One business unit may be exclusively using a customer list that has potential for other divisions. Associating an exclusive list with one business unit is not recommended. Such a practice can psychologically block seeing the potential from broader application.

The process for taking an inventory of intellectual property is described as *mapping*. Intellectual property can stretch over many aspects of a corporation like a river that sustains life through entire regions of a country. It is not appropriate to identify a river with the inventory account of one U.S. state. Likewise, it is also inappropriate to identify many types of intellectual properties with one of the company plants, divisions, or subsidiaries. The process of mapping starts with a comprehensive list that identifies the various types of intellectual property. Then a mechanism is derived to show the many places where, in the organization, each of these assets is used. The *map* should be flexible, allowing the location of property use to be broadly defined, but also including identification of other applications. The usage location, defined as the primary activity or physical location of use, can be defined to run among products, divisions, or manufacturing locations. Different organizations will find that their own circumstances dictate how usage locations should be defined.

The questions to be answered in the mapping process are basic:

1) What intellectual property do we possess?
2) Where is it being used?

After these questions are answered, a great many new possibilities can be considered: Where else can we use the property? Can it be licensed? Is it being properly protected? Can it be contributed to a joint venture? Can it be traded to fill an intellectual property gap? Should an idle property be sold off for cash?

Once the basic questions are answered, new possibilities might appear for more fully exploiting these assets. Strategic planners that assess the profit centers and profit opportunities of large companies will find many aspects of mapping intellectual property familiar. However, the focus is shifted to intellectual property and away from business units.

Provided below is a brief outline of the steps needed to begin and complete the mapping process. The steps include:

1) Identification
2) Location
3) Coordination with strategic plans
4) Routing for internal exploitation
5) Identifying gaps
6) Routing for external application.

This chapter will focus on providing guidance about what to look for and where to find intellectual property—identification and location.

IDENTIFICATION

Keystone patents and flagship trademarks are easy to identify. But buried in the organization are many other gems just waiting to be discovered. Start with a list of all of the patents and trademarks of the company from the legal department. Then begin to think like a detective. BUT do not limit yourself to the list. Some very valuable intellectual property in the form of know-how can lurk unnoticed. Make inquiries throughout the company by interviewing managers from all divisions at all levels. It is important to get into the lower ranks of the organization because most of the best insights come from the bottom to the top. Show everyone the complete list of patents and trademarks, and find out which are being used. Also find out why unused patents and trademarks are not being incorporated into activities. Ask everyone—employees, customers, suppliers—*What makes our product, company, or service special?* and *Why are customers buying our goods?* Do not fall into the trap of only asking the marketing people why customers buy. They have prejudices, just like the engineering, customer service, and manufacturing people will. So ask everyone. The answers will range all over the place, but a few answers will lead to the discovery of unrecognized intellectual property. These are the intellectual property assets that can lead to new opportunities. These are the assets that a comprehensive inventory effort must discover. Examples include secret formulas, process procedures, quality control secrets, customer lists, incentive plans, databases, supplier agreements, employee training methods, and other intangible items never imagined.

> Xerox found that their internal training program was highly regarded by outsiders. They made an entire business by selling training programs to other companies.

The search must include line functions and staffing functions. Corporate databases can be just as valuable as keystone patents. Marketing plans can also be significantly valuable. They can also have great potential for application to other aspects of the business. The search must include extensive field work, but cannot omit the all too familiar backyard of corporate headquarters.

> A Wisconsin power company spent millions to develop a new computer system that coordinated power production activities with customer utilization and billing.

It was a sophisticated program, and other utilities could enjoy its benefits without becoming a competitive threat. Wisconsin Power set up a subsidiary, and licensed the new company to market the computer program.

British Technology Group calls itself the largest licenser of technology in the world. According to BTG chief executive Ian Harvey: "We believe that many corporations doing R&D use only 20 to 30 percent of the technology they have developed. The remainder lies unused for a variety of reasons." (*Global Technology-Asset Management: A New Survival Skill for the 1990s,* by Jeffrey L. Staley, *Technology Transfer,* Fall 1991). If Mr. Harvey is correct, this technology deserves to be found and exploited. If it is not useful for the present strategic plans, then sell it, license it, joint venture with it. Do something with it. Because, to paraphrase a well-known slogan—"Intellectual property is a terrible thing to waste."

Presented below is a list of intellectual property and intangible assets. Not all will possess the potential for further exploitation. Some will have mild potential; others could be great success stories. Each department of a corporation can be a treasure trove of exploitable property:

Engineering

Governmental approvals and acquisition expertise

Governmental regulation compliance

Quality control testing procedures and equipment

Design efficiencies

Product defect statistics

Assembled engineering work force

Research & Development

Research programs
Patented technology applications
Patented technology
Prototypes
Embryonic research
Assembled research work force

Manufacturing

Production practices
Knowledge about factors affecting quality
Assembled manufacturing work force
Order backlog
Spare parts annuity
License agreements
Process patents
Material handling technology
Vendor and supplier list
Just-in-time raw materials delivery techniques
Automated inspection procedures and equipment

Distribution & Marketing

Brands and trademarks
Advertising and media programs
Packaging research
Assembled sales staff and representatives

Retail accounts and shelf space

Statistics on loyal customer buying history

Competitor analysis

Copyrights on sales material

Distribution rights to other products

Finance & Administration

Management information systems

Long-term and favorable lease arrangements

Assembled work force

Copyrights on computer software

Mortgage portfolios

Unique incentive programs

Here is a description of some of the intellectual property to be found from a mapping program. Not all of it will have the potential for enhanced exploitation, but some of it will. A few possibilities are discussed.

ASSEMBLED WORK FORCE

In many businesses, the presence of a skilled work force that is knowledgeable about company procedures and possesses expertise in certain fields is vital to the continued profitability and growth. Access to some of these professionals can be used to leverage a company into a strategic alliance. It is common in the pharmaceutical industry for one partner to conduct product research and get government approvals, while the other partner is responsible for large-scale manufacturing and marketing. Expertise is needed in research, manufacturing, and marketing. A full assessment of the special skills of the entire work force from all departments can be an unmatched proprietary asset. Successful corporations are very much like individuals. They develop areas of focused expertise, but are weak in other areas of life. Compounding the problem is that people of similar interests and expertise flock together. Managers with primary interests in research tend to like and hire people with similar strengths. In other companies, the dominant personality might be marketing. When this occurs, the company develops an unmatched expertise in an important business function. Instead of dooming the company because of its overspecialization, the dominant tendency attracts other companies possessing complementary specialties. Once a company recognizes its specialties, new possibilities can be discovered by looking for others that might like to joint venture.

CAPTIVE SPARE PARTS ANNUITY

The continued purchase of replacement parts for capital equipment that have already been sold to customers can be an extraordinarily profitable portion of a business. If a company manufactures and sells complex capital equipment like aircraft, defense equipment, computer equipment, and other items requiring a substantial customer investment, then the customer purchasing the original item must continually return to the manufacturer for replacement parts and accessories. Typically, these items are sold at a healthy premium price contributing healthy profit margins. Premium pricing of these parts reflects the near monopoly position that the original equipment manufacturer possesses as the only source for these parts.

The term *captive* is used to describe the nature of the relationship with the customers. Once the original equipment is purchased, few options exist as sources for spare and replacement parts. The term *annuity* refers to the regularity of receiving orders. The continued receipt of orders is a function of the life of the original equipment and the age of the equipment that the company has placed with its customers. In some businesses, the original piece of equipment is sold at an extremely low level of profit or at break-even in order to capture the monopoly position for regular maintenance and accessory parts. The sale of spare parts, replacement parts, and accessories can be a substantial portion of a business. Some companies can estimate the amount of sales from this component of the business very accurately, and can therefore plan ahead to achieve the greatest amount of profitability. Sales of new equipment may be hurt during economic downturns, but replacement parts are usually very resilient. Unique opportunities for strategic alliances exist with spare parts annuities.

> The Sikorski helicopter division of United Technologies was an attractive joint venture partner to Dow Chemical. The helicopter company possesses a large backlog of spare parts contracts associated with aircraft that has sold to customers. The new joint venture will combine Dow's sophisticated composite materials technology with the business already booked by United Technologies.

COMPUTER SOFTWARE

Valuable computer software can be related to a company product or can represent internal controls that enhance the efficiency of operations. Lotus Development Corporation has copyrighted products like "Lotus 1-2-3" that serve as the foundation of their business. Federal Express has internal software and procedures that allow customers to ascertain the location of shipments in less than an hour. Federal Express uses this software to control operations, and also as a strong selling point to differentiate it from competitors.

Computer software is currently protected under copyright laws which only protect the expression of an idea, and not the idea itself. Aggressive competition in all areas of product software abound, including programs for spreadsheets, accounting systems, word processing, database management, and utilities.

Successful software products are usually a strong foundation from which to launch accessory software, products, and services. These can be handled internally or licensed out.

> The Microsoft basic intellectual property, the DOS operating system, has taken the company into a large product line of application programs, hardware accessories, programming books, and magazines.

COPYRIGHTS

Copyrights are legally protected expressions of an idea, including films, books, articles, software, television programs, and other works. Decades of repeat sales are often possible. Copyrights are also excellent candidates for many forms of strategic alliances.

> The "Teenage Mutant Ninja Turtles" started as a comic book. The characters are now part of Nintendo software, bedroom linens, lunch boxes, books, feature films, childrens' clothing, school supplies, and too many other things to consider. Mattel has, for the first time, licensed "BARBIE" for a line of girls' bedroom linens and clothing. Dr. Seuss's "Cat in the Hat" is sold on video cassette. Bill Blass has his own line of chocolate candies.

The point is that copyrights can get companies into many other businesses.

CUSTOMER LISTS

A list of established customer relationships comprised of individuals who repeatedly order from the company can have extraordinary value. The information contained in such lists usually includes the preferences of the customer, the buying patterns of the customer, and the history of purchases that have been received from the customer. In a sense, a list of loyal customers who regularly provide the company with sales is similar to the captive parts and annuity. An opportunity exists by developing other products for sale to this loyal customer list. If needed, these products can be licensed. Also, the list can be a substantial asset for contributing to a joint venture. Loyal customers cost a lot to nurture, and creating a customer list from scratch takes time. Whenever a customer list exists, a valued piece of property exists for expanded exploitation.

DISTRIBUTION NETWORKS

Many manufacturing companies do not possess an extensive staff of sales individuals. Instead, a network of independent distributors is used to find customers and get orders. These distributors receive a commission on each sale. They also can be a vital source of customer information. Many product enhancement ideas have come from customers through comments made to representatives of the distributor. Development of a distribution network can require an extensive amount of time as prospective distributors are identified, interviewed, qualified, and educated about the products that they will carry.

An established distribution network is many times the primary reason for product failure. New products from small companies often fail before the customer has a chance to vote on their commercial worthiness. If a new product cannot get to the shelves, the manufacturer will never realize any sales. Distribution networks are a strong bargaining chip when negotiating with a potential licenser, especially when the licenser does not have a similar means to reach consumers.

TRADEMARKS

Identifying a trademark or brand most often is easily accomplished. Take a look at the patent office files. For a short list of valuable names, look at the type on the packaging of company products. Then, it is just a matter of determining, through consumer focus groups, the names, and marks that can be exploited elsewhere, inside and outside of the company, without harming the core brand value. But before this intellectual property category is checked off the list, consider the potential for revitalizing unused trademarks.

> When BUICK decided to return to its roots, it decided, rather than create a new image, the company would build contemporary cars that possess the Buick heritage of spaciousness, comfort, and upscale features. Two of the new models recently introduced by the car maker take their names from elite carriages of the 1950s. The names "ROADMASTER" and "LaSALLE" still carry a powerful image of serene success. Buick did not need to hire a consultant to create a new name, or even a new image; they only needed to open a file drawer and look at forgotten intellectual property with new eyes.

It is important to look everywhere and ask everyone about intellectual property. Be sure to check the discard pile . . .

> The "POST-IT " notes are based on a glue that 3M developed for another purpose. The original plan for the glue (glue that sticks and resticks without leaving a mess) failed. Imaginative application of this *failed* technology created a huge business.

LOCATION

The physical location at which the intellectual property resides is not as important as the product or divisional location in which the property is used. The choices of how to assign locations include products, services, divisions, operating executives, and countries. It is important to show current applications and all potential applications. As such, the same intellectual property should be on several lists. This function of the mapping process is important because it serves as a means for organizing the inventory of intellectual property. It shows where the intellectual property is being used and where it may be needed.

STRATEGIC PLAN COORDINATION

A well-defined strategic plan answers the questions: "*Where are we going, and how are we going to get there?*" Intellectual property is the vehicle that will take you to the future completion of your plan. With the map in one hand and the strategic plan in another (you remember the strategic plan, don't you? It is that big, dusty tome holding the cafeteria door open), a comparison should quickly reveal opportunities for enhanced exploitation of the mapped intellectual property. The comparison can also show where some of the discovered intellectual property is redundant or unneeded.

Routing For Internal Exploitation

When you find something that works well, duplicate it. A comparison of high-profit business units and the intellectual property map should identify the keystones of success. Once they are discovered, an examination is needed as to how the keystone intellectual property can be leveraged into another, underperforming business unit.

Identification Of Gaps

The comparison should also quickly show that underperforming business units are lacking intellectual property. The successful units will be associated with intellectual property. The slow movers will conspicuously lack intellectual property. When this is discovered, go get the missing piece through licensing, joint venture, or development.

Routing For External Exploitation

Sometimes a perfectly good piece of intellectual property will be discovered that does not fit into any aspect of the strategic plan. This situation is similar to owning prime real estate that the company no longer needs. Enhanced exploitation in this situation can be accomplished by selling the intellectual property to an unrelated entity or by licensing. It might also be traded for access to someone else's intellectual property that can fill a gap that exists elsewhere in the organization.

MAPPING IS A HUGE ENDEAVOR

The process can quickly become overwhelming in large corporations. This, however, is more reason to begin mapping intellectual property sooner instead of later. The project can be made manageable:

- Cut the process into smaller pieces. Map trademarks first or patents first. Then move on to know-how, marketing plans, customer databases, and training courses.
- Conduct the mapping process for one division at a time, and later weave the separate reports together into an integrated map.
- Hire outside consultants for tackling the field work.

The process can indeed be managed. The most important thing is to get going.

BENEFITS

Mapping intellectual property is a lot like taking stock of an investment portfolio. More shares of winning investments may be added, and poor performers can be liquidated. Some of the possible benefits from mapping intellectual property include:

- Successful marketing strategies can be discovered and duplicated for other product categories that are sold to other markets.
- Customer lists of one division may be discovered as very useful to unrelated divisions.
- Technology gaps may be discovered, and valuable joint ventures can be established to fill the void.

- Trademark banners may be used more prominently, becoming more important than specific brand names.
- Technology in a specific division may solve problems in an unrelated division.
- Unused, but valuable technology may be found and exploited through licensing.
- Unused, but valuable technology may be rediscovered and used internally.
- Trademarks, like "ROADMASTER," can be reactivated.
- New opportunities for growth and profit may be discovered in your own backyard.

A ROUND LITTLE WHITE EXAMPLE

The remainder of this chapter will illustrate how to analyze a product to discover the presence of some types of intellectual property. We will do this by considering the complex business of making and selling golf balls. We will utilize only publicly available information, primarily related to the TITLEIST brand, in order to demonstrate how far one can go in this analysis using only annual reports, advertising materials, and industry data.

INDUSTRY REVIEW

The 1991 U.S. Industrial Outlook reported that golf equipment sales are $1.5 billion annually, and that the growth rate of sales between 1985 and 1991 has been 22%. TITLEIST is a branded product line of the Acushnet division of American Brands, Inc. Acushnet sells almost 120 million golf balls each year. Most of its $336 million in sales revenues is from golf balls.

NATURE OF THE PRODUCT

Understanding the product should start with a review of advertising materials. How do manufacturers describe their products?

> "MAXFLI"—Ask the top tour professionals which ball they play. . . ask Ian Woosnam, Ian Baker-Finch, Steve Ballesteros, ask Fred Couples which ball helped capture the Ryder Cup—Maxfli HT—The premier balata ball on the planet. . . . It's got the feel, it's got the accuracy, it's got the wind control, it's got the durability, and its got more wins worldwide than any other golf ball."

> "TITLEIST HVC"—"The first two-piece distance ball worthy enough to earn the stamp of Titleist. It's the product of five years of development and testing, at the world's most sophisticated golf ball manufacturing facility . . . HVC is 33% more accurate off the tee and up to twice as accurate off the irons than other two-piece distance balls."

> "SLAZENGER 480-INTERLOK"—"Rips through the maze of technology . . . Announcing a breakthrough of ball aerodynamic science and core technology . . . distance generating and trajectorially controlling . . . A dynamic core . . . four different dimple sizes . . . flight stability."

> "TOP-FLITE"—"Three new 90 and 100 golf balls which give you an unmatched combination of spin, feel and incredible Top-Flite distance . . . Our scientists have also created and patented two new cover materials that are both durable and elastic: ZYLIN 90 and ZYLIN 100 . . . give yourself the same edge Top-Flite has always enjoyed. Technical superiority."

These are only a few of the claims broadcast by golf ball manufacturers, yet they all run along similar lines: more distance, more control, durable cover, more accuracy. These claims leave the impression that the manufacturers have terrific secrets that let golfers hit their balls hundreds of yards farther than anyone else and with greater accuracy. But wait a minute, golf balls are also closely regulated.

GOLF BALL REGULATIONS

The physical characteristics of golf balls are regulated by the United States Golf Association, which runs an extensive testing program to ensure that golf courses and equipment conform to USGA standards. From the *1992 Rules of Golf, Appendix III,* we can learn the common standards that apply to golf balls.

1992 Rules of Golf, Appendix III

- The weight of the ball shall be no greater than 1.620 ounces avoirdupois (45.93 gm).
- The diameter of the ball shall be not less than 1.680 inches (42.67 mm) . . . test being carried out at a temperature of 23± 1°C.
- The ball must not be designed, manufactured, or intentionally modified to have flight properties which differ from those of a spherically symmetrical ball.
- Each ball type will be tested using 40 pairs . . . launched spinning about a specified axis . . . differences in carry and time of flight . . . must be less than 3.0 yards and 0.20 seconds . . .
- The velocity of the ball shall not be greater than 250 feet per second when measured on apparatus approved by the USGA . . . within a tolerance of 2% at 23± 1°C.

- The ball, when tested on USGA approved approach, . . . shall not cover a distance in carry and roll exceeding 280 yards plus a tolerance of 6%.

These specific and rigidly applied requirements bring into question the previously mentioned manufacturer claims. Speed, distance, shape, and weight are all fairly rigidly defined.

PRODUCT PRICING

What is the retail price, per ball, of golf balls? As of 1992, our survey in retail stores shows that golf balls can vary greatly in price, even though their performance can only vary by prescribed amounts.

Brand	Price/Each
SPALDING "X-OUTS"	$0.67
SPALDING EXECUTIVE	0.78
MAXFLI PLUS	0.83
WILSON PRO STAFF	0.83
RAWLINGS ROCKET	0.83
SPALDING TOP-FLITE	0.93
SPALDING ELITE	1.00
MAXFLI DDH	1.00
SPALDING TOP-FLITE PLUS II	1.06
MOLITOR	1.08
MAXFLI DDH II	1.25
FLYING LADY	1.25
WILSON ULTRA	1.41
HOGAN LS	1.50
MAXFLI MD LD	1.58

Brand	Price/Each
HOGAN EDGE	1.66
PINNACLE GOLD	1.66
WILSON STAFF	1.66
SPALDING TOP-FLITE TOUR	1.75
TITLEIST DT	1.75
TITLEIST HVC	1.75
TITLEIST TOUR	2.08

PRODUCT CHARACTERISTICS

What are golf balls like? For this, we look to the published literature and/or advertising materials. Access to company manufacturing procedures is the better place to look for this information, but outsiders are restricted as to the information that is available. Still, we learn that there are many different ways to manufacture a golf ball. The centers can be hard or liquid-filled. The cover materials can be hard, soft, elastic, and colorful. The number of dimples ranges around 300 per ball. The compression of the balls offers different responses when struck with a club. Here are some of the differences in how golf balls are manufactured.

Construction

Center—hard

Center—soft, liquid-filled

Two piece construction—center/cover

Three piece construction—center/windings/cover

Cover material—SURLYN

—LITHIUM SURLYN

—ZYLIN
—Balata
—LITHIUM Balata
—ZYLIN 90

Dimples—pattern
—sized
—number (318–492)

Compression—75 lb per sq. inch
—80
—90
—100
—105

PRODUCT MANUFACTURE

From a pamphlet contained in a package of a dozen TITLEIST balls, we learn:

> *Wound Core*. The wound core ball (also called three-piece ball) consists of the center, the windings, and the cover. The center is hollow-filled or solid, and the cover is Balata or SURLYN.
>
> Balata balls have a hollow center filled with a liquid or paste material. The center of a "TOUR" ball is filled to a precise weight with a nontoxic solution of water, corn syrup, and salt.
>
> Liquid-filled centers are frozen so that they will stay round during the winding process.

Windings. The center is wound to a predetermined size to optimize velocity and spin.

Cover. There are two basic types of cover material. Balata was once a natural material which has been replaced by a synthetic one. Balata covers are preferred by better players who look for better control and feel. The cover is soft and flexible, which compresses against the club face, giving high spin to the ball.

The most widely used cover is an ionomer plastic resin, most commonly called SURLYN, developed by DuPont 20 years ago. It is harder and more durable than balata. The new lithium-based SURLYN is an improvement over sodium- or zinc-based compounds.

Manufacturing. Two methods are used—injection molding and compression molding.

Injection molding holds the core in a mold with pins while the cover material is injected. Before cooling, the pins are extracted and the ball is ejected.

Compression molding starts with SURLYN covers in half-shells. The core is placed inside, and the other half of the cover is placed over it. The assemblies are subjected to high temperatures and pressures which fuse them together. This is a more expensive method, but gives better quality results.

Aerodynamics. The dimple pattern can determine the ball's aerodynamic characteristics. A ball is subject to all of the physical laws of any flying body. The ball encounters lift and drag, and the dimples create a thin blanket of turbulence around the ball, which reduces drag.

TITLEIST's icosahedron dimple pattern is patented, and as the advertisements say, *"optimizes distance and control."*

Spin Rate. The spin rate dramatically affects ball control, or the golfer's ability to purposely draw or fade (curve to the left or right) a shot or stop the ball quickly on landing. The spin rate is determined by the softness of the cover because the club face can *grip* the ball and impart its movement to the ball.

ANALYSIS

So what do we have from this analysis? A summary of our investigation might include:

1) Golf balls are a product which, by virtue of USGA regulations, has many of the characteristics of a commodity.
2) It is very difficult to achieve product differentiation from advertising, emphasizing distinct advantages that other balls lack.
3) Golf balls are a product of relatively low unit cost and price.
4) Heavy advertising and promotion expenditures are required to maintain or improve market position.
5) Endorsements by celebrities are a common advertising strategy.
6) There appear to be two predominant manufacturing techniques and a limited variety of materials.

WHAT ARE THE INTANGIBLE ASSETS?

Most important for maintaining market share is continued support of the image associated with the different trademarks.

This is advanced by association with celebrity endorsements. TITLEIST, as an example, is sold in pro shops, and is not found in discount or mass market outlets. It retains an elite image by appearing to cater to the "carriage trade." This image is tied to the TITLEIST name. So we have identified a very important intellectual property in the trademark.

What about advertising claims? Maybe the methods used to convey impressions to golfers is more important than actual performance. For the most part, the golf balls deliver parity performance. We should carefully investigate the advertising programs in existence.

Are materials important? Only in part. Materials technology could easily be developed that would allow average golfers to drive golf balls across state lines, but they would not be useful. USGA rules clearly limit the *capabilities* that a golf ball can possess. Materials that optimize the USGA-allowed characteristics while imparting durability for the average hacker are indeed valuable, but breakthrough proprietary materials and designs do not seem to be in evidence currently. All of the manufacturers use pretty much the samc materials and manufacturing processes but there has been considerable controversy in the past concerning patent infringement related to cover materials. But knowledge gained from continued use of the same old materials might be transferred to application of golf ball materials to other consumer products. Anyone else using SURLYN might like to have a peek at the materials testing information developed by golf ball manufacturers.

Dimple designs have been patented, but even if a dimple design would allow a golf ball to hover over a par three green, it would not be allowed by the USGA. Dimple designs are not a total write-off, though, in the search for enhanced exploitation. Maybe the dimple design could have application elsewhere—paddle balls, aircraft fuselage design, automobile front ends, super-train aerodynamics improvement, or other aerodynamic applications.

Manufacturing techniques are an area worth lengthy investigation. When a company is making 119 million items every year (as does TITLEIST), there is a tremendous motivation to save every penny possible in production costs, especially if you have established a trademark that allows you to maintain a premium price. A saving of $0.02 per ball equals $2.4 million straight to the bottom line. Areas of intellectual property in manufacturing include better manufacturing speed; techniques to make for fewer rejects; and processes that require lower investments in manufacturing equipment, and the use of lower cost materials. In this case, we would carefully examine every aspect of the manufacturing process. Is there know-how built into the machinery? Is there special know-how in the skills of the manufacturing personnel? How is the raw material handled? What contracts are in place for its procurement?

Since many of the golf balls are the same and companies use well-recognized brand names, then maybe larger market shares are derived from having a better distribution network. A computerized inventory control that quickly restocks retailers could keep more products on the shelf, keep retailers happy, and move more products to customers. If a unique distribution network is discovered, where else in and out of the organization might it be exploited? Talk to the marketing people about why sales are made and the distribution channels.

SUMMARY

Ask questions, and intellectual property will be discovered. Be imaginative, and new uses will be developed. The first step, however, is to find out what you possess.

Appendix A

Investment Rate of Return Requirements

This Appendix provides an overview of some of the ways that appropriate investment rates of return can be derived and then incorporated into the compensation that investors demand for accepting risk. Licensing transactions and joint venture deals are also forms of investment that should be judged using the same framework that incorporates the dynamics of risk and investment return into valuation decisions.

The foundation of investment value can be summarized as the present value of the expected stream of economic returns over the remaining economic life of the investment that is under analysis. Value is derived by discounting future economic benefits at an appropriate rate of return that reflects the risks associated with realizing the forecasted stream of benefits.

Economic returns must be determined with consideration for:

- the amount of the returns
- the form in which they will be provided
- the timing of the returns
- the trend expected in the amount of returns
- the duration of the economic returns.

A comprehensive discussion of modern investment theory goes beyond the scope of this book. Complete books and careers are dedicated to the study of the relationship between risk and return. Indeed, significant differences of academic opinion exist as to the proper measure of risk, as well as the proper measure of return. This Appendix has been included to acquaint the reader with the basic concepts of risk and return, and the vital role that these concepts play in determining the value of intellectual property and proper royalty rates. A bibliography is included that provides a rich collection of books and articles that should be studied to further appreciate the relationship between risk and return.

INVESTMENT RISK

Investment risk, whether that of a stock portfolio or an investment in intellectual property, is comprised of four broad components:

- Purchasing power risk
- Business risk
- Interest rate risk
- Market risk

Investors expect a return on all investments, and require compensation for the various components of risk.

Purchasing Power Risk

Even if the expected stream of economic benefits from an investment could be determined with absolute certainty, risk still exists with regard to the purchasing power of the future dollars that are expected to be received. There always exists the risk that inflation will intensify and consume any gains that may be realized from investment performance.

The Consumer Price Index shows that between 1946 and 1986, inflation averaged 4.4%. If this rate could be expected to continue in the future at this same level, then investment planning could include an element in the rate of return requirements to assure that this amount of inflation were incorporated into the contemplated investment returns. In a sense, the purchasing power risk would be eliminated.

Unfortunately, there were periods within the 40-year span between 1946 and 1986 with unanticipated swings of inflation. It is the unanticipated changes that introduce investment risk. The following table provides a sample of the level of inflation during selected time periods.

Selected Inflationary Periods

Period	Inflation Rate
1946–1986	4.4%
1950–1959	2.2%
1960–1969	2.4%
1970–1979	7.2%
1980–1986	6.1%

Even though inflation has averaged 4.4% since World War II, the investment rate of return requirements that were based upon this average were never quite correct during the selected periods. This represents risk, and a portion of investment rates of return on all types of investment properties must include an element that compensates for this risk component.

Interest Rate Risk

This risk element presents uncertainty similar to purchasing power risk. Alternate forms of investment such as corporate bonds, treasury securities, and municipal debt provide another investment opportunity with which an intellectual property investment must compete. If the future brings with it higher returns that are available from investments of lesser risk, then the value of the intellectual property investment may be diminished.

Business Risk

This element of risk is very specific to the company or intellectual property that is being studied. It involves the ability of the company to maintain customer loyalty, to achieve enough earnings to meet operating and debt expenses, to meet competitor challenges, and ultimately the risk associated with achieving a return for the equity and debt investors. Incorporated into this element of risk are the business cycle risks associated with specific industries, product liability obligations, and work force harmony.

A very significant business risk pertaining to technological intellectual property involves the existence of competitive technology that may shortly emerge. Remaining economic benefits that can be derived from the existing technology may be cut short by superior technology. This risk could limit the time frame over which initial investments are recovered.

Market Risk

A unique and often unkind element of risk is, in large part, associated with "market psychology." Irrespective of any fundamental changes in the expected performance of an investment, market risk reflects the fluctuation in the demand for a specific type of investment. On October 19, 1987, the stock market plunged in value by over 500 points as measured by the Dow Jones Industrial Average. There was no fundamental change in economic outlooks or the declaration of a world war. Yet, the value of all investments plunged. This is indeed an example of the risk that is classified by market risk.

An additional component of market risk is the risk associated with investment marketability. An investment for which an active market exists is more valuable, all else being equal, than an investment for which no active market exists.

Market risk is therefore comprised of market psychology risk and the risk of illiquidity: the ability to convert the investment into cash.

REQUIRED RATE OF RETURN COMPONENTS

There are three primary components integrated within the required rate of return:

Risk-free rate

Expected rate of inflation
Risk premium

The risk-free rate is the basic value of money assuming that there is no risk of default on the principal and that the expected earnings stream is guaranteed. Under this scenario, the investor has only sacrificed the use of the money for a period of time. Typically, the rate on long-term treasury securities serves as a benchmark for the risk-free rate.

Because investors are interested in a real rate of return, a portion of the required rate of return must include an amount that is sufficient to offset the affects of inflation. Therefore, the rate of return at which long-term treasury securities have been traded to yield represents two components of the required rate of return: the real risk-free rate and the expected inflation rate. On May 8, 1992, the Federal Reserve Bank of St. Louis reported that the average rate provided by long-term treasuries was 7.9%. Assuming that the long-term outlook for inflation is expected to be 4%, then the real, risk-free rate of return that is demanded by investors is presently about 3.9%. Unfortunately, most investments are not risk free, and must provide additional return to compensate for the risks that are associated with business risk. This is typically referred to as the risk premium. It represents compensation for the possibility that actual returns will deviate from those that are expected. Evidence can be easily found that higher rates of return are required by investors where higher levels of risk are present. By focusing on the yield that is provided by different fixed income securities, this principle can be demonstrated. The table below compares the yield on selected security investments as reported by the Federal Reserve Bank of St. Louis on May 8, 1992.

Investment	Yield %
Treasury bill (6 month)	3.78%
Treasury bill (1 year)	4.07
Long-term treasury securities	7.90
Corporate bonds, rated AAA	8.37
Corporate bonds, rate BAA	9.22

The yield differential between the six-month and one-year treasury bills represents the risk associated with purchasing power losses because the safety of principal and interest in both cases is guaranteed by the U.S. Government. The long-term fixed income securities are represented by treasury securities and two corporate issues with different ratings. While they are all subject, for the most part, to the same purchasing power risks, the safety of principal and interest is different. The higher the risk, the higher the rate of return that investors expect.

RATE OF RETURN MODELS

Having discussed the factors that affect rates of return and the components, a review is provided of a variety of methods used to determine the required rate of return.

Briefly described are five different approaches that are commonly used as a means to develop a required rate of return. They are:

- Dividend growth model
- Built-Up method
- Capital asset pricing model
- Arbitrage pricing theory
- Venture capital

Dividend Growth Model

The formula for valuing a share of preferred stock presents a simple version of the dividend growth model:

$$\text{Value} = \frac{\text{Dividend}}{\text{Required rate of return}}$$

The dividend stream is known with certainty, having been contractually set. It is promised to continue into perpetuity at the established level. This eliminates the complex assignment of trying to determine the rate at which the dividend will grow. The growth rate is zero.

If the value of the preferred share of stock is known and the dividend is known, then the equation is easily solved for the unknown value and provides an indication of the required rate of return.

$$\text{Required rate of return} = \frac{\text{Dividend}}{\text{Value}}$$

The resulting rate is the rate of return that investors are requiring for investments that provide a fixed dividend into perpetuity, possessing characteristics of risk similar to the specific issue being valued.

Preferred stock is not riskless. The dividends are paid only after debt obligations are satisfied. The indicated rate could be used as a benchmark for any investment that promises a fixed cash flow stream into perpetuity, possessing the same characteristics of risk and to the same degree (this model also assumes that there does not exist the risk that the preferred shares will be called by the issuing corporation).

Application of the dividend growth model to common stock is more complex, but if properly applied, can provide a meaningful indication of the required rate of return for equity investments with certain characteristics of risk.

In the case of common stock, the future level of the cash streams and the rate at which they might grow is not known with certainty. Expansion of the model used to value preferred stock is presented below:

$$V = \frac{D_1}{(1 + i)} + \frac{D_2}{(1 + i)^2} + \frac{D_3}{(1 + i)^3} + \cdots$$

where

V = the value of the common stock
D = the amount of dividend during each successive time period
i = the required rate of return on the stock.

The value of the stock is presented as the discounting of all future dividends. Rather than attempt to determine the amount of dividends that will be paid in each future year, an assumption is generally made regarding the rate at which the current dividend will grow. Introduction of this factor into the model along with algebraic wizardry provides a useful form for the dividend growth model:

$$V = \frac{D_0(1 + g)}{i - g}$$

The value of the stock is related to the growth of the current dividend, D_0, at the growth rate, g, capitalized at the required rate of return, i. If the value of V, D_0, and g can be determined, then the required rate of return, for an equity investment possessing comparable characteristics of risk, can be derived.

An important assumption is that the growth rate selected will be constant into the future. Also, the growth rate must be a value that is less than the required rate of return. This last requirement may seem to be too restrictive. What about a company that is growing at a fantastic pace? If the growth rate is indeed going to continue at the fantastic rate indefinitely, then the dividend growth model is not useful. It is important, however, to consider the realistic likelihood of being able to sustain abnormally high growth rates forever.

In many cases where reasonable estimates can be made for the value of the investment and the growth rate of the cash flow, an indication of the required rate of return can be calculated.

The dividend growth model is most useful for defining appropriate rates of return for intellectual property that is close to the mature portion of its economic life and is already proven as commercially viable. At this point of the life cycle, future growth rates are more predictable, and the overall market for the product or service with which the property is associated is well defined. One of the other rate of return models may turn out to be more appropriate for fast emerging intellectual property.

Built-Up Method

This method is very subjective, but can be used to directly reflect the amount of risk that is associated with the major risk factors that we have discussed. The method lists each of the components of risk, and assigns an amount of return to compensate for each risk component. An example is presented below:

Built-Up Rate of Return

Risk Component	Require Return
Risk-free rate of return	3.0%
Purchasing power	4.5%

Risk Component	Require Return
Market risk	4.0%
Interest rate risk	2.0%
Business risk	5.0%
Total required rate of return	18.5%

This method is quite attractive because it addresses each of the risk components individually, and can reflect an individual investor's own perceptions of the relative degree of risk presented by each of the components. Unfortunately, specific quantification of the exact amount of return that is necessary to compensate for each risk component is not easily quantifiable.

Too much conservatism in setting the rates can make an otherwise viable investment appear too risky. A rosy outlook can encourage investment in a project for a rate of return that is too low in relation to the risk that was accepted.

The built-up method is rarely used because of the unreliability associated with setting of the specific rates.

Capital Asset Pricing Model

The capital asset pricing model (CAPM) is one of several factor models. These models associate the proper rate of return to various investment factors. In the case of CAPM, the appropriate rate of return is considered to be determined by one factor: the volatility of returns relative to the returns that can be achieved by a broad market portfolio.

Presented below is the equation that describes the model:

$$R_e = R_f + B\,(R_m - R_f)$$

where

R_e = the equity rate of return
R_f = the risk-free rate of return
R_m = the rate of return provided by the overall market portfolio of investments

B = beta, a measure of the volatility for a specific investment relative to the market portfolio.

Application of CAPM is traditionally associated with assessing the risk and return for specific stock positions taken by investors. The risks and return of a particular stock are related to its asset base, industry position, and competitor attacks, as well as to changes in inflation and other economic forces.

The capital asset pricing model (CAPM) can be used to estimate the required rate of return for specific intellectual property by analyzing the required rates demanded by investors on specific stocks that operate in the same industry as that in which the intellectual property plays. Analysis of stocks of companies that are dominated by the type of intellectual property being studied will more directly reflect required rates of return for intellectual property in specific industries.

CAPM and Beta

Beta is a measure which indicates a company's susceptibility to changing conditions. These changes include inflation rate trends, monetary policy, world oil prices, and other factors that affect the rates of return on the entire market. Beta is a broad measure of the amount of risk possessed by a specific investment when compared to the diversified risk of a broad market portfolio.

If the stock of a company fluctuates more than the price of the broad market portfolio, then the stock, and the underlying business assets, are more susceptible to macroeconomic shifts than a broad market portfolio. If the stock's price over the past is more stable than the broad market, then the stock is considered less risky.

A common stock that has a beta of 1.0 moves in perfect unison with the overall broad market. If the market rises by 10%, then the specific stock with beta equal to 1.0 will also rise 10%. This stock is no more or less volatile than the broad market. Where beta is less than 1.0, the underlying stock moves in the same direction as the market, but to a smaller degree, and is less volatile than the overall market and less risky. Where beta is greater than 1.0, the underlying stock moves in the same direction as the market, but to a larger degree, and is more volatile than the overall market and is riskier.

Beta values are calculated for specific stocks by many investment advisory services and brokerage houses such as Merrill Lynch, Value Line, Standard & Poor's, and The Media General Financial Weekly.

A risk measure for valuing intellectual property can be determined by studying the betas of publicly traded companies that are highly dependent upon the same type of intellectual property for which a value is desired. If the risk of comparable and public companies in the same industry is the same as those affecting the subject intellectual property, then a study of their betas can serve as a risk benchmark.

CAPM and Ibbotson Associates, Inc.

The studies conducted annually by this company have examined total long-term returns as comprised of dividends, interest payments, and capital appreciation. The investments studied include all New York Stock Exchange stocks, corporate bonds, and U.S. Treasury securities; bonds, bills, and notes.

Using these studies, the return from investment in a broad market portfolio, R_m, can be determined for insertion into the CAPM model.

Critics of CAPM point to several assumptions that must be accepted for the model to be useful:

1) The rate of return for the broad market, R_m, must be established in an efficient market where all available information is properly reflected in the price of financial securities.
2) The broad market portfolio can be defined and measured accurately.
3) All elements of systematic risk can be captured by the beta factor.

Arbitrage Pricing Theory

This theory asserts that an asset's risk is related to more than the type of investment risk. APT attributes total return to the sensitivity of investment returns to *unanticipated* changes in five factors:

1) default risk
2) the term structure of interest rates
3) inflation

4) the long-run expected growth rate of profits for the economy
5) residual market risk

The arbitrage pricing theory can be expressed by the equation below:

$$R = E + (B_1)(F_1) + (B_2)(F_2) + (B_3)(F_3) + (B_4)(F_4) + e$$

where

R = the actual return on an asset
E = the expected return on an asset
B_n = the asset's sensitivity to a change in F_n
F_n = a specific economic factor
e = the return attributed to idiosyncratic factors specific to the asset.

Determination of the sensitivity of asset returns to each economic factor is not an easy task. Stock price movements are not easily traced to a given factor because so many different economic and idiosyncratic forces affect the stock price movement.

The capital asset pricing model is appealing because the sensitivity factor, beta, can be readily determined. Yet, this model denies the sensitivity of returns to specific factors for specific investments.

Presently, implementation of the inferences of APT theory can be accomplished by requiring premium rates of return on investments where the expected returns can be significantly affected by unanticipated changes in the identified economic factors. The important lesson of the APT studies that support this model is the realization that certain investments are more sensitive than others to unanticipated changes in specific economic factors.

Unexpected inflation might have only a minor effect on the profits of certain consumer product industries where it is relatively easy to pass along the inflationary costs in the form of higher product pricing. Other industries, where product pricing is very inelastic, could be significantly affected by inflation.

Investments in firms and industries that use a high degree of leverage are very sensitive to unanticipated interest changes, and are therefore sensitive to default risk: the risk of principle or interest expense default.

Many industries are nondiversified, and are very sensitive to unanticipated changes in the general prosperity of the overall economy. As valuation and royalty rate decisions are contemplated, the sensitivity of the intellectual property investments to unanticipated changes in many of these factors is an important consideration.

Venture Capital

So far, this Appendix has discussed how to determine appropriate rates of return for an equity investment where risk quantification is possible by comparative analysis. CAPM and APT are typically used where commercial viability of the investment is either already proven or highly likely. Rates of return for investments possessing similar risk characteristics serve as the basis for the development of an appropriate rate.

Investments in emerging technology carry much higher risks with considerable potential for complete loss of the initial investment. In addition to the risks previously discussed such as inflation, competition, changing economic climates, and the like, emerging technology carries additional risks.

Additional risks include the possibility that laboratory scale success may not survive the transition to pilot plant production, or that pilot plant scale successes may not be economically successful at full scale levels of commercial production. Embryonic technology investments may not even be defined past the pencil and paper stage of development where laboratory experimental success is not even assured.

These types of intellectual property investments involve substantial risks, and investors expect substantial "paydays" if the commercial viability ever materializes. Seed money for such risky investments is provided more and more by venture capitalists. Sometimes the word "venture" is replaced with "vulture" because of the seemingly extraordinary rate of returns that these investors require. But considering the high potential in these cases for a complete loss of millions of dollars of seed money, the required investment returns are not really out of line.

At various stages of development, the venture capital required rate of return changes with the amount of risk that is perceived at each stage. Presented below is an estimate of the amount of return required at different development stages:

Venture Capital Rates of Return

Stage of Development	Required Rate of Return
Start-up	50%
First stage	40%
Second stage	30%
Third stage	25%

The various levels of venture financing can be expressed as follows:

- **Start-up** is a company with an idea and not much else. This is the riskiest level of embryonic intellectual property investment and requires the largest amount of return. The funds are used for basic research and possibly development of a prototype. Revenues at this stage are not even part of management goals.
- **First stage** companies may have a prototype that has proven its capabilities, but further development is required before commercial scales of production can be achieved. Positive net cash flows may still be several years away.
- **Second stage** companies may have experienced success in the commercial production of the product or service, but expansion of market penetration requires substantial amounts that a bank may be unwilling to provide. At this point, the ability to make a profit may be already proven, but rapid expansion requires more than present operations can provide.
- **Third stage** financing begins to blur with fast growth companies that can get limited bank loans or additional funds from a public

offering. Strong profit levels may be consistently achieved, but more funds are needed for national or global expansion.

Venture capital companies are not long-term investors. They typically try to get out of the investment in five–seven years with a three- to tenfold increase in the original investment. This is usually accomplished by selling its interest in the developed company to a larger corporation or taking the developed company public.

WEIGHTED AVERAGE COST OF CAPITAL

The discussion thus far has presented various concepts and methods that help define the rate of return on equity investments. But investments are usually financed by a combination of equity and borrowed funds.

Corporate investments typically must pass hurdle rates in order to be considered as viable opportunities. Since debt and equity funds are used to finance these investments, the return that is provided must be sufficient to satisfy the interest due on the debt, and also provide a fair rate of return on the equity funds. The hurdle rate must be this weighted average cost of capital, at a minimum.

A corporation that is financed with both debt and equity might have a capitalization structure that is comprised of 25% debt and 75% equity. A good bond rating might allow the corporation to finance debt at 9%. An appropriate equity rate, as determined from one of the models above, might be 15%.

Shown in Figure A.1 is the weighted average cost of capital. The tax deductibility of interest expense makes the after-tax cost of debt only 60% of the stated interest rate for corporations that pay a combined state and federal income tax of 40%. Equity returns are in no way tax deductible. When the cost of these capital components is weighted by their percentage of the total capital structure, a weighted average cost of capital of 12.6% is the result. This is the amount of return that the company must earn, at a minimum, on its investment, fixed equipment purchases, acquisitions of competitors, or intellectual property.

A multinational corporation, for which a 12.6% weighted average cost of capital is appropriate, may be a well-diversified "basket" of

Business Enterprise Weighted Cost of Capital					
Invested Capital Component	Amount ($ Millions)	Percent of Invested Capital	Cost of Capital	After tax Cost of Capital	Weighted Average Cost of Capital
Equity	75.0	75.0%	15.0%	15.0%	11.3%
Debt	25.0	25.0%	9.0%	5.4%	1.4%
Total	100.0	100.0%			12.6%

Required Rate of Return Among Assets					
Asset Category	Amount ($ Millions)	Percent of Invested Capital	Return Required	Weighted Return Required	Percent of Total Return
Net Working Capital	20.0	20.0%	7.0%	1.4%	11.2%
Fixed Assets	30.0	30.0%	11.0%	3.3%	26.3%
Intangible Assets	50.0	50.0%	15.7%	7.9%	62.5%
Total	100.0	100.0%		12.6%	100.0%

Figure A.1 Business Enterprise Weighted Cost of Capital and Required Rate of Return Among Assets

investments. Some of the investments may be more risky than others. Overall, the rate of return that these investments must earn is 12.6%.

If we apply this concept to a small company or an isolated subsidiary of a multinational company, the weighted average rate of return requirement can also be allocated among the assets that are employed within the defined business enterprise. The allocation is conducted with respect to the amount of investment risk that each component represents to the business enterprise.

The weighted average cost of capital for a small company or subsidiary would comprise an equity and debt rate which reflects the risk and return dynamics that are unique to the industry of the defined business enterprise.

As discussed in previous chapters, the business enterprise is the sum of the fair market value of the invested capital (debt and equity). This is also represented by the sum of net working capital (monetary assets), tangible assets, and the intangible assets. Just as the weighted average cost of capital (WACOC) is allocated among the debt and equity components of the invested capital, it is also possible to allocate a portion of the WACOC to the asset components.

Shown in Figure A.1 is an allocation of the weighted average cost of capital for a business enterprise allocated among the business assets. The various rates of return assigned to each of the assets reflect their relative risk. The relative returns provided by each asset category are also indicated.

Appropriate Return on Monetary Assets

The monetary assets of the business are its net working capital. This is the total of current assets minus current liabilities. Current assets are comprised of accounts receivable, inventories, cash, and short-term security investments. Offsetting this total are the current liabilities of the business such as accounts payable, accrued salaries, and accrued expenses.

Working capital is considered to be the most liquid asset of a business. Receivables are usually collected within 60 days, and inventories are usually turned over in 90 days. The cash component is immediately available, and security holdings can be converted to cash with a telephone call to the firm's broker. Further evidence of liquidity is the use of accounts receivable and/or inventories as collateral for loans. In addition, accounts receivable can be sold for immediate cash to factoring companies at a discount of the book value.

Given the relative liquidity of working capital, the amount of investment risk is inherently low. An appropriate rate of return to associate with the working capital component of the business enterprise is that which is available from investment in short-term securities of low risk levels. The rate available on 90-day certificates of deposit or money market funds serves as a benchmark.

Appropriate Return on Tangible Assets

The tangible or fixed assets of the business are comprised of production machinery, warehouse equipment, transportation fleet, office buildings, office equipment, leasehold improvements, and manufacturing plants. An indication of the rate of return that is contributed by these assets can be pegged at about the interest rate at which commercial banks make loans, using the fixed assets as collateral. While these assets are not as liquid as working capital, they can often be sold to other companies. This marketability allows a partial return of the investment in fixed assets of the business should the business fail. Another aspect of relative risk reduction relates to the strategic redeployment of fixed assets. Assets that can be redirected for use elsewhere in a corporation have a degree of versatility which can still allow an economic contribution to be derived from their employment, even if it is not from the originally intended purpose.

While these assets are more risky than working capital investments, they possess favorable characteristics that must be considered in the weighted average cost of capital allocation.

Fixed assets that are very specialized in nature must reflect higher levels of risk which, of course, demands a higher rate of return. Specialized assets are those which are not easily redeployed for other commercial exploitation or liquidated to other businesses for other uses.

Appropriate Return on Intangible Assets and Intellectual Property

Intangible assets are considered to be the most risky asset component of the overall business enterprise. These assets may have little, if any, liquidity and poor versatility for redeployment elsewhere in the business. This enhances their risk. Customized computer software that is installed and running on a company's computer may have very little liquidation value if the company fails. The investment in a trained work force may be altogether lost, and the value of other elements of a going concern is directly related to the success of the business. A higher rate of return on these assets is therefore required.

Since the overall return on the business is established as the weighted average cost of capital, and since reasonable returns for the monetary and tangible assets can be estimated, we are then in a position to derive an appropriate rate of return to be earned from the intangible assets.

The following equation presents the means by which the 16% rate was derived for the intangible assets in our example:

$$\text{WACOC} = \frac{V_m}{V_{bev}}(R_m) + \frac{V_t}{V_{bev}}(R_t) + \frac{V_i}{V_{bev}}(R_i)$$

where

WACOC is the weighted average cost of capital for the overall business enterprise

V_m, V_t, V_i are the fair market values of the monetary, tangible, and intangible assets, respectively

R_m, R_t, R_i are the relative rates of return associated with the business enterprise asset components

V_{bev} is the fair market value of the business enterprise, which is the total of V_m, V_t, and V_i.

A little algebraic wizardry, and we can solve this equation for the appropriate rate of return on the intangible assets:

$$R_i = \frac{\text{WACOC}(V_{bev}) - R_m(V_m) - V_t(R_t)}{V_{bev}}$$

If the WACOC that is developed is for a diversified multinational corporation, the proper rate that should be used in conjunction with a specific intellectual property investment could be far greater. The WACOC represents an overall return from the diversified investments or asset base of the business. The rate attributed to a specific intellectual property must reflect the various risks associated with the division within which the specific property is used.

Thus, the process may first require determination of an appropriate WACOC for the whole business, followed by a determination of a WACOC for each operating division, working towards the business segment in which a specific intellectual property resides in a "top-down" approach.

The example that was presented yielded a 12.6% WACOC. This was based upon use of an equity rate of return of 15%. Such a rate would imply that the business is commercially viable, and that the associated intellectual property has also been proven. Embryonic and emerging intellectual property possesses more risks, and as such, would most likely be analyzed using a venture capital rate of return.

Overall, the business enterprise is comprised of various types of assets, each possessing different degrees of investment risk that correlates with the weighted average cost of capital.

REFERENCES

Smith, Gordon V. and Russell L. Parr, *Valuation of Intellectual Property and Intangible Assets* (New York: John Wiley & Sons, 1989).

Parr, Russell L., *Investing in Intangible Assets—Finding and Profiting from Hidden Corporate Value* (New York: John Wiley & Sons, 1991).

Copeland, Tom, Tim Koller, and Jack Murrin of McKinsey & Company, Inc., *Valuation—Measuring and Managing the Value of Companies* (New York: John Wiley & Sons, 1990).

Cohen, Jerome B., Edward D. Zinbarg, and Arthur Zeikel, *Investment Analysis and Portfolio Management,* 4th Ed. (Homewood, IL: Richard D. Irwin, Inc., 1982).

Harrington, Diana R., "Stock Prices, Beta, and Strategic Planning," *Harvard Business Review,* May–June 1983, p. 157

Reilly, Frank K., *Investment Analysis and Portfolio Management,* 2nd Ed. (Chicago, IL: Dryden Press, 1985).

Levine, Sumner N., Editor-in-Chief, *Financial Analyst's Handbook, Portfolio Management* (Homewood, IL: Dow Jones-Irwin, 1975).

Maginn, John L. and Donald L. Tuttle, Editors, *Managing Investment Portfolios, A Dynamic Process* (Boston, MA: Warren, Gorham and Lamont, 1983).

Gray, III, William S., *The Historical Record—Insights for Forecasting Expected Return and Risk* (Homewood, IL: Institute of Chartered Financial Analysts, Dow Jones-Irwin, 1985).

Roll, Richard and Stephen A. Ross, "The Arbitrage Pricing Theory Approach to Strategic Portfolio Planning," *Financial Analysts Journal,* May–June 1984.

Jereski, Laura, "Too Much Money, Too Few Deals," *Forbes,* March 7, 1988, p. 144.

Berry, Michael A., Edwin Burmeister, and Marjorie B. McElroy, "Sorting Out Risks Using Known APT Factors," *Financial Analysts Journal,* March–April 1988, p. 29.

Appendix B

Financial and Business Information Sources

We are often asked about how one can obtain the financial information that can be used in the return on investment models we recommend. It can be a special problem for those who are evaluating a licensing transaction *into* an industry with which they are unfamiliar. The same problem can arise when evaluating the suitability of a joint venture partner from the financial viewpoint. The only answer is to become familiar with a new industry—What drives it, who are the major players, what is its outlook, what is its vulnerability? We therefore offer the following sources that are available.

A STARTING POINT

We suggest the following references, since many of the information sources are arranged by Standard Industrial Classification (SIC) code.

Executive Office of the President, Office of Management and Budget, *Standard Industrial Classifications Manual.*

Congressional Information Service (a private firm), *American Statistics Index: A Comprehensive Guide and Index to the Statistical*

Publications of the United States Government. This is a very comprehensive index of U.S. government sources.

FINANCIAL DATA

Armed with the SIC code of the industry to be researched, one can first extract the names of the companies within that industry, and then view their financial performance in the following sources which are cited in their hard-copy format, although many are also available in electronic form.

Moody's Investors Services, 99 Church Street, New York, NY 10007.

This firm publishes several series of information that provide detailed balance sheet and income statement data on a current and historical basis, together with a company background and securities.

Industrial Manual—Annual two-volume publication that provides information on companies listed on the New York and American Stock Exchanges.

Moody's Industrial News Reports—Published twice each week to update on a current basis the *Industrial Manual*.

Public Utility Manual—Contains similar information on over 475 electric and gas utilities, gas transmission companies, telephone and water companies.

Public Utility News Reports—Published twice weekly, and updates the annual *Manual*.

International Manual

Bank and Finance Manual

Municipal & Government Manual

OTC Industrial Manual

Transportation Manual

Bond Survey—Published weekly; provides an economic overview and review of current bond offerings, changes in ratings, and yields of various bond groupings.

Standard & Poor's Corporation, 25 Broadway, New York, NY 10004.

This firm publishes balance sheet and income statement data, as well as company information and industry data in several forms:

Corporation Records—Company history and historical financial information.

S & P Reports—Current financial and market data on:

- New York Stock Exchange companies
- American Stock Exchange companies
- Over-the-counter companies

The Outlook—Published weekly, provides selected information on industries and individual companies.

Statistical Service, Current Statistics—Published monthly and annually; provides bond prices and yields, earnings, preferred stock prices, and stock price indexes for industry groups.

Stock Guide—Provides abbreviated financial information on over 5,300 common and preferred stock issues.

Bond Guide—Summarizes information on over 6,700 bond issues.

Earnings Guide—Provides consensus of Wall Street earnings estimates on over 3,300 publicly traded stocks.

Industry Surveys—Two-volume annual publication with market data and forecasts by industry groupings.

Value Line Publishing, Inc., 711 Third Avenue, New York, NY 10017.

This firm's offerings include a wide range of investor-related information:

The Value Line Investment Survey—Composite industrial data and yields of various types of bonds and debt.

Investment Survey—Individual financial information on approximately 1,600 companies

Value/Screen II—A computerized version of the investment surveys, providing this financial information on disk monthly with software to manipulate it.

C.A. Turner Utility Reports, P.O. Box 650, Moorestown, NJ 08057.

Financial Statistics of Public Utilities

I/B/E/S—Institutional Brokers Estimate System, Lynch, Jones & Ryan, 345 Hudson Street, New York, NY 10014.

Monthly Comments—Observations and earnings estimates on individual companies, as well as industry groups.

Capital Publications, Inc., 1101 King Street, P.O. Box 1454, Alexandria, VA 22313-2054.

Blue Chip Economic Indicators— Monthly publication summarizing what economists are projecting about the U.S. outlook.

Company Annual Reports.

Ibbotson Associates, 8 South Michigan Avenue, Suite 700, Chicago, IL 60603.

Stocks, bonds, bills, and inflation

National Quotation Bureau, Inc., The Harbor Side Financial Center, 600 Plaza III, Jersey City, NJ 07311-3895.

The NQB Monthly Price Report—Monthly publication of stock prices of over-the-counter and other small stock issues.

Prentice Hall, Tax & Professional Practice Division, Englewood Cliffs, NJ 07632.

Almanac of Business and Industrial Financial Ratios—Provides balance sheet and income statement financial ratios for all major U.S. industry groups.

The Robert Morris Associates, One Liberty Place, 1650 Market Street, Suite 2300, Philadelphia, PA 19103-7398.

Annual Statement Studies—Provides summaries of balance sheet and income statement statistics for 382 industries identified by titles and SIC codes.

RMA also publishes a wide variety of information on *lending and credit analysis*, as well as international lending practices and credit information.

Disclosure, 5161 River Road, Bethesda, MD 20816.

Subscription and on-demand access to documents filed at the Securities and Exchange Commission for nearly 15,000 U.S. and foreign companies.

Gale Research Company, Book Tower, Detroit, MI 48226.

Ward's Business Directory of U.S. Private and Public Companies—Summary description and financial data on approximately 133,000 companies.

CompuServe, 5000 Arlington Centre Blvd., P.O. Box 20212, Columbus, OH 43220.

CompuServe is an on-line database system that provides access to an extraordinary amount of business information for more than 10,000 public companies, including business descriptions, stock price information, and financial statements. The system also provides access to newspaper and magazine archives which can be searched by keyword.

ECONOMIC DATA

U.S. Bureau of the Census, *Current Population Reports.*

Every five years, the Bureau publishes economic census data on Agriculture, Mineral Industries, Manufacturing, Retail Trade, Wholesale Trade, Transportation, Governments, Construction Industries, and Service Industries.

Bureau of Labor Statistics, *Monthly Labor Review.*

OBERS Area Economic Projections (1985).

Federal Reserve Bank of St. Louis, P.O. Box 66953, St. Louis, MO 63166-6953.

U.S. Financial Data—Weekly review of U.S. economic activity with yields and interest rates on selected securities.

U.S. Department of Commerce.

U.S. Industrial Outlook— Annual publication covering international economic outlook, as well as industry reviews and forecasts for all major industry groups.

INTERNATIONAL DATA

U.N. Yearbook of International Trade Statistics
U.N. Demographic Yearbook
UNESCO Statistical Yearbook
International Monetary Fund:
Government Finance Statistics Yearbook
Balance of Payments Statistics
Direction of Trade Statistics
The Economist (private publication)

SOURCES OF SOURCES

Where to Find Business Information, **John Wiley & Sons, Inc., 1982.**

Lists sources of business information by subject. As an example, under the heading "Energy, Solar—World Solar Markets," one finds a reference to a monthly report which monitors worldwide solar energy use published by the *Financial Times* in London.

Other sample references include "Exploration and Economics of the Petroleum Industry," "Fusion Power Report," and "Pharmaceutical Marketletter."

Instant Information, **Joel Makower and Alan Green, 1987, Tilden Press, Inc.**

Provides lists of organizations arranged by state, as well as an index by organization and subject.

Provides the name and address of the organization, as well as a brief description of its activities. Examples are entries ranging from the Naval Blood Research Laboratory in Boston to the Pilgrim Society in Plymouth, MA.

***Corporate Libraries*—Many large corporations maintain libraries and information services which are available to the public, and which, of course, are concentrated in the industrial interests of the company. Other examples are the Cast Iron Soil Pipe Institute in McLean, VA, and the Brown Swiss Cattle Breeders Association of the USA in Beloit, WI.**

***Litigation Services Resource Directory*, John Wiley & Sons, Inc., 1992.**

This is an annual publication which lists books, encyclopedias, and magazine or journal articles grouped by subject, as well as professional and technical associations and institutes.

***Encyclopedia of Business Information Sources*, Paul Wasserman et al., 1988, Gale Research Company, Book Tower, Detroit, MI 48226.**

***Directory of Industry Data Sources, The U.S. and Canada*, 1982, Ballinger Publishing Company, Cambridge, MA 02138.**

***Executive's Business Information Source Book*, Phil Philcox, 1990, Prentice-Hall, West Nyack, NY 10995-9900.**

***Manufacturing USA: Industry Analyses, Statistics, and Leading Companies*, Arsen J. Darnay, 1989, Gale Research, Inc., Detroit, MI 48277-0748.**

***The Business Information Source Book*, Gustav Berle, 1991, John Wiley & Sons, Inc., New York.**

***Thomas Register*, Thomas Publishing Company, One Penn Plaza, New York, NY 10001.**

Twenty-six volumes listing companies by Products and Services, cross-indexed to Company Profiles, and Catalog Files. Also offered in regional format and electronically. If one wants to know who makes what, this is the place to start.

***Encyclopedia of Business Information Sources*, Gale Research.**

Approximately 21,000 citations of all types arranged by subject.

***Handbook of Business Information: A Guide for Librarians, Students, and Researchers*, Diane Wheeler Strauss, 1988, Libraries Unlimited, Inc., Englewood, CO.**

A comprehensive source of sources.

***Corporate Technology Directory (CORPTECH)*, Corporate Technology Information Services, Inc., 12 Alfred Street, Suite 200, Woburn, MA 01801-9998.**

Information on approximately 35,000 companies that manufacture or develop high-technology products. Four volumes published annually, cross-referenced by business, product, and location.

DIALOG, Dialog Information Services, Inc., 3460 Hillview Avenue, Palo Alto, CA 94304.

Through its DIALOG information service, this firm offers a huge array of on-line databases, from general business data to specific company and industry information. Searching is facilitated, and one can collect a great deal of information in a short time.

Appendix C

Licensing Transaction Examples and Royalty Rates

Recent examples of licensing transactions are presented below, categorized by industry. The majority show that royalties payments are typically based on a percentage of sales. Sometimes, the royalty rate is a flat amount. Sometimes, the royalty rate changes over time or is tied to an aggregate amount of royalty payments. Sometimes, license fees are high, low, or not part of the deal at all. In general, industry norms and rules-of-thumb cannot be detected and should be avoided. The following information was obtained from ***Licensing Economics Review*** of Moorestown, NJ.

AUTOMOTIVE

General Motors and Chrysler charge toy car model makers like Revel, Ertl, and Monogram between 4 and 6% of sales as a royalty for using car designs in the manufacture of model car kits.

Mercedes Benz AG licenses technological know-how to Ssangyong Motor Company of Korea for use in manufacturing small trucks, vans, diesel engines, and transaxles. Ssangyong committed to invest $1 billion by 1996 to build the necessary manufacturing plants. Mercedes will received 80 million marks as a down payment, and a running royalty of 2% of sales per unit.

CHEMICALS

Fibercem Incorporated licensed its fiber optic chemical sensor technology to Sippican, Incorporated for use in environmental markets in the areas of ocean, ground, and surface water detection and monitoring. Fibercem will also continue to market the technology in the same markets under its own label. Sippican agreed to pay a licensing fee of $25,000, and also agreed to pay an additional $500,000 for sensor research and development funding in three payments. In addition, Sippican agreed to pay a 5% royalty on its gross sales of Fibercem-developed products, along with a 3% royalty on "accessory" products that are made for use with a Fibercem sensor. Fibercem indicated that it will manufacture sensors for both its own product lines and that of the licensee. Sippican is a privately owned corporation located in Marion, MA, specializing in oceanographic instrumentation.

Southwall Technologies, Inc. granted a license to produce transparent conductive thin films and flexible circuit base materials using proprietary sputtering technology to Mitsui Toatsu Chemicals, Inc. The license agreement is an extension of an ongoing relationship between the two companies. Mitsui agreed to pay a $3.8 million fee for the license, which provides the company with exclusive manufacturing rights for certain electronic products in Japan. The license agreement also calls for the payment of annual royalties based on product sales. The royalty rate, in any calendar year, on products that are covered by the license is calculated on a sliding scale as follows: 5% on the first $5 million of sales, 4% on the next $5 million, and 3% on any other sales in a calendar year. Beginning in 1996, Mitsui will guarantee annual minimum royalty payments of $300,000, with the minimum amount escalating at a rate of 5% each year until the expiration date of the license agreement at the end of 2006.

COMPUTER SOFTWARE

Wisconsin Public Service Corporation, a public utility, has licensed management information software to WPS Development, Incorporated, and will receive a royalty equal to 10% of all software licensing fees received by WPS Development, Incorporated. The software program is known as the IFM system involving numerous computer applications useful for natural gas, electric, sewer, water, and other utilities. Wisconsin Public Service Corporation is not involved in the business of developing and marketing or otherwise servicing computer program designs. As such, WPS Development, Incorporated has entered into a license agreement whereby it can sublicense the IMF system to others. The agreement runs until December 31, 1996.

CONSTRUCTION

Insituform of North America, Incorporated announced that NuPipe International, a wholly owned subsidiary, has signed an exclusive agreement to license a trenchless pipeline rehabilitation technology to Nordisk Rorrenovering AB of Sweden. American Underground Technology Limited, in Australia, will also receive an exclusive agreement to use the technology in Australia. The licensees paid an initial licensing fee that was undisclosed, and each has agreed to pay royalties of 8% on new contract volume, subject to a minimum royalty payment, throughout the life of the 20-year license agreement. The NuPipe process begins with a folded pipe manufactured from PVC which has been stored on a reel and is heated at the installation sight. The heat makes the replacement pipe flexible so that it can be inserted into an existing manhole and pulled into place. A special rounding device is inserted in the upstream end of the NuPipe and propelled by pressure to the termination point. The rounding device expands the NuPipe tightly against the walls of the host pipe. Rehabilitated systems achieve a strong, seamless, jointless, corrosive-resistant PVC pipe that is installed in an existing underground system without requiring excavation.

Lucky-Goldstar Group, of South Korea, signed a $10 million contract with Sinar Mas Group to make polyvinyl chloride products. A 50–50 joint venture was formed, and will be called P.T. Sinar Lucky Plastics Industry. A plant will be built in Indonesia, and it will produce polyvinyl chloride pipe. The products will provide Indonesia with construction materials for water supply and sewage facilities. Lucky-Goldstar will provide the manufacturing, production, and facilities design technology. Sinar will pay a running royalty of 2.5% of net sales over the next five years.

Utilex Corporation and Dow Corning signed a definitive agreement under which Utilex became the exclusive licensee of the Dow Corning Cablecure technology. The cablecure process uses a proprietary method to treat and restore failing underground electric cables. Under terms of the agreement, Utilex paid $2 million in cash, and will pay a royalty of 50% of the pretax profits from the sale of cablecure services. Utilex also issued warrants to Dow Corning to purchase up to 353,846 additional shares of its common stock at an exercise price of $8.13 per share. The warrants will become exercisable if revenues from cablecure business reach certain milestones during the first eight years of the agreement. This agreement is unique because the running royalty payment is based on a split of profits rather than a percentage of revenues. This agreement adds another proprietary technology to the Cablecure repertoire of skills for renovating underground utility infrastructures possessed by Utilex. The company provides services for the replacement and renovation of underground utilities in the United States and Canada through a network of regional sales and service centers. It also conducts operations in Europe and Asia through its wholly owned subsidiary in the U.K. and through business associates throughout Europe and Japan.

COPYRIGHTS AND TRADEMARKS

The African National Congress (ANC) is South Africa's biggest and oldest anti-apartheid movement. It announced that it is going commercial. ANC is seeking to license its familiar green, gold, and black colors to clothes designers, book publishers, and jewelry makers. The organization is looking for a wide range of business opportunities to boost funds, and expects to get a 15% royalty on sales of items that use its logo.

Hilton Hotels is planning to license the use of the venerable "WALDORF-ASTORIA" name for use on up-scale consumer goods such as home furnishings, china, glassware, table linens, upholstery, wall coverings, cookbooks, entertainment guides, and food products. Licensees are being sought who will use design elements of the art deco hotel and pay royalties on sales at the 7–10% level.

Jennifer Convertibles Inc. has established Jennifer Chicago, LP, to open 20 licensed Jennifer Convertible stores in the Chicago area.

Jennifer Convertibles Inc. will receive a royalty of 5% of the partnership and sales. Jennifer Convertibles is the largest specialty retailer of convertible sofas in the nation. The company attributes its success and growth to a strategy that offers stylish quality furniture at reduced prices in a variety of price points to serve a large demographic market.

Marriott Corporation is planning to establish 46 airport restaurant/bars over the next five years that will be modeled after the best known bar in America—*Cheers*. Two locations are already in operation—Detroit Metropolitan Airport and Minneapolis–St. Paul International Airport. New locations will be located in the United States, New Zealand, and Australia. The restaurants are arranged just like the television program set, and include two robots that mimic the bar banter of television show characters Norm Peterson and Cliff Clavin. Marriott is paying a royalty of 4% to Paramount Pictures on all food and drink sales.

Major League Baseball makes a lot of money from licensing. For most of baseball's 150-year history, licensing was merely a sideline. In 1985, total retail sales of licensed merchandise was about $200 million. The merchandise involved tacky jackets, hats, equipment, mugs, blankets, and other paraphernalia that displayed logos and uniform reproductions of baseball teams. Today, over 300 licensees market 3,000 different items with baseball team logos and designs. The total retail sales is expected to top $1.8 billion this year. The royalty rate on wholesale revenues equals approximately 8.5%. Each team gets about $2.6 million. The merchandise sold still includes tacky trinkets and caps for children, but has expanded to include high-priced items sold on the racks of Nordstrom, Bloomingdales, and Saks Fifth Avenue.

Pen Corporation is a leading designer and manufacturer of quality decorated paper tableware, paper party accessories, invitations, gift wrap products, stationery, and giftware. Under its "Beach" and "Contempo" trademarks, the company produces and markets an extensive line of napkins, table covers, cups, plates, towels, trays, and coasters in a variety of coordinated designs, themes, and colors. The company works directly with leading design studios such as Gloria Vanderbilt, Bob Van Allen, Gear, Saloomey, Laurette, Betty Whitiker, Joan Luntz, Mary Quant, and J.G. Hook. Pen Corporation also produces and markets children's party tableware and accessories such as horns, hats, and blowouts which often feature licensed characters from the Disney Company, Children's Television Workshop (Sesame Street), Warner Brothers, and Marvel Entertainment Group. Pen Corporation typically pays royalty rates that run from 5 to 10% of the invoiced price of the tableware and accessories on which the licensed characters appear.

Rutgers, Harvard, Notre Dame, UCLA, Penn State, Florida State, and most other major universities allow their college logos and names to be placed on sweatshirt, pennants, hats, license plate holders, chairs, tie bars, and a myriad of other consumer products for a royalty of between 5 and 7.5% of sales.

Time Warner, Inc.'s *Batman* sparked a merchandising frenzy in 1989, selling an estimated $500 million of Bat paraphernalia. Ever since, movie studios have been trying to make repeat performances by licensing movie products. The strategy is a simple way, at little cost, for a studio to get a significant return to the bottom line. Originally, the idea of licensing movie products started out as a way to generate interest in a movie to encourage the sale of more tickets. The trend has evolved into an important revenue stream for studios which receive 5–10% of wholesale product prices from licensees for the privilege of manufacturing and selling a licensed character.

Western Publishing Company is the largest creator, publisher, manufacturer, and marketer of children's books in the United States. Included are storybooks for children between the ages of two and eight marketed as "Golden Books" and "Little Golden Books." In addition, the company markets sound storybooks and musical storybooks for children ages three and up that are marketed under the "Golden Sound Story" trademarks. The company also markets children and adult games. These games include classics such as Bingo, Checkers, Chess, Backgammon, and Dominoes under the Golden and Whitman trademarks. The company also sells crayons featuring licensed characters, prerecorded audio cassette tapes, and prerecorded audio cassette tapes that are packaged with books. The products of the company often feature popular characters that are licensed from other companies, including the Disney Company, Children's Television Workshop (Sesame Street), Mattel Incorporated, and Warner Brothers. Royalty rates paid by Western Publishing Company Incorporated generally range from 6 to 10% of the invoiced price of the merchandise that features licensed characters and properties. Most license agreements require advance royalty payments and minimum royalty guarantees. The license agreements also typically include editorial standards that cover the use of the characters and properties, and which allow for the agreements to be canceled if Western Publishing fails to meet the contractual obligations.

ELECTRONICS

Gamma Electronic Systems Incorporated has signed a license agreement with Fusan Laboratory Incorporated for the exclusive distribution rights to B.A.S.E. audio technology, a patented system regarding a psychoacoustical technique which brings a natural sonic ambiance to audio material. It has a wide range of applications in professional recording studios, broadcasting stations, film sound tracks, and consumer audio playback systems. The terms of the agreement include up-front licensing fees, minimum annual performance criteria, and a minimum of 3% royalty on sales. The B.A.S.E. system has been used on movie productions, including *The Hunt for Red October, Total Recall,* and *Star Trek V.*

IBM receives royalties from dozens of Taiwanese companies that pay a royalty of 3% of sales for AT and XT clones that are sold in the United States. The royalty rate for sales of clones that are sold outside of the United States is 2% of sales.

MTC Electronic Technologies Company, Ltd. acquired all rights to an ac–dc voltage converter with isolation capabilities. The converter was designed to be configured as an integrated circuit device, and is composed of discrete electronic components. MTC acquired its exclusive worldwide rights to the converter through a 70% owned subsidiary, which simultaneously sold rights for the converter to MTC in exchange for royalties equal to 6% of the net sales of the converter. The remaining 30% of the worldwide rights is owned by engineers who designed the converter. The converter device is designed to perform the functions of a traditional power transformer, as well as to convert voltage from ac to dc. Traditional power transformers are inefficient, heavy, and costly. Two power transformers are traditionally employed in electronic devices, with one used to step voltages up and down, while the other is used for isolation. The converter accomplishes both tasks. In addition to being smaller and saving on space and weight, the converter is designed to be more efficient. The commercial status of the product is embryonic. The company has not done customer-based testing nor has it finalized production plans or completed any market research.

Ovonic Battery Company, Inc. entered into license agreements involving their battery technology. The company has granted Sylva Industries, Ltd., a division of Gold Peak Industries of Hong Kong, a nonexclusive license to make small consumer batteries in Hong Kong, Singapore, Taiwan, The People's Republic of China, Malaysia, and Indonesia. The license also allows Sylva to use and sell the consumer batteries worldwide. The agreement requires Sylva to pay Ovonic an initial payment of $1 million. In addition, Sylva will pay running royalties of 3.5% of net sales until five years after the expiration of an improvement period and 2.0% of net sales thereafter for the remainder of the license. Ovonic Battery Company, Inc. is a subsidiary of Energy Conversion Devices, Inc. Ovonic batteries, unlike conventional batteries, contain no toxic materials, and have over twice the energy of nickel cadmium (NiCd). The batteries also can be made in any size, ranging from button cells to batteries for energy storage at utilities. In addition, the batteries do not have a memory effect. The battery technology of Ovonic is based on nickel metal hybrid technology. Some of the companies around the world that are converting to this new technology include Varta Batterie A.G., Gates Energy Products, Hitachi Maxell, Ltd., and Sovlux. The company has also formed joint ventures with entities in Russia and India.

Symbol Technologies Inc. has formed a joint venture with Olympus Optical Company Ltd. to sell and support bar-code data capture products in Asia. The joint venture will be called Olympus Symbol Inc., and will be financed on an equal basis by both partners. Symbol Technologies Inc. will receive a 10% royalty on revenues from the venture, in addition to its equity ownership stake. After five years of operation, the royalty rate will drop to 7.5%.

Symbol Technologies Inc. licensed its one-piece integrated laser scanning terminal for reading bar codes and collecting data to Electromagnetic Systems Inc. for a royalty on sales of 7.5%

Texas Instruments has earned more than $900 million in royalties from technology licenses in less than ten years. In fact, the licensing operations of TI are more profitable than its core business, which is subject to the extreme competitive pressures found in the electronics industry.

FOOD

AquaSciences International exclusively licensed its in-store bottle water purification vending systems to Critical Industries Inc. Critical will promote, market, install, and service the AquaNatural Systems. AquaSciences receives a $0.02 per gallon royalty for each gallon sold, a percentage of sales on products, and a percentage of licensing and royalty revenues internationally over the 20-year duration of the license agreement. AquaSciences also said that it would continue its ongoing research and development of water purification technologies. The company said that the marketing plan calls for the installation of about 2,800 systems in the United States during the first three years. It estimates that this would result in the sale of over 100 million gallons by the third year of the agreement. Plans include licensing of the AquaNatural System internationally, with concentration on Europe and Mexico.

Golden Valley Microwave Foods Incorporated signed a licensing agreement that settled an outstanding patent infringement case with Hunt-Wesson Incorporated, a wholly owned subsidiary of Conagra Incorporated. The license covers the use of Golden Valley's patented microwave popcorn packaging technologies. Under terms of the agreement, Golden Valley immediately began to receive a cash royalty of one penny on each bag of microwave popcorn sold by Hunt-Wesson, including its Orville Redenbacher's brand. Payments will be split between Golden Valley and its original licensee, General Mills Incorporated. Golden Valley's portion of the cash royalties are expected to exceed $2 million on an annual basis.

Vitafort International Corporation designs nutritionally enhanced food and beverage products, and then plans manufacturing and marketing systems for the new products. Vitafort has licensed the technology associated with a new line of eggs with increased polyunsaturated fats to Nulaid Food Inc. Vitafort will receive a royalty of $0.05 per carton of a dozen eggs, and $0.01 per pound on sales of egg byproducts.

MEDICAL

Disease Detection International (DDI) has provided a nonexclusive license to Meridian Diagnostics Incorporated that will allow Meridian to manufacture and sell six rapid diagnostic test kits for pregnancy, strep throat, toxoplasma rubella, cytomegalovirus, herpes simplex I, and herpes simplex II. DDI received a $110,000 license fee, and another $100,000 as an advance against future royalties, which are set at 6% of Meridian sales.

Future Medical Technologies International purchased a patented device that filters microorganisms from body fluids from Human Medical Laboratories, Inc. Future Medical made an advance cash payment of $372,000 and 150,000 shares of unregistered common stock. Future Medical will also pay a 3% royalty based upon net profits, with a lifetime cap of $5 million.

Future Medical Technologies Incorporated and the University of Maryland at College Park entered into licensing and collaboration agreements. The agreements give Future Medical exclusive worldwide rights to test and commercialize recently developed nonagar-based media formulations for use in detecting and/or selectively growing salmonella. Future Medical believes that incorporating this new media into the company's microbiological "Qualture" product line will offer a unique advantage not usually available in a market which is estimated to perform 12 and 15 million tests annually. The rights that have been granted to Future Medical are subject to a royalty-free nonexclusive license permitting the United States Government to practice all licensed inventions for U.S. Government purposes. During each of the four years of the license agreement, Future Medical will pay annual royalty rates of 2, 3, 4, and 5% of net sales, respectively, for all licensed products that the company sells. In the fifth and subsequent years, under the license agreement, Future Medical will pay an annual royalty of 6% of net sales for all licensed products sold by the company. If sales of the licensed products are made by any authorized sublicensee of Future Medical, then Future Medical will pay to the University 50% of all revenues received from sublicensees. Future Medical Technologies Incorporated markets a device (the "Qualture") that is designed to separate and filter microorganisms from specimens of urine, blood, spinal, joint, and other body fluids for identification, quantification, and presumptive diagnosis of infectious diseases accomplished in a time period substantially less than present conventional procedures.

Molecular Biosystems, Inc. (MBI) amended its supply and license agreement with E.I. du Pont De Nemours & Company which covers proprietary nucleic acid probe technologies that are owned by MBI. The renegotiated agreement was originally established in April 1986.

Previously, du Pont had an exclusive license, but under the new agreement, will only retain a nonexclusive right to these technologies. MBI will continue to manufacture nucleic acid probe agents for du Pont as it did under the previous agreement. The royalty rate on du Pont's net sales was lowered from 5.5 to 4% to reflect the change of du Pont's licensing rights from exclusive to nonexclusive. This represents a reduction in the royalty rate of 27%. Molecular Biosystems, Inc. is a San Diego, CA, company recognized as a leading biomedical firm developing proprietary medical products that diagnose human disease. The company is also a leading developer and supplier of direct, nonradioactively labeled nucleic acid probe products. The company is also developing diagnostic imaging products including Albunex, an injectable contrast agent for use in ultrasound imaging.

Pfizer Incorporated obtained a license to manufacture and sell Water-Jel sterile burn dressing products in the U.S. and Canada from Trilling Medical Technologies Incorporated. Pfizer agreed to pay a royalty of 5% on sales of Water-Jel products, and 5% on sales of any new products that are developed using the technology. Also, Pfizer promised to pay a 2% royalty on net sales on each new Pfizer product which makes use of Trilling's nine licensed trademarks. The entire deal fell through within six months when Trilling received notification of possible patent infringement by the licensed technology from an unaffiliated company. Pfizer immediately withdrew from the deal. Whoever said that patent protection was the most important component to a license deal was not kidding.

Roche Molecular Systems licenses the use of Polymerase Chain Reaction (PCR) diagnostic technology for 9% of sales. PCR technology replicates a single DNA strand millions of times in under two hours, allowing scientists to amplify and identify certain DNA segments. It also has strong potential for identifying infectious diseases, genetic diseases, cancer, and food testing applications.

Surgidyne Inc. has provided a unit of Baxter Healthcare Corporation with exclusive worldwide marketing rights for its autotransfusion products. The products involve capturing a surgical patient's blood during an operation and reusing the blood during and after the operation. The licensed system employs a battery-powered vacuum controller with disposable collection and reinfusing products. Baxter will pay Surgidyne a royalty of 20% on sales up to $2 million in royalties, after which the royalty rate on sales drops to 5%.

Index

INDEX